The Talmud of the Land of Israel

Chicago Studies in the History of Judaism
Edited by Jacob Neusner

The University of Chicago Press
Chicago and London

Talmud Yerushalmi. English.

The Talmud of the Land of Israel

A Preliminary Translation and Explanation

Volume 33 Abodah Zarah

Translated by Jacob Neusner

Jacob Neusner is University Professor and Ungerlieder Distinguished Scholar of Judaic Studies at Brown University. He is the author of numerous works, including *Judaism: The Evidence of the Mishnah,* published by the University of Chicago Press.

The University of Chicago Press, Chicago 60637
The University of Chicago Press, Ltd., London

Printed in the United States of America

89 88 87 86 85 84 83 82 5 4 3 2 1

Library of Congress Cataloging in Publication Data

Talmud, Yerushalmi. Avodah zarah. English.
Abodah zarah.

(The Talmud of the land of Israel; v. 33)
(Chicago studies in the history of Judaism)
Bibliography: p.
Includes index.
1. Talmud Yerushalmi. Avodah zarah—Commentaries.
I. Neusner, Jacob, 1932– . II. Title.
III. Series: Talmud Yerushalmi. English; v. 33.
IV. Series: Chicago studies in the history of Judaism.
BM498.5.E5 1982, vol. 33 296.1′2405 81-23124
[BM506.A15E5] AACR2
ISBN 0-226-57693-0

In memory of
Hyman Shanok

1906–1980

Contents

Foreword ix

Introduction to Abodah Zarah 1

1 Yerushalmi Abodah Zarah, Chapter One 7

2 Yerushalmi Abodah Zarah, Chapter Two 50

3 Yerushalmi Abodah Zarah, Chapter Three 110

4 Yerushalmi Abodah Zarah, Chapter Four 153

5 Yerushalmi Abodah Zarah, Chapter Five 188

Abbreviations and Bibliography 223

Index of Biblical and Talmudic References 225

General Index 229

Foreword

This translation into English of the Talmud of the land of Israel ("Palestinian Talmud," "Talmud Yerushalmi") is preliminary and provisional, even though it is not apt to be replaced for some time. It is preliminary, first, because a firm and final text for translation is not in hand; second, because a modern commentary of a philological and *halakhic* character is not yet available; and, third, because even the lower criticism of the text has yet to be undertaken. Consequently, the meanings imputed to the Hebrew and Aramaic words and the sense ascribed to them in this translation at best are merely a first step. When a systematic effort at the lower criticism of the extant text has been completed, a complete philological study and modern dictionary along comparative lines made available, and a commentary based on both accomplished, then the present work will fall away, having served for the interim. Unhappily, as I said, that interim is apt to be protracted. Text-critics, lexicographers, and exegetes are not apt to complete their work on Yerushalmi within this century.

The purpose of this preliminary translation is to make possible a set of historical and religions-historical studies on the formation of Judaism in the land of Israel from the closure of the Mishnah to the completion of the Talmud of the land of Israel and the time of the composition of the first *midrashic* compilations. Clearly, no historical, let alone religions-historical, work can be contemplated without a theory of the principal document and source for the study, the Palestinian Talmud. No theory can be attempted, however tentative and provisional, without a complete, prior statement of what the document appears to wish to say and how its materials seem to have come to closure. It follows that the natural next steps, beyond my now-finished history of Mishnaic law and account of the Judaism revealed in that history, carry us to the present project. Even those steps, when they are taken, will have to be charted with all due regard to the pitfalls of a translation that is preliminary, based upon a text that as yet has not been subjected even to the clarifying exercises of lower criticism. Questions will have to be shaped appropriate to the parlous state of the evidence. But even if the historical and religions-historical program were to be undertaken in the Hebrew language instead of in English, those who might wish to carry on inquiries into the history of the Jews and of Judaism in the land of Israel in the third and fourth centuries would face precisely the same task we do. No one can proceed without a systematic account of the evidence and a theory of how the evidence may and may not be utilized. Further explanation of the plan and execution of this work will be found in volume 34, pp. x–xiv. The glossary, abbreviations, and bibliography for the whole series, are in volume 34, pp. 225–31.

It remains only to thank those who helped with this volume.

My student, Mr. Roger Brooks, checked my translation against the Leiden manuscript and the *editio princeps* and saved me a great deal of tedious work in so doing. He also uncovered more than a few points requiring attention and correction. I am grateful for his hard and careful work. Professor Baruch A. Levine of New York University served as the critical reader for this volume. I am thankful for the many corrections and observations supplied by him, and still more, for his willingness to take time out to study this tractate and so improve my work on it. I retain full responsibility for whatever unsolved problems and deficiencies may remain.

Mr. Brooks looked up all the biblical verses in this tractate, saving me much work. Miss Winifred Bell typed them. Mrs. Marie Louise Murray typed the entire manuscript and did so with unusual care and a high standard of accuracy. She also contributed corrections of various details. I could not have done this work without the help of these loyal co-workers.

J.N.

Introduction to Abodah Zarah

The Mishnah tractate Abodah Zarah supplies rules and regulations for carrying out the fundamental scriptural commandments concerning the destruction of idols and all things having to do with idolatry. It follows that while the tractate deals with facts and relies upon suppositions that Scripture does not supply, its basic viewpoint and the problem it seeks to solve derive in fact from the Mosaic code. Before proceeding, we had best review those general statements that Scripture does make:

Ex. 23:13

Take heed to all that I have said to you; and make no mention of the names of other gods, nor let such be heard out of your mouth.

Ex. 23:24

When my angel goes before you, and brings you in to the Amorites, and the Hittites, and the Perizzites, and the Canaanites, the Hivites, and the Jebusites, and I blot them out, you shall not bow down to their gods, nor serve them, nor do according to their work, but you shall utterly overthrow them and break their pillars in pieces.

Ex. 23:32–33

You shall make no covenant with them or with their gods. They shall not dwell in your land, lest they make you sin against me; for if you serve their gods, it will surely be a snare to you.

Ex. 34:12–16

The Lord said to Moses, "Come up to me on the mountain, and wait there; and I will give you the tablets of stone, with the law and the commandment, which I have written for their instruction." So Moses rose with his servant Joshua, and Moses went up into the mountain of God. And he said to the elders, "Tarry here for us, until we come to you again; and, behold Aaron and Hur are with you; whoever has a cause, let him go to them."

Then Moses went up on the mountain, and the cloud covered the mountain. The glory of the Lord settled on Mount Sinai, and the cloud covered it six days; and on the seventh day he called to Moses out of the midst of the cloud.

Deut. 7:1–5

When the Lord your God brings you into the land which you are entering to take possession of it, and clears away many nations before you, the Hittites, the Girgashites, the Amorites, the Canaanites, the Perizzites, the Hivites, and the Jebusites, seven nations greater and mightier than yourselves, and when the Lord your God gives them over to you, and you defeat them; then you must utterly destroy them; show no mercy to them. You shall not make marriages with them, giving your daughters to their sons or taking their daughters for your sons. For they would turn away your sons from following me, to serve other gods; then the anger of the Lord would be kindled against you, and he would destroy you quickly. But thus shall you deal with them: you shall break down their altars, and dash in pieces their pillars, and hew down their Asherim, and burn their graven images with fire.

Deut. 7:25–26

The graven images of their gods you shall burn with fire; you shall not covet the silver or the gold that is on them, or take it for yourselves, lest you be ensnared by it; for it is an abomination to the Lord your God. And you shall not bring an abominable thing into your house, and become accursed like it; you shall utterly detest and abhor it; for it is an accursed thing.

Deut. 12:2–3

You shall surely destroy all the places where the nations whom you shall dispossess served their gods, upon the high mountains and upon the hills and under every green tree; you shall tear down their altars, and dash in pieces their pillars, and burn their Asherim with fire; you shall hew down the graven images of their gods, and destroy their name out of that place.

The tractate, which proposes to realize these commandments in ordinary life, is in three parts, moving from the general to the specific. It deals first with commercial relationships, second, with matters pertaining to idols, and finally with the very urgent issue of the prohibition of wine of which part has served as a libation to an idol. There are a number of unstated principles before us. What a gentile is not likely to use for the worship of an idol is not going to be prohibited. What may serve not as part of idolatry but as an appurtenance thereto is prohibited for Israelite use but permitted for Israelite commerce. What serves for idolatry is prohibited for use and for benefit. Certain further assumptions about gentiles, not pertinent specifically to idolatry, are expressed. Gentiles are assumed routinely to practice bestiality, bloodshed, and fornication, without limit or restriction. This negative image of the gentile finds expression in the laws before us. The outline of the tractate follows.

Commercial relationships with gentiles (1:1–2:7)

A. *Festivals and fairs.* 1:1, 2

1:1 For three days before gentile festivals it is forbidden to do business with them. Ishmael: Three days afterward also.

1:2–4 These are the festivals of gentiles. A city in which there is an idol—in the area outside of it, it is permitted to do business.

B. *Objects prohibited even in commerce.* 1:5–2:2

1:5 These are things that it is forbidden to sell to gentiles.

1:6 In a place in which they are accustomed to sell small cattle to gentiles, they sell them (the consideration being use of the beasts for sacrifices to idols).

1:7 They do not sell them bears, lions, or anything that is a public danger. They do not help them build a basilica, scaffold, stadium, or judges' tribunal.

1:8–10 They do not make ornaments for an idol, sell them produce that is not yet harvested, sell them land in the Holy Land.

2:1 They do not leave cattle in gentiles' inns, because they are suspect in regard to bestiality.

2:2 They accept healing for property (e.g., animals) but not for a person.

C. *Objects prohibited for use but permitted in trade.* 2:3–9

2:3 These things belonging to gentiles are prohibited, and the prohibition concerning them extends to deriving any benefit from them at all: wine, vinegar, earthenware that absorbs wine, and hides pierced at the heart.

2:4–6 Skins of gentiles and their jars, with Israelite wine collected in them—they are prohibited, the prohibition extends to deriving benefit, so Meir. Sages: Not to deriving benefit.

2:7 On what account did they prohibit cheese made by gentiles?

2:8 These are things of gentiles that are prohibited, but the prohibition does not extend to deriving benefit from them: milk, bread, oil, etc.

2:9 These are things that to begin with are permitted for Israelite consumption.

Idols (3:1–4:7)

A. *General principles.* 3:1–9

3:1 All images are prohibited, because they are worshiped once a year, so Meir. Sages: prohibited is only one that has an emblem of authority.

3:2–3 He who finds the sherds of images—lo, these are permitted.

3:4 Discourse with idolator.

3:5 Gentiles who worship hills and valleys—the hills or valleys are permitted, but what is on them is forbidden.

3:6 If one's house-wall served also as the wall of a temple and it fell down, one may not rebuild it.

3:7–9 There are three states in regard to idolatry. What is built for idolatrous purposes is forbidden. What is improved is forbidden until the improvement is removed. What merely happens to be used for an idol is permitted once the idol is removed.

B. *The Asherah.* 3:10–14

3:10 What is an *asherah?*

3:11–13 Use of an *asherah*-tree.

3:14 Desecrating an *asherah*-tree.

C. *The Merkolis.* 4:1–2

4:1–2 Three stones beside a Merkolis (= Hermes) are forbidden, so Ishmael.

D. *Nullifying an idol.* 4:3–7

4:3 An idol that had a garden or bathhouse.

4:4–6 An idol belonging to a gentile is prohibited forthwith. One belonging to an Israelite is forbidden only once it has been worshiped. How one nullifies an idol.

4:7 If God does not favor idolatry, why does he not wipe it away?

Libation wine (4:8–5:15)

4:8 They purchase from gentiles the contents of a winepress that has already been trodden out, for it is not the sort of wine that gentiles use for a libation until it has dripped down into the vat.

4:9 Israelites tread a winepress with a gentile, but they do not gather grapes with him.

4:10–11 A gentile who is found standing beside a cistern of wine—if he had a lien on the vat, it is prohibited. If he had no lien on it, it is permitted.

4:12 He who prepares the wine belonging to a gentile in a condition of cleanness and leaves it in his domain.

5:1–2 He who hires an Israelite worker to work with him in the preparation of libation wine—the Israelite's salary is forbidden.

5:3 Libation wine that fell on grapes—one may rinse them off, and they are permitted. If the grapes were split and absorbed wine, they are prohibited.

5:4–6 A gentile who, with an Israelite, was moving jars of wine from place to place—if the wine is assumed to be watched, it is permitted. If the Israelite told the gentile he was going away for any length of time, the wine is prohibited.

5:7 The same point, now in the context of eating at the same table.

5:8 A band of gentile raiders who entered a town peacefully—open jars are forbidden, closed ones permitted.

5:9–10 Israelite craftsmen, to whom a gentile sent a jar of libation wine as salary, may ask him to pay in money instead, only if this is before the wine has entered their possession. Afterward it is forbidden.

5:11–12 Libation wine is forbidden and imparts a prohibition on wine with which it is mixed in any measure at all. If it is wine poured into water, it is forbidden only if it imparts a flavor.

5:13 Libation wine that fell into a vat—the whole of the vat is forbidden for benefit. Simeon b. Gamaliel: All of it may be sold except the value of the volume of libation wine that is in it.

5:14–15 A stone winepress that a gentile covered with pitch—one dries it off, and it is clean. One of wood; one of earthenware.

The opening unit unfolds in a fairly orderly way, from a prologue on the special problems of fairs to the general matter of things an Israelite may not even buy or sell, as against things he may not use but may trade (**I**.B, C). The second unit lays down some general principles about images, then presents special ones on two specific kinds of idols (**II**.B, C) and at the end asks the logical, necessary question about how one nullifies an idol entirely. The third unit is a very long essay about libation wine and its effect upon Israelite-gentile commerce. I do not see any coherent subdivisions of this sizable discussion, which goes over the same ground time and again.

1 Yerushalmi Abodah Zarah Chapter One

1:1

[39a/A] *Before the festivals of gentiles for three days it is forbidden to do business with them,*

[B] *[1] to lend anything to them or to borrow anything from them,*

[C] *[2] to lend money to them or to borrow money from them,*

[D] *[3] to repay them or to be repaid by them.*

[E] *R. Judah says, "They accept repayment from them, because it is distressing to him."*

[F] *They said to him, "Even though it is distressing to him now, he will be happy about it later."*

[G] *R. Ishmael says, "Three days before them and three days after them it is prohibited."*

[H] *And the sages say, "Before their festivals it is prohibited, but after their festivals it is permitted."*

[**I**.A] R. Ḥama bar ʿUqbah derived scriptural support for all of those [statements about the interval of three days during which it is prohibited to do business with gentiles prior to a festival of theirs] from the following verse: "[Come to Bethel and transgress; to Gilgal and multiply transgression;] bring your sacrifices every morning, your tithes on the third day" (Amos 4:4).

[B] Said to him R. Yosé, "If so, then even in the exilic communities [the rule should be the same].

[C] "Yet it has been taught in a Tannaitic tradition: '**Nahum the Mede says, "One day in the exilic communities [before their festival] it is prohibited [to do business with gentiles, and not**

the three days specified by M. A.Z. 1:1, which apply only to the Holy Land]" ' [T. A.Z. 1:1A]."

[D] Why so?

[E] There [in Babylonia] they looked into the matter and found out that [the pagans] prepare their requirements [for celebrating a festival] in only a single day, so they forbade business dealings with them for a single day. But here [in the Holy Land] they looked into the matter and found out that they prepare their requirements [for celebrating a festival] in a full three days, so they forbade business dealings with them for a full three days.

[F] How then does R. Yosé interpret the cited verse of Scripture, "Bring your sacrifices every morning [etc.]"?

[G] Concerning the reign of Jeroboam does Scripture speak.

[H] Once Jeroboam took up the reign over Israel, he began to entice Israel [toward idolatry], saying to them, "Come and let us practice idolatrous worship. Idolatry is permissive."

[I] That is the meaning of the following verse of Scripture: "[Because Syria with Ephraim and the son of Remaliah has devised evil against you, saying,] 'Let us go up against Judah and terrify it, and let us conquer it for ourselves and set up the son of Tabeel as king in the midst of it' " (Is. 7:5–6).

[J] Said R. Abba, "We have searched through the whole of Scripture and have found no instance in which his name was Tabeel. But [the meaning is] that he does good for those who serve him."

[K] The Torah has said, "I chose him [the tribe of Levi] out of all the tribes of Israel to be my priest, to go up to my altar, to burn incense, to wear an ephod before me (1 Sam. 2:28)."

[L] And idolatry says, "[He also made houses on high places,] and appointed priests from the fringe element [MQṢWT] of the people[, who were not of the Levites] (1 Kings 12:31)."

[M] Said Rabbi, "Not from the thorns [QWṢYM] that were among the people, but from the refuse [PSWLT] that was among the people."

[N] The Torah has said, "You shall not let the fat of my feast remain until the morning" (Ex. 23:18).

[O] But idolatry has said, "Bring your sacrifices every morning" (Amos 4:4).

[P] The Torah has said, "[When you offer a sacrifice of peace-offerings to the Lord, you shall offer it so that you may be accepted]. It shall be eaten the same day you offer it, or on the morrow[; and anything left over until the third day shall be burned with fire]" (Lex. 19:5–6).

[Q] And idolatry has said, ". . . your tithes on the third day" (Amos 4:4).

[R] The Torah has said, "You shall not offer the blood of my sacrifice with leavened bread" (Ex. 23:18).

[S] And idolatry has said, "Offer a sacrifice of thanksgiving of that which is leavened" (Amos 4:5).

[T] The Torah has said, "When you make a vow to the Lord, your God, you shall not be slack to pay for it[; for the Lord your God will surely require it of you, and it would be a sin in you. But if you refrain from vowing, it shall be no sin in you. You shall be careful to perform what has passed your lips, for you have voluntarily vowed to the Lord your God what you have promised with your mouth]" (Deut. 23:21–23).

[U] And idolatry has said, "And proclaim freewill offerings, publish them" (Amos 4:5).

[V] Said R. Yudan, father of R. Mattenaiah, "The intention of [a verse of] Scripture [such as is cited below] was only to make mention of the evil traits of [39b] Israel.

[W] " 'On the day of our king [when Jeroboam was made king] the princes became sick with the heat of wine; he stretched out his hand with mockers' (Hosea 7:5).

[X] "On the day on which Jeroboam began to reign over Israel, all Israel came to him at dusk, saying to him, 'Rise up and make an idol.'

[Y] "He said to them, 'It is already dusk. I am partly drunk and partly sober, and the whole people is drunk. But if you want, go and come back in the morning.'

[Z] "This is the meaning of the following Scripture, 'For like an oven their hearts burn with intrigue; all night their anger smolders[; in the morning it blazes like a flaming fire]' (Hosea 7:6)."

[AA] " 'All night their anger smolders.'

[BB] " 'In the morning it blazes like a flaming fire.'

[CC] "In the morning they came to him. Thus did he say to them, 'I know what you want. But I am afraid of your sanhedrin, lest it come and kill me.'

[DD] "They said to him, 'We shall kill them.'

[EE] "That is the meaning of the following verse: 'All of them are hot as an oven. And they devour their rulers' (Hos. 7:7)."

[FF] [Concurring with this view,] R. Levi said, "They slew them. Thus do you read in Scripture [to prove that 'the princes became sick' (HḤL) means 'the princes killed' (ḤLL)], 'If anyone is found slain [ḤLL] (Deut. 21:1).' "

[GG] Rabbi does not [concur. He maintains that] they removed them from their positions of power [but did not kill them].

[HH] "On the day of our king the princes became sick with the heat of wine" (Hosea 7:5)—it was the day on which the princes became sick.

[II] What made them sick? It was the heat of the wine, for they were thirsting for wine.

[JJ] "He stretched out his hand with the mockers."—

[KK] When he would see an honorable man, he would set up against him two mockers, who would say to him, "Now what generation do you think is the most cherished of all generations?"

[LL] He would answer them, "It was the generation of the wilderness [which received the Torah]."

[MM] They would say to him, "Now did they themselves not worship an idol?"

[NN] And he would answer them, "Now do you think that, because they were cherished, they were not punished for their deed?"

[OO] And they would say to him, "Shut up! The king wants to do exactly the same thing. Not only so, but [the generation of the wilderness] only made one [calf], while [the king] wants to make two."

[PP] "[So the king took counsel and made two calves of gold] and he set up one in Bethel, and the other he put in Dan (1 Kings 12:29)."

[QQ] The arrogance of Jeroboam is what condemned him decisively [or: certified him as a leper].

[RR] Said R. Yosé bar Jacob, "It was at the conclusion of a sabbatical year that Jeroboam began to rule over Israel. That is the meaning of the following verse: '[And Moses commanded them.] At the end of every seven years, at the set time of the year of release, at the feast of booths, when all Israel comes to appear before the Lord your God at the place which he will choose, you shall read this law before all Israel in their hearing' (Deut. 31:10–11).

[SS] "[Jeroboam] said, 'I shall be called upon to read [the Torah, as Scripture requires]. If I get up and read first, they will say to me, 'The king of the place [in which the gathering takes place, namely, Jerusalem] comes first.' And if I read second, it is disrespectful to me. And if I do not read at all, it is a humiliation for me. And, finally, if I let the people go up, they will abandon me and go over to the side of Rehoboam the son of Solomon.'

[TT] "That is the meaning of the following verse of Scripture: '[And Jeroboam said in his heart, Now the kingdom will turn back to the house of David;] if this people go up to offer sacrifices in the house of the Lord at Jerusalem, then the heart of this people will turn again to their Lord, to Rehoboam, king of Judah, and they will kill me and return to Rehoboam, king of Judah' (1 Kings 12:27–28).

[UU] "What then did he do? 'He made two calves of gold' (1 Kings 12:28), and he inscribed on their heart, '. . . lest they kill you' [as counsel to his successors].

[VV] "He said, 'Let every king who succeeds me look upon them.' "

[WW] Said R. Huna, " '[The wicked go astray from the womb, they err from their birth speaking lies. They have venom like the venom of a serpent, like the deaf adder that stops its ear, so that it does not hear the voice of charmers] or of the cunning caster of spells (Ps. 58:5). Whoever was associated with him [Jeroboam] he [Jeroboam] cast a spell over him [in the sin of the bull-calves]."

[XX] Said R. Huna, " '[Hearken, O house of the king! For the judgment pertains to you; for you have been a snare at Mizpah, and a net spread upon Tabor.] And they have made deep the pit of Shittim[, but I will chastise all of them]' (Hos. 5:1–2). For [Jeroboam] deepened the sin. He said, 'Whoever explains [the meaning of what has been inscribed on the bull-calves] I shall kill.' "

[YY] Said R. Abin bar Kahana, "Also in regard to the Sabbaths and the festivals we find that Jeroboam invented them on his own. That is the meaning of the following verse: 'And Jeroboam appointed a feast on the fifteenth day of the eighth month like the feast that was in Judah, and he offered sacrifices upon the altar[; so he did in Bethel, sacrificing to the calves that he had made]' (1 Kings 12:32).

[ZZ] "Thus he did in Bethel, having sacrifices made in a month that he made up on his own. This is as you read in Scripture, 'In addition to the Sabbaths of the Lord' (Lev. 23:23). [So Jeroboam confused the people by establishing his own calendar for Bethel, keeping the people from pilgrimages to Jerusalem in such a way.]"

[**II**.A] [If] one transgressed [the rule against doing business with gentiles three days before a pagan festival] and did business with one [of them], it is permitted [to derive benefit from the proceeds].

[B] R. Jacob bar Aḥa, R. Yosé in the name of R. Yoḥanan: "And [that is the rule for proceeds gained] even on the day of the pagan festival itself."

[C] And there is a Tannaitic tradition to the same effect: Under what circumstances? In the case of a gentile whom the Israelite does not know [is it prohibited to do business prior to a festival]. In the case of a gentile whom [the Israelite] knows, it is permitted, because it is as if he flatters them.

[D] It was taught in a Tannaitic teaching: [If one] entered a town and found the people celebrating, he celebrates with them, because it is only as if he flatters them.

[E] A certain *quaestor* honored Yudan the patriarch with a chest filled with dinars [in celebration of his festival]. [Yudan] took one of them and sent back the rest.

[F] He asked R. Simeon b. Laqish [whether it was permitted to derive benefit from the dinar he had accepted, since it was given to him in celebration of a pagan festival].

[G] He said to him, "Send any benefit derived from that coin[, that is, whatever you buy with it] to the Dead Sea[, for it is prohibited to benefit from the coin]."

[H] Now lo, you have a case in which this is post facto [as in the rule of A, above], and lo, you have a case in which this derives from someone whom the Israelite knows [as in the rule of C, above]. And yet has R. Simeon b. Laqish given instructions to send any benefit derived from that coin to the Dead Sea!

[I] Said R. Abbahu, "And I too—did not Rabban Gamaliel son of Rabbi inquire of me about the law governing going to a fair [in celebration of a pagan god], and I prohibited him from going?"

[J] And has it not been taught in a Tannaitic tradition: **They go to a [gentiles'] fair and purchase from them boy-slaves and girl-slaves [T. A.Z. 1:8C: "because he is as one who rescues these from their power"]?**

[K] R. Simeon b. Laqish said, "It is not the end of the matter [that one is permitted to go in order to purchase] Israelite slaves, but [it is permitted to go in order to purchase] even gentile [slaves], because in doing so one brings them under the wings of the Presence."

[L] What is then [the explanation of why Simeon ben Laqish prohibited Yudan from making use of the coin the gentile gave him in honor of the pagan festival]?

[M] Rabban Gamaliel [at the time of his inquiry] was a young man, and R. Abbahu wanted to set a fence about him [that he should not become accustomed to participating in pagan festivals].

[N] But R. Yudan the patriarch was an adult.

[O] Still, R. Simeon b. Laqish [for his part also] wished to set a limit to the matter.

[**III**.A] It is easy [to understand why sages have prohibited] lending anything to them [M. 1:1B]. But [why should it be forbidden] to borrow something from them?

[B] It is because [the borrower] then owes [the lender] gratitude[, which pleases the lender].

[C] It is easy to understand why sages have prohibited lending money to them. But [why should it be forbidden] to borrow money from them?

[D] It is because [the borrower] then owes [the lender] gratitude.

[E] It is easy to understand why [it should be prohibited] to pay them back a debt one owes. But [why should it be forbidden] to accept repayment for a debt owed by them?

[F] So that the idolator should not have occasion to say [that his idol] has assisted him [in paying back his debts, and the Israelite should thus be in the position of causing the idolator to feel gratitude to the idol].

[G] R. Ba bar Ṭablai in the name of Rab: "If it was an unsecured loan, it is permitted [to accept repayment for it on the occasion of a pagan festival]."

[H] And it has thus been taught in a Tannaitic teaching: An unsecured loan is witnessed solely by witnesses [orally]. A secured loan is one for which there is a bond of indebtedness.

[I] Even a loan secured by a bond is one which is insecure, for it is not at every moment that a man has the good fortune to collect what is owing to him.

[J] What then is [the definition of an unsecured loan]?

[K] An unsecured loan is one for which there is no security, and a secured loan is one which is covered by security [a pledge]. [The former may be collected on a pagan festival, the latter may not.]

[L] There is an extant Tannaitic tradition within the former definition: An unsecured loan is before witnesses[, not with a bond]. A secured loan is with a bond.

[**IV**.A] There we have learned: *[A woman may prepare her wedding adornments on the intermediate days of a festival.] R. Judah says, "She should not use lime, since this makes her ugly"* [M. M.Q. 1:7F–G] [and this prohibition applies even though later on the woman will be beautified, for on the festival itself it is disfiguring. So on the occasion of the festival we do not take account of later advantage].

[B] R. Ḥaninah and R. Mana—one said, "Concerning lime that the woman removes on the festival itself do the sages dispute, but concerning lime that she removes after the festival [there is no dispute], for it is forbidden [on the festival to make use of lime that imparts its benefit only afterward]."

[C] The other said, "Concerning lime that the woman removes after the festival itself do the sages dispute, but concerning lime that she removes on the festival [there is no dispute], for it is permitted."

[D] Now we do not know which one said this and which one said that.

[E] Now [let us infer the position of each] from that which R. Ḥaninah, R. Yosé in the name of R. Yoḥanan said: "R. Judah is consistent with his established position, as R. Judah has said in that case, 'Disfiguring for a moment is disfiguring [and is prohibited], so did he say in the present case that what is painful for a moment is painful [at the moment, even though he will be happy about it later, thus M. A.Z. 1:1E, F]."

[F] [In the light of R. Ḥaninah's observation about the position of R. Judah, then, we may infer] that it is he who said, "Concerning lime that the woman removes on the festival itself do the sages dispute, but concerning lime that she removes after the festival [there is no dispute], for it is forbidden." [For Judah will prohibit the lime removed during the festival, since it is disfiguring at *that* time, and this is without regard to the fact that later on—even on the festival itself—the woman will be glad she had put the lime on her skin.]

[V.A] **Israelite workmen who were working with a gentile at the time of their festival—in the case of [their doing so] in an Israelite's household, it is prohibited [to work on the occasion of the festival] [Tosefta; permitted]. In the case of [doing so] in a gentile's household, it is permitted [Tosefta: prohibited].**

[B] **R. Simeon b. Eleazar says, "[Tosefta: If he was hired by the day, whether working in the household of an Israelite or working in the household of a gentile, it is prohibited. If he was hired as a contractor, working in the household of an Israelite is permitted. Working in the household of a gentile is prohibited.]"** [The continuation of the discussion below indicates that the Tosefta's text is taken for granted by the Talmud, even though it is not cited in the printed text.]

[C] **"Under what circumstances? In the case of working on what is plucked [Tosefta: as yet unplucked]. But as to working on what is not yet plucked [Tosefta: plucked], it is prohibited.**

[D] **"And in another town, one way or the other, it is permitted" [T. A.Z. 1:3B–I].**

[E] What is the meaning of "one way or the other" [just now stated at D]?

[F] [It is permitted in another town for the Israelite to work for the gentile on the occasion of the festival] whether the crops are plucked or not yet plucked, whether as a day laborer or as a contractor [as at B].

[G] Said Rabbi, "No. Whether the crop is plucked or not yet plucked, [it is permitted] only on the condition that [the Israelite works] as a contractor [but not as a day laborer, in which circumstance he is paid for work done on the pagan festival and his salary is thus part of the remuneration deriving from idolatry]." [So Rabbi differs from Simeon b. Eleazar.]

[H] R. Simeon bar Borsenah in the name of R. Aḥa: "In regard to rules for the Sabbath, for mourning, and for the governance of idolatry, the law is in accord with the rulings of R. Simeon b. Eleazar."

[**VI**.A] *[R. Ishmael says, "Three days before them and three days after them it is prohibited for Israelites to do business with gentiles"]* [M. A.Z. 1:1G]. Associates state the reasoning of R. Ishmael. It is because of the [continuing celebration of] the meal associated with the festival [so, as the eating and carousing continue, Israelites should have no part of the matter, even after the festival day itself].

[B] Said R. Ba, "Since [the pagan] knows that it is prohibited for you to do business with him, it diminishes the celebration of his festival" [and that is the basis of Ishmael's reasoning that even after the festival one may not do business, for even on the festival the pagan will be concerned that later on he will be deprived of the benefit of Israelite trade].

[C] What is the difference between the two [explanations of R. Ishmael's position]?

[D] Selling [to a gentile even prior to the festival] things that do not last.

[E] In accord with the position of associates, it is prohibited to do so, and in accord with the position of R. Ba it is permitted to do so[, for in the former case, the fact that the articles will not last is immaterial, whereas in Ba's reasoning it is crucial. Associates will regard selling things that do not last as contributory to the pleasure of the festival, while Ba will not regard that as a critical issue. (Pené Moshe provides alternative explanations of C–E, which should be consulted *ad loc.*)].

[F] Said R. Yudan, "A verse of Scripture supports the position stated by associates: 'Now on the twenty-fourth day of this month [Tishri, after Sukkot] the people of Israel were assembled with fasting and in sackcloth and with earth upon their heads. [And the Israelites separated themselves from all foreigners and stood and confessed their sins]' (Neh. 9:1–2).

[G] "Now why is it not said that they did so on the twenty-third [since Sukkot ends on the twenty-second]? It was because of the [continuing celebration of] the meal of the festival [of Sukkot, which the people observed prior to that day. So the day after the festival ended was deemed a continuation of the celebration of the festival, and on this account the day of sackcloth and mourning was postponed until the twenty-fourth. The same reasoning applies to gentile festivals].

[H] "Now if you should propose that [they postponed the fast] because the twenty-third was the Sabbath [and not because of the aftereffects of the festival, as I claim], you in fact cannot do so. [For the twenty-third of Tishri cannot fall on the Sabbath, for, if it should,] you will then find the great fast [the Day of Atonement] coinciding with a Sunday[, and we do not observe two Sabbaths—the regular Sabbath and the Day of Atonement—in succession. If then the court observes that the Day of Atonement will coincide with a Sunday, they add a day to the prior month of Elul so that the Day of Atonement will fall on a Monday. So it cannot be because of the Sabbath, and the stated reason is the only valid explanation."]

[I] Now what difference does that make [and why should the Day of Atonement *not* fall on a Sunday]?!

[J] And did not R. Ḥoniah make light of someone who transferred [the Day of Atonement] from its anticipated time [on a Sunday]?

[K] Said R. Yoḥanan bar Madayya [39c], "I calculated the matter, and it in fact was *not* on the Sabbath [that is, the twenty-third of Tishri in the time of Ezra did not coincide with the Sabbath, and the reason of associates is valid]."

The Talmud approaches the Mishnah through a protracted exercise in scriptural exegesis. The matter of idolatry, in the Talmud's mind, begins with the Israelite version, specifically, the two calves erected by Jeroboam. Consequently, a rather roundabout route is taken at the outset to make possible the introduction of Jeroboam and the Scriptures deemed relevant to him. Once these verses come into view, at **I**.G, the true focus and thus intent of the whole also become clear. Jeroboam's idolatry and the reasons for it are relevant because the Talmud wishes to take up Israelite participation in idolatry and the reasons for it. If this interpretation is sound, then what the Mishnah's rule has triggered is the notion that Israelites might participate in pagan celebrations. Since the Mishnah's intent is to prohibit any possible benefit from such participation, the Talmud then makes its comment on those who might contemplate the matter to begin with. That is why, I think, the Israelite version of idolatry is introduced at the outset. The specific verses chosen for discussion, dealing with Jeroboam and deriving also from Amos and Hosea, then are treated within their own discipline and framework. I see no trace of an effort to introduce distinctively contemporary considerations into the exegesis of the cited verses.

The five units (**II–VI**) that take up the details of the laws of the Mishnah pericope begin in the consideration of a rather general question about the disposition of profits gained in the violation of the Mishnah's law. From that point the specific exegesis of the Mishnah's materials begins. **III** turns to M. 1:1B–C. **IV** then proceeds, by a rather circuitous route, to M. 1:1E–F, using the materials in a remarkably subtle and interesting juxtaposition of two discrete cases, related in their most fundamental supposition. The exegesis of both cases is advanced in their juxtaposition. **V** takes up a pericope of the Tosefta relevant to the Mishnah. Then **VI** proceeds to the exegesis of Ishmael's position at M. 1:1G.

1:2

[A] *These are the festivals of gentiles:*

[B] *[1] Kalends, [2] Saturnalia, [3] Kratesis [the commemoration of the empire],*

[C] *and [4] the emperor's anniversary, [5] his birthday, "and [6] the day of his death," the words of R. Meir.*

[D] *And sages say, "In any case of death rites in which there is a burning, there is idolatry, and in which there is no burning, there is no idolatry."*

[**I**.A] Rab said, "Their testimonies [spelling the word for festivals at M. 1:2A with an ʿayin]."

[B] And Samuel said, "Their calamity [with an ʾalef]."

[C] He who claims that the word is spelled with an ʿayin [as "their testimonies,"] draws evidence from the following verse: "Let them bring their witnesses to justify them" (Is. 43:9).

[D] And he who claims that the word is spelled with an ʾalef, as "their festivals," draws evidence from the following verse: "For the day of their calamity (ʾYDM) is at hand" (Deut. 32:35).

[E] Rab said, "They add a piece [ʾBR] to a town [in connection with the Sabbath limits]."

[F] Samuel said, "They augment from within [ʿBR]."

[G] The one who said, "They add" understands the law to mean that they augment the city with a limb [ʾBR].

[H] The one who said, "They augment from within [ʿBR] compares the matter to a pregnant woman [MʿWBRT]." [The Leiden MS and *editio princeps* read: ʿWBRH.]

[I] Rab said [in reference to the Mishnah pericope, They say a blessing over a flame only once they make use of (or: derive pleasure) from its light], "They derive pleasure [YʾWTW]."

[J] And Samuel said, "They make use [YʿWTW]."

[K] The one who maintains that the correct reading is with an 'alef derives evidence from the following verse: "Only on this condition will we consent (N'WT) to you" (Gen. 34:15).

[L] The one who maintains that the correct reading is with an ʿayin cites the following verse: "That I may know how to sustain [ʿWT] with a word him who is weary" (Is. 50:4).

[**II**.A] Rab said, "Kalends did the first man found.

[B] "When he saw that the nights were getting longer, he said, 'Woe is me. Perhaps him concerning whom it is written, "He shall bruise your head, and you shall bruise his heel" (Gen. 3:15)—perhaps he is going to come and bite me.'

[C] " 'Even the darkness is not dark to thee, [the night is bright as the day; for darkness is as light with thee]' (Ps. 139:12).

[D] "When [the first man] saw that the days were growing longer, he said, 'Kalendes—*Kalondeo!* Praise be to God!' "

[E] Now this view is in accord with the position of the one who said that it was in Tishri [in the autumn] that the world was created [so that Adam saw the nights growing longer, but did not know that, after 21 December, the days would again begin to grow longer].

[F] But in accord with the opinion of the one who maintained that in Nisan the world was created, Adam already knew [that it was normal for the days to grow shorter in the fall, longer in the spring, so there was no need to fear, and this account of the origin of Kalends then is not credible].

[G] Said R. Yosé b. R. Bun, "Who is of the opinion that it was on the New Year [of Tishri] that the world was created? It is Rab, for it has been taught in the verses associated with the sounding of the shofar [on the New Year] of the school of Rab [that the world was created on the New Year, as follows]: 'This day is the beginning of your works [of creation], a memorial to the first day [of creation].' It follows that the world was created on the New Year." [It follows that Rab is consistent in assigning the origin of Kalends to the time when the world was created in the autumn, and Adam's fear upon observing that the days were growing shorter and his joy upon noting that they were again growing longer.]

[B] *and a gentile who made a banquet for his son—*

[C] *it is prohibited for only that day, and in regard to that individual alone [to enter into business relationships of any sort, as listed at M. 1:1].*

[**I**.A] [Is the stated prohibition of business dealings with an individual gentile on the specified occasions applicable] to that day alone, or [does it apply] to that day from one year to the next?

[B] [The solution to the problem is clear,] for it has been taught: "The day on which he shaves off his beard and the day on which his son shaves off his beard—it is forbidden [and that cannot be deemed an annual festival, for two distinct days are subject to discussion, and if it were annual, both would be celebrated on the same day (Pené Moshe)].

[C] But you may interpret the cited tradition to mean that both of them shaved on the same day [so the foregoing interpretation does not solve the problem].

[D] And has it not been taught: [The days of] his banquet and the banquet of his son are forbidden [with the same consequences as are spelled out at B]?

[E] But you may interpret the cited tradition to mean that both of them shaved at one time when they got married.

[F] And has it not been taught: his birthday and the birthday of his son are forbidden? Now do you have the possibility of claiming that both of them were born simultaneously?

[G] You may interpret the cited tradition to mean that [the father] did not suffice [to celebrate his birthday] on the specified day before a son was born to him, so he celebrated [both birthdays] at one time.

[**II**.A] It has been taught in a Tannaitic teaching [T. B.Q. 7:8]: **One should not send [to his fellow] jugs of wine that already have been sold to a storekeeper,** for this is as if to impose upon him an empty claim [for in opening many jugs as if to honor a guest, in fact there is no loss]. **One should not pressure his fellow to come as his guest when he does not want to do so. He should not overwhelm his fellow with gifts knowing that he will not accept them.**

[B] What is the meaning of the use of "gifts" [instead of "presents," that is, TQRWBT instead of MTNWT]?

[H] R. Yoḥanan did not hold that same opinion, but [maintained] that [there is a different origin for Kalends, as follows:] the kingdom of Egypt and the kingdom of Rome were at war with one another. They declared, "Now how long are we going to kill one another in battle? Come and let us make a rule that whichever kingdom will say to its chief general, 'Fall on your sword [and kill yourself],' and [whose general] will listen to that command—[that kingdom] will seize the power [over both of us] first.' [Now] the Egyptian [general] did not hearken to them.

"The [general] of the Romans was a certain old man. Now his name was Januarius. He had twelve sons. They said to him, 'Now if you will hearken unto us [and fall on your sword], we shall make your sons dukes, hyparchs, and generals.' So he hearkened to them [and fell on his sword and he died]. Thus then did his sons cry out for him, 'Kalendes Januarius!' From the day following and onward, they mourned for him, 'The black day!' "

[I] Said R. Yudan of En-Todros "Whoever sows lentils on that day—they will not flourish."

[**III**.A] Rab said, "[Doing business with gentiles three days before] Kalends is forbidden in the case of all [gentiles]."

[B] R. Yoḥanan said, "It is forbidden only [to do business] with those who worship on that day."

[C] [Supply: Rab said,] "Saturnalia is forbidden in the case of all [gentiles]."

[D] R. Yoḥanan said, "With reference to both Kalends and Saturnalia, it is forbidden only [to do business] with those who worship on that day."

[E] Associates asked whether the wives of those who worship are deemed equivalent to those who worship [so that one may not do business with the wives, even if the women themselves do not observe the holy day].

[F] R. Abbahu asked about the status of [a place named] Taqsis in Caesarea.

[G] Since there are many Samaritans, it is deemed to be tantamount to a place of the worship of idolatry.

[H] But as to Taqsis in the town of Duqsis it is necessary to make inquiry.

[I] R. Bibi sent R. Zeira to buy him a small web at the fair of the Saturnalia of Beishan. He came to R. Yosé [to find out whether this was permitted]. He considered giving him instruction in accord with the position of R. Joshua b. Levi [that it was] permitted to do so, but he gave him instruction in accord with the opinion of R. Yoḥanan [that it was] forbidden.

[**IV**.A] [Supply: *Kalends*] Rab said, "Kalends comes eight days before the winter solstice, and Saturnalia is eight days afterward."

[B] Said R. Yoḥanan, "Peroqto is the beginning of the season."

[C] R. Ba in the name of Rab: "There are three festival seasons in Babylonia, and three festal seasons in Media. The three festal seasons in Babylonia are Mahuri, Kanauni, and Banauta. The three festal seasons in Media are Nausardi, Tiriasqi, and Mahirkana."

[D] R. Huna in the name of R Naḥman b. Jacob: "Nauros [new year] is on the second of Adar in Persia, on the twentieth of Adar in Media."

[E] Saturnalia means "hidden hatred" [*Sina'ah ṭemunah*]: [The Lord] hates, takes vengeance, and punishes.

[F] This is in accord with the following verse: "Now Esau hated Jacob" (Gen. 27:41).

[G] Said R. Isaac b. R. Eleazar, "In Rome they call it Esau's Saturnalia."

[H] Kratesis: It is the day on which the Romans seized power.

[I] Now has this opinion already been assigned [to Kalends, by Yoḥanan who said that the day on which Rome seized power is Kalends, not Kratesis]?

[J] Said R. Yosé b. R. Bun, "It [celebrates] the second time [that Rome seized power]."

[K] Said R. Levi, "It is the day on which Solomon intermarried with the family of Pharaoh Neccho, king of Egypt. On that day Michael came down and thrust a reed into the sea, and pulled up muddy alluvium, and this was turned into a huge pot, and this was the great city of Rome. On the day on which Jeroboam set up the two golden calves, Remus and Romulus came and built two huts in the city of Rome. On the day on which

Elijah disappeared, a king was appointed i
no king in Edom, a deputy was king" (1 K

[L] The emperor's anniversary: "On the third da
Pharaoh's birthday, he made a feast for all his
40:20).

[M] His birthday and the day of his death: To this p
nah pericope refers] to public [celebrations]. Fron
forward it refers to individual [celebrations, which
bidden when accompanied by idolatrous rites].

[N] Now it has been written, "You shall die in peace. An
were burned for your fathers, the former kings who w
fore you, so men shall burn spices for you and lament
(Jer. 34:5).

[O] And thus does the Mishnah teach: In the case of any deat
rites in which there are incense and burning, there is idola
and in which there are no incense and burning, there is no
idolatry [cf. M. 1:2D].

The Mishnah's listed festivals are of two sorts, public and private, as **IV**.M observes. The latter are anniversaries of the reigning emperor. Kalends was the Roman new year; Saturnalia was a December *mardi gras;* and Kratesis marked the commemoration of the conquest of the eastern provinces by the Roman empire. C's items are clear as specified. The sages do not disagree with C[4], [5]. D means that to Meir should be attributed only B[6], as I have indicated. The reasoning of the sages is clear as given. The Talmud's treatment of the Mishnah's materials begins at **II** with some stories about the origins of the named holy days. **III** then quite logically proceeds to laws governing those same days. **IV** appears to intend a systematic glossing of the Mishnah's list; that is surely the case at **IV**.H, L, and M. The order of these materials generally is gloss, law, story, rather than as it is before us.

1:3

[A] *[1] On the day on which [a gentile] shaves off his beard and lock of hair, [2] on the day on which he came up safely from an ocean voyage, [3] on the day on which he got out of prison,*

[C] [It is the sort of invitation extended after the fact, when there is no space for more guests, when the pretended host says,] "Wash, sit in the corner over there" [when in fact there is no room].

[D] And in Jerusalem [there was the custom of] turning the buckle from the right to the left shoulder [as an indication that there was no more space properly to receive guests].

[**III**.A] It has been taught in a Tannaitic teaching: **A city in which Israelites and gentiles live—if the gentiles contribute to the charity collectors, they collect the funds from them and from Israelites, and they provide support for the poor of the gentiles just as they do for the poor of Israelites. They visit the sick of the gentiles just as they do for the sick of Israelites. They comfort the mourners of gentile deceased just as they do for the mourners of Israelite deceased. They bury the dead of gentiles just as they do for the dead of Israelites. They bring in the utensils of gentiles and the utensils of Israelites—[all] on account of peace** [T. Git. 3:13–14 (not verbatim)].

[B] The [Israelite] folk of Girda asked R. Ami, "As to the day on which gentiles make a feast, what is the law [about doing business with them]?"

[C] He considered permitting it to them on the grounds of maintaining peace [in relationships, in line with A].

[D] Said to him R. Ba, "And did not R. Ḥiyya teach: 'The day of a banquet of gentiles it is forbidden [to do business with them]'?"

[E] Said R. Ami, "Were it not for R. Ba, we should have ended up permitting their idolatrous practices. So blessed is the Omnipresent who has kept us distant from them!"

1:3A refers to personal holidays, A[1] to the offering to an idol of the first growth of a beard or a lock, a puberty rite; the others are clear as specified. C gives the rule covering all these items (A–B). **I** raises the question of the extent of the application of the prohibition of M. 1:3A[1], B. The question is left moot. **II** is totally out of place. The point of citing **III**.A is clear at B–E, which through a story set the limits of what may be done in the interests of peace. Surely **III**.D falls well within the frame of the Mishnah's position on the same question.

1:4

[A] *A city in which there is an idol—*

[B] *[in the area] outside of it it is permitted [to do business].*

[C] *[If] an idol was outside of it, [in the area] inside it is permitted.*

[D] *What is the rule as to going to that place?*

[E] *When the road is set aside for going to that place only, it is prohibited.*

[F] *But if one is able to take that same road to some other place, it is permitted.*

[G] *A town in which there is an idol,*

[H] *and there were in it shops that were adorned and shops that were not adorned—*

[I] *this was a case in Beth Shean, and sages ruled, "Those that are adorned are prohibited, but those that are not adorned are permitted."*

[**I**.A] *[A city in which there is an idol]*—lo, [if the idol is] inside of [the city], it is forbidden [to do business in that city].

[B] Now is it merely because there is a single statue in the city that it should be forbidden to do business in that city?

[C] R. Simeon b. Laqish said, "It was in connection with a market[-day] that they have taught this rule."

[D] And what is the difference between the rule [applying when the idol is] inside of the [city] and [when the idol is] outside of it [if we speak of a market-day]?

[E] [When the idol is] inside of [the city], it is a case in which the [idol] derives benefit from the imposts [levied on the business done at the fair, and so it is] forbidden. [But when the idol is] outside [of the city], it is permitted [to do business] because [the temple of idolatry] does not derive benefit from the imposts [levied in connection with the fair].

[F] And if [the idol] was outside of it [but still] derived benefit from the imposts [levied on account of the fair], also [doing business when the idol is] outside of it is forbidden.

[**II**.A] Now has it not been taught: **"They go to a fair and purchase from there boy-slaves and girl-slaves and cattle [T. A.Z. 1:8C]?**

[B] R. Simeon b. Laqish said, "It is not the end of the matter that they may purchase Israelite slaves, but even gentile slaves [one may purchase at a fair held in honor of idolatry], for one brings them under the wings of the Presence." [So M. 1:4 prohibits what this tradition would encourage.]

[C] Now has it not been taught: "If one has purchased from there a suit of clothing, it is to be burned; a beast, it is to be hobbled; coins—they are to be taken to the Salt Sea"?

[D] Now one may explain burning a suit of clothes, tossing coins into the Salt Sea, or hobbling a beast.

[E] But has it not been taught: **They go to a fair and purchase from there boy-slaves and girl-slaves and cattle?** R. Simeon b. Laqish said, "It is not the end of the matter that they may purchase Israelite slaves, but even gentile slaves [one may purchase at a fair held in honor of idolatry], for one brings them under the wings of [39d] Heaven."

[F] One should interpret this opinion to apply to one Israelite [who purchases] from another Israelite[, in which case there is no celebration of the pagan festival and no contradiction with our Mishnah pericope].

[G] But has it not been taught: He who sells his slave to gentiles—the proceeds are prohibited? [Now, where did this Israelite get the slave? That is, if it was from a gentile, how did the first Israelite sell the slave to the gentile, who then sold it to another Israelite? For it is forbidden for the first Israelite to sell his slave to the gentile.]

[H] Here too one should interpret the case to speak of an Israelite purchasing from another Israelite.

[**III**.A] An Israelite who is on his way to a fair—they purchase [goods] from him, because it is as one who saves [property] from [gentiles'] possession. But when he is on his way back, it is forbidden to do so, for whatever he has in hand has been given to him on account of idolatry. And in the case of gentiles, one way or the other, whether they are going to the fair or whether they are coming back from the fair, it is permitted [to do business with them] [cf. T. A.Z. 1:15].

[B] R. Ba son of R. Ḥiyya bar Ba in the name of R. Yoḥanan: "If [the gentile was] the innkeeper, it is permitted [to buy from him]."

[C] R. Zeira asked, "Is the rule that in the case of a fair it is forbidden to do business with a gentile, but in the case of a gentile innkeeper [PWNDQ] it is permitted to do so? [That makes no sense.] Is it possible that R. Yoḥanan laid down such a rule in connection with trading in goods [PRGMṬY']?"

[D] R. Ba son of R. Ḥiyya bar Ba in the name of R. Yoḥanan: "If it was the case of an innkeeper, it is permitted [to do business] in connection with trading in goods."

[E] Said R. Yoḥanan, R. Abbahu in the name of R. Yoḥanan: "If one has exchanged a beast for an idol, [the beast] is prohibited. [The supposition is that the meaning of the case is as follows: If a gentile exchanged a beast for an idol, the beast is prohibited for Israelite use.]"

[F] R. Ḥisda asked, "If [the gentile] had bowed down to the beast itself, it would not have been forbidden[, for a beast is not forbidden for an ordinary Israelite's use merely because a gentile has worshiped it]. Now because the beast has been exchanged for an idol, will the beast then be forbidden? [This is incommensurate to the case.] Perhaps [R. Yoḥanan stated the rule] in the case of a business agreement that came into force before the holding of festival[, in which case the beast is forbidden for a specified period and not for all time, as we had originally thought]."

[G] R. Zeira, R Abbahu in the name of R. Yoḥanan: "If one has traded a beast for an idol, it is forbidden in the case of a business deal that was entered into before a fair."

[H] Said R. Abbahu, "It is forbidden to make up a band of [Israelite] traders in connection with a fair."

[I] And there is a Tannaitic tradition to the same effect: **[A person should not do business with a gentile on the day of his festival, nor on such an occasion should one talk frivolously,] nor should one ask after his welfare in a situation that is taken**

into account. But if one happened to come across him in a routine way, he asks how he is with all due respect [T. A.Z. 1:2].

[**IV**.A] R. Ḥiyya bar Vava sent someone to buy him a sandal at the fair in Tyre.

Said to him R. Jacob bar Aḥa, "Now are you among those who buy things at a fair?"

He said to him, "Now have you never in your life purchased pressed olives?"

He said to him, "But that is different, for R. Yoḥanan said, 'They have not prohibited [buying at a fair] something that is necessary to sustain life.' "

[B] R. Simeon b. Yoḥanan sent and asked R. Simeon b. Yoṣedeq, "Have you ever looked into the character of the fair held at Tyre?"

[C] He replied, "Yes, and [if] you give me two litras of pepper for my stock[, I'll answer your question]!"

[D] So [instead, he personally] went up [to the fair at Tyre] and found written there, "I, Diocletian the emperor, have founded the fair of Tyre for the fortune of Archeleus, my brother, for eight days" [so the fair was indeed for the sake of idolatry].

[E] R. Isaac bar Naḥman asked R. Ḥaninah about the character of the fair at Gaza.

[F] He said to him, "Now have you ever gone to the fair at Tyre? And did you see an Israelite and a gentile as partners in a single pot, without scrupling that the gentile has stirred the pot[, and Israelites may not eat food cooked by gentiles]?"

[G] Now had he asked him a question of one sort, and the other had replied to him in this way?

[H] But the reason was that, since R. Ḥaninah would never say a word that he had not heard in his life [from his teacher], on that account, while the one asked him one thing, he replied with another.

[I] Came R. Yosé b. R. Bun, Abba bar Hana in the name of R. Yoḥanan: "They prohibited a fair only in the case of one of the character of that at Botnah."

[J] And it has been taught along these same lines in a Tannaitic tradition: There are three fairs, the fair at Gaza, the fair at

Acre, and the fair at Botnah, and the most debased of the lot of them is the fair at Botnah.

[K] What is the law as to going there?

[L] If one were a wayfarer, it is prohibited to do so, but if he were a resident of that town, it is permitted to do so.

[M] A caravan is permitted to do so, for it is surely the normal way of a caravan to travel hither and yon.

[**V**.A] *[And there were in it shops that were adorned and shops that were not adorned* (M. 1:4H)].—With what are they adorned?

[B] R. Yoḥanan said, "With myrtle."

[C] R. Simeon b. Laqish said, "With any sort of decorative leaves."

[D] In accord with the opinion of R. Yoḥanan, all [such shops adorned with myrtle] are prohibited.

[E] In accord with the opinion of R. Simeon B. Laqish, prohibited are only the shops bearing additional decorations[; since it was routine to decorate the shops anyhow, only the ones with additional wreaths may not be patronized].

[F] What would be a practical illustration of such a case?

[G] If the storekeeper was accustomed to put out five baskets [of produce], and he put out ten [on a given day], if you say that he put out the extra ones as a decoration on account of the feast day of the idol, it is prohibited to patronize the shop. If you say that he did so merely for displaying his wares for sale, it is permitted to patronize the shop.

The opening unit, **I**, undertakes an exegesis of the Mishnah's language. The second one then goes on to deal with the substance of the Mishnah's clearcut prohibition of doing business with idolatry. Unit **II** points out that there are conditions under which some hold that it is permitted to attend a fair. The solution to the problem is not successful. Some sort of lower criticism surely is needed to deal with the repetition of A–B at E. What is clear is that the Talmud wishes to point out discrete trends of thought on the topic of the Mishnah. **III** then adds amplifying materials, specifically analyzing a sequence of rules relevant to but independent of the Mishnah. After the opening item, A, all of **III**'s materials come from Yoḥanan, involving questions of clarification from Zeira, Abbahu, and Ḥisda. The purpose of unit **IV** is to supply some cases on the conduct of various rabbinical authorities in regard to fairs. Here we see criticism of a far more lenient position than the Mishnah and the antecedent clarifications of the Mishnah suggest were available. Finally, proceeding onward, **V** takes up M. 1:4H's rule and provides some useful clarifications. In all the Talmud is coherent and well arranged.

1:5

[A] *These are things [that it is] forbidden to sell to gentiles:*

[B] *[1] fir-cones, [2] white figs [3] and their stalks, [4] frankincense,*
and [5] a white cock.

[C] *R. Judah says, "It is permitted to sell him a white cock among other cocks.*

[D] *"And when it is all by itself, one cuts off its spur and sells it to him,*

[E] *"for [idolators] do not offer to an idol one that is lacking [a spur]."*

[F] *And as to everything else, [if] they are left without specification [as to their proposed use], it is permitted, but [if] they are specified [for use for idolatry], it is prohibited.*

[G] *R. Meir says, "Also fine dates, Ḥaṣab and Nicolaus dates is it prohibited to sell to gentiles."*

[**I**.A] Simeon bar Ba in the name of R. Yoḥanan: "*White figs* on their stalks, *fir cones* with their attachments."

[B] *Frankincense:* It has been taught in a Tannaitic tradition: **If it was a bundle, it is permitted [to sell to gentiles]. And how much is a bundle? R. Judah b. Beterah says, "A bundle of frankincense is no less than five varieties" [T. A.Z. 1:21A–C].**

[C] If [the customer] was a priest, it is forbidden to sell to him[, since he will certainly use the frankincense for idolatry]. [If he is] a physician, it is permitted. [If he is] a wholesale merchant, it is permitted. [If he is] a merchant suspect of idolatrous practices, it is forbidden.

[**II**.A] We repeat in the Mishnah pericope [the version]: *A white cock.*

[B] R. Ḥiyya repeated [for his version of] the Mishnah pericope: A cock of any sort.

[C] The present version of the Mishnah [specifying a white cock] requires also the version of R. Ḥiyya, and the version of R. Ḥiyya requires also the [present] version of the Mishnah.

[D] [Why both?] If we repeated [the present version of the Mishnah], and we did not repeat the version of R. Ḥiyya, we should have reached the conclusion that the sages state the rule only in regard to a white cock, but as to any sort of cock other than that, even if this was all by itself [M. 1:5D], it is permitted. Thus there was need for the Mishnah version of R. Ḥiyya.

[E] Now if one repeated the version of R. Ḥiyya, and we did not repeat the version before us in the Mishnah, we should have ruled that the rule applies only in the case of an unspecified cock [requested by the purchaser], but [if the purchaser requested] a white cock, then even if this was all by itself, it would be prohibited [to sell such a cock].

[F] Thus there was need for the Mishnah version as it is repeated before us, and there also was need for the Mishnah version as it is repeated by R. Ḥiyya.

[G] Said R. Bun bar Ḥiyya, "[In Ḥiyya's view, if a gentile said, 'Who has] a cock to sell,' one may sell him a white cock, [so Ḥiyya differs from, and does not merely complement, the version of the Mishnah pericope]."

[H] [Now if the gentile should say, "Who has] a white cock to sell," we then rule that if the white cock is by itself, it is forbidden, but if part of a flock of cocks, it is permitted to sell it to him. [This clearly is the position of the Mishnah pericope, so there is no dispute at all, merely complementary traditions, as argued at D–E (Pené Moshe).]

[**III**.A] R. Bun bar Ḥiyya raised the following question: "[If] one saw a flock of cocks pecking at a dung heap, and there was a white cock among them, and [a gentile] said, 'To whom do these belong?' [what is the rule]?

[B] "Do we rule that it is as if he completed [the sentence, 'To whom does the white cock belong?' in which case it is as if he wanted only that one, and it is then forbidden to sell him the lot, or do we rule that, since he did not make explicit his interest in the white cock, one may sell him the whole lot?" The question is not answered].

[C] [If the cock] was lacking a spur naturally, does one rule that one lacking by nature do the pagans offer for idolatry [or not]?

[D] "And when you offer blind animals in sacrifice [is that no evil? And when you offer those that are lame or sick, is that no evil?]" (Malachi 1:8)

[E] Thus does [Scripture] state that they do offer to idolatry one that is [naturally] lacking a spur.

[**IV**.A] *R. Meir says, "Also fine dates, Ḥaṣab and Nicolaus dates, it is prohibited to sell to gentiles"* (M. 1:5G).

[B] R. Ḥama bar ʿUqbah said, "[He refers to] caryota [dates]."

[C] R. Eleazar b. R. Yosé said, "It is a species [in its own right], and its name is Ḥaṣada."

[D] [If] one transgressed and sold [these kinds of dates, what is the rule as to the disposition of the proceeds]?

[E] The rule is in accord with that which R. Eleazar said [below, at M. 1:7], "If one transgressed and built [a building with them, for use as a basilica], [the proceeds nonetheless are] permitted, and so here too, [if] one transgressed and sold [them the prohibited kinds of dates, the proceeds are] permitted."

The Talmud's principal interest, unit **II**, is in the reading of M. 1:5B[5]. Ḥiyya presents a version of the Mishnah that omits the specification of a *white* cock. His version then will allow the sale of no cocks, white or otherwise. Rather than attempt to read M. 1:5B[5] in the light of M. 1:5C–D (which then requires the specification of a *white* cock, for otherwise, Judah's point of difference is incomprehensible), the Talmud takes a different route. It attempts to work things out by harmonizing the two readings and showing that each version is important by itself as well as in relation to the other. This approach is rejected by Ḥiyya's son, who insists that between the two readings there is a clear difference in substance. The themes of the materials of unit **II** (M. 1:5B–E) are carried forward in unit **III**, which takes up two points. First, Bun bar Ḥiyya asks about the interpretation of language used by a gentile in purchasing cocks. Second, an acute question is addressed to M. 1:5D. Unit **IV**, like unit **I**, simply provides some clarification of the language and rule of the Mishnah. In all the treatise is concise but by no means simple.

1:6

[A] *In a place in which they are accustomed to sell small cattle to gentiles, they sell them.*

[B] *In a place in which they are accustomed not to sell [small cattle] to them, they do not sell them.*

[C] *And in every locale they do not sell them large cattle, calves, or foals, whether whole or lame.*

[D] *R. Judah permits in the case of lame ones.*

[E] *And Ben Beterah permits in the case of horses.*

[**I**.A] [Now since the Mishnah pericope states that it is permitted to sell small cattle to gentiles, does it follow that] it is permitted to raise them [to begin with in the Holy Land]?

[B] Said R. Ba, "[The Mishnah speaks of raising small cattle in a place such as] Mehir, which is sixteen mil by sixteen mil[, a wilderness area in the Holy Land in which it is permitted to do so]."

[C] They proposed to rule: He who stated that it is permitted to sell them maintains that it is permitted to set them aside, and he who stated that it is prohibited to sell them maintains that it is prohibited also to set them aside [in corrals of gentiles, cf. M. 2:1A].

[D] R. Jonah, R. Eliezer in the name of Rab: "And even in accord with the one who maintained that it is permitted to sell them, it still is forbidden to set them aside."

[E] What then is the difference [in the opinion of that party, D] between selling them and setting them aside?

[F] When one actually sells the beast to a gentile, it becomes tantamount to a beast belonging to a gentile. But when he sets it aside for a gentile, it remains tantamount to a beast belonging to an Israelite and [the gentile] is suspect [concerning such a beast, on the count of bestiality].

[**II**.A] *In a place in which they are not accustomed to sell [small cattle] to them, they do not sell them [M. A.Z. 1:6B].*

[B] What is the reason [for this rule]? Because one thereby removes the small cattle [from the category of obligation to the rule requiring that the first] fleece [be given to the priest].

[C] But take note of the case in which it was a goat [so there is no fleece].

[D] [Then the reason is] that one removes [the beast from the obligation to give] the firstborn [to the priest].

[E] But take note of the case in which it was a male.

[F] [The reason then is] that one removes the beast from the obligation to give [to the priest] the gifts [of the cheeks and maw when it is slaughtered].

[G] If that is the operative reasoning, then one should not sell wheat to a gentile, because one removes it from the obligation of giving the dough-offering [of bread made from the wheat to the priest]; one should not sell wine and oil to a gentile, because one removes them from the very obligation of there being a blessing [before they are consumed].

[**III**.A] *And in every locale they do not sell them large cattle [calves, or foals, whether whole or lame]* (M. 1:6C).

[B] What is the reason for this ruling? Because in the case of a large beast there is the possibility [that the gentile will work the beast on the Sabbath and so impose on the Israelite, who retains responsibility,] the liability for a sin-offering.

[C] But in the case of a small beast, there is no possibility of incurring liability for a sin-offering [for the stated reason does not apply].

[D] But does [the gentile] not milk or shear [the small beast]?

[E] One should say: in the case of a small beast, the liability falls upon the beast, but in the case of the large beast, it falls upon the one who works it[, and the gentile's deeds with the beast are the Israelite's responsibility].

[F] Still, once the Israelite sells the beast to the gentile, does the beast not become tantamount to the beast of a gentile [so that the Israelite no longer has to scruple about what the gentile does with the beast on the Sabbath? So what concern is there that the Israelite incur liability for a sin-offering?]

[G] R. Ami, the Babylonian, in the name of the rabbis there [(in Babylonia) states the reason]: "Sometimes [the Israelite] sells [the beast] to a gentile in order to try the beast out, and the gentile may then return the beast after three days, so it turns out that the gentile performs a prohibited act of labor [on the Sabbath] with a beast belonging to an Israelite."

[H] If that is the operative ruling, then if it is for a test, it should be prohibited, but if it is not for a test, it should be permitted.

[I] The one [has been prohibited] because of the other.

[**IV**.A] [If] one transgressed [the law in a locale in which it is prohibited to sell such beasts to gentiles] and sold [such a beast to a gentile], do they impose a fine upon him [so depriving the Israelite of the use of the proceeds]?

[B] Just as the sages impose such a penalty on the Israelite in the case of the violation of a law [e.g., deliberately blemishing a firstling so that the priest has no claim to it], so they impose a penalty on him for the violation of a custom [operative in a given locale].

[C] And how do we know that they impose such a penalty upon a person for violating [what is merely] a local custom?

[D] [There is this precedent.] A certain person sold a camel to an Aramaean. The case came before R. Simeon b. Laqish, who imposed a penalty on him of twice the proceeds, so that [the Israelite] would go after the [Aramaean purchaser] and recover the camel.

[E] Said R. Yosé b. R. Bun, "[Simeon b. Laqish] imposed the fine on the middleman [40a], [and not on the Israelite who had sold the beast to the middleman], and they used to insult [the child of the middleman], "A son of the Aramaeans' agent!""

[F] [In imposing such a fine, even though, in law, the man was exempt from such a fine,] R. Simeon b. Laqish was in accord with R. Judah.

[G] For it has been taught in a Tannaitic tradition in the name of R. Judah:

[H] **R. Judah says, "He who receives a beast from a gentile and it produced a firstling estimates its value and gives half of its value to the priest. If he handed one over to him under contract, lo, this one estimates it, and hands over the entire price to a priest." And sages say, "Since the finger of a gentile is mixed up in the matter, it is free of the law of the firstling [and there is no obligation to give the priest anything]."** [So it follows that Judah is willing to impose a penalty for entering an illicit agreement with the gentile, even in such a case in which, so far as the law is concerned, there is no obligation at all (cf. T. Bekh. 2:1G–I).]

[I] [It is not that Simeon b. Laqish merely is in agreement with the basic position of Judah.] R. Simeon b. Laqish goes further than the position of R. Judah.

[J] The ruling of R. Judah is made because of violation of the laws of the firstling [which derive from the Torah], while the ruling of R. Simeon b. Laqish is made because of violation of the laws against raising small cattle [which do not derive from the Torah; nonetheless, even for violation of such minor matters, Simeon b. Laqish is willing to impose a drastic fine for violation of those laws].

[**V**.A] *R. Judah permits in the case of lame ones* [M. 1:6D].

[B] R. Judah ruled only in regard to a lame beast that is not subject to healing [so it will not be used for labor on the Sabbath].

[C] They said to him, "Now is it not so that the gentile may bring a male to her, and the male will crouch over her, and she will give birth [so why may we permit the sale of a lame beast]?"

[D] He said to them, "But I for my part have made such a ruling only in the case of a male horse which is not subject to healing."

[E] They said to him "Now is it not so that the gentile may then bring a female to him, and the male will crouch over her, and the female will give birth? [So how can you permit even in this case, for the embryo will be born and will be worked on the Sabbath?]"

[F] R. Abin in the name of the rabbis from there [Babylonia]: "That is to say that it is prohibited to make available for sale [to gentiles] the embryo [of an unborn beast]."

[G] There we have learned (M. Bekh. 1:1): *He who purchases the unborn offspring of the ass of a gentile, and he who sells it to him (even though one is not permitted to do so), and he who is a partner with him; and either he who receives asses from him under contract to rear them and share in the profit, or he who delivers asses to him under contract to rear them and share in the profit—[the fetus, when born] is exempt from the law of the firstling.*

[H] R. Haggai asked before R. Yosé, "Now has it not been stated that it is prohibited to set before them for sale any sort of embryos? [So such a transaction is null.]"

[I] He said to him, "R. Abin in the name of rabbis from over there already has made that same point before you: 'That is to say that it is prohibited to make available for sale to gentiles the embryo [of an unborn beast].' "

[**VI**.A] *Ben Beterah permits in the case of horses* [M. 1:6E].

[B] Ben Beterah has stated this rule only in connection with a male horse, who will kill its owner in battle.

[C] And some say that the ruling applies to a male horse, which runs after females [and so is dangerous].

[D] And some say that the ruling applies to a male horse, which stands still when it urinates [and is not reliable].

[E] What is the difference among the several rulings adduced in explanation of the position of Ben Beterah?

[F] A castrated horse.

[G] The one who maintains that Ben Beterah speaks of a horse that runs after females will hold that this one will not run after females[, so one may now sell it to a gentile].

[H] And the one who maintains that Ben Beterah's ruling applies to a horse that stands still when it urinates, this one also will stand still when it urinates.

[I] [In explanation of the blanket prohibition of sages,] R. Tanḥum bar Ḥiyya [said], "When it gets old, one harnesses it to the millstones[, so the Israelite will bear responsibility for the beast's laboring on the Sabbath]."

[J] R. Yosé b. R. Bun in the name of R. Huna: "Ben Beterah and R. Nathan—both of them have laid down the same ruling [that a living creature bears its own weight, so one is not responsible for its movements on the Sabbath. Ben Beterah will not be concerned at the movements of the beast on the Sabbath, on which account he permits the sale of the beast. Nathan does not regard moving a beast from one domain to another on the Sabbath as culpable. Both concur, therefore, that the living beast bears its own weight. The contrary view assigns that rule solely to a human being]. Thus it has been taught:

[K] "If one has brought out [on the Sabbath, from private to public domain] a domesticated beast, wild beast, or fowl, whether living or dead, he is liable.

[L] "Rabbi Nathan says, '[If the beast was brought across one domain to another when it was] dead, [the one who did so] is liable. [But if it was] alive, he is exempt.' " [So Nathan maintains that a living beast, like a living person, is deemed to carry its own weight, and one is not liable for leading such a beast from one domain to another, any more than one is liable for carrying a living person who is able to transport himself.]

[M] And the rabbis maintain that the one who does so is liable for a sin-offering.

[N] Now do they reply to him in line with his mode of reasoning? Thus did they answer him: "In accord with your reasoning, we maintain that it is [prohibited to sell a horse to a gentile] because of the requirement to preserve the beast's Sabbath rest [and so harnessing the beast to a millstone must be prevented, and on this account, there will be liability for a sin-offering, when the horse gets old and is harnessed for work, even on the Sabbath. From our position there is a liability for a sin-offering on the quite distinct count specified by us, namely, the beast's movements across the line from private to public domain].

[O] "Thus I too claim that when the beast gets old, they will harness him to the millstones."

[VII.A] **Rabbi says, "I say that it is prohibited [to sell horses to gentiles (M. 1:6E)].**

[B] **"First, because one may not sell them weapons of war [and a horse is a weapon of war].**

[C] **"Second, because one may not sell them a large beast** [M. 1:6C; T. A.Z. 2:3I–K]."

[D] And so it has been taught in a Tannaitic teaching:

[E] [Selling] a large wild beast is tantamount to [selling] a small domesticated beast.

[F] And who has repeated this tradition? Rabbi[, who maintains that the same reasons that prohibit selling the domesticated beast apply to a large wild beast. Therefore it is forbidden to sell to a gentile a wild beast just as it is prohibited to sell a large domesticated beast].

[G] But so far as the sages are concerned?

[H] R. Bisna, R. Ḥanan bar Ba in the name of Rab: "A large wild beast is tantamount [only] to a large domesticated beast [and the rule depends upon the local practice, as specified in the Mishnah pericope]."

The Talmud systematically takes up each of the clauses of the Mishnah pericope. The discourse is orderly and to the point, a model for the Talmud's approach to commentary upon the Mishnah. Unit **I** raises a secondary question, flowing from the Mishnah's rule. In unit **II** there is a sustained effort to supply a credible reason for the Mishnah's ruling. The basic mode of thought in this instance is to explain what a gentile will not do, which, from the law's viewpoint, must be done with the animal in question (or vice versa). This same consideration will appear below, at **IV**, **V**, and **VI**. **II** and **III** form a single protracted discussion, following a uniform pattern of thought, which **V** carries forward. While appearing to be intruded, **IV** raises a secondary issue, recurring later on, concerning the disposition of funds received from selling to gentiles beasts that one should not sell to them. The discussion adduces in evidence a precedent and then identifies a Tannaitic authority whose opinion stands behind the precedent. Continuing the inquiry begun at **II**, unit **V** asks about the reasoning behind Judah's position. No sustained effort goes into showing that Judah has a viable viewpoint; discussion veers off in a different direction. Ben Beterah's view, **VI**, is given a number of explanations. But the Talmud's real interest is in a completely extraneous issue, introduced at J. In fact two distinct positions are relevant to Ben Beterah. One is that we are concerned that the beast not be worked on the Sabbath, I. The other, also relevant, is that the beast's movements on the Sabbath, from private to public domain, will not be the responsibility of the owner; there is no violation of the Sabbath law if a creature that can carry its own weight is moved by another party from one domain to another. The sages *vis-à-vis* Nathan apply that principle solely to a human being. N–O then explain the relevance of the antecedent materials. The sages maintain that, even in accord with the reasoning of Ben Beterah on the issue of whether a beast is deemed to bear its own weight, Ben Beterah's basic position on selling a beast to a gentile still is invalid, because of the paramount consideration of the beast's not laboring on the Sabbath. Unit **VII** then returns us to the explanation of the prohibition of selling horses to gentiles.

1:7

[A] *They do not sell them [1] bears, [2] lions, or [3] anything that is a public danger.*

[B] *They do not build with them [1] a basilica, [2] scaffold, [3] stadium, or [4] judges' tribunal.*

[C] *But they build with them [5] public bathhouses or [6] private ones.*

[D] *[Once] they reach the vaulting on which they set up an idol, it is forbidden [to help build any longer].*

[**I**.A] [Since the Mishnah specifies, at A(3), that Israelites may not sell to gentiles anything that is a danger to the public,] lo, [it follows that it is] permitted to sell them anything that is not a danger to the public.

[B] The Mishnah [is in accord with the opinion of the one who will permit accommodation of that which is not a public danger,] who taught in the following Tannaitic tradition:

[C] **He who witnesses [the performances of] sorcerers and enchanters, or of a moqion, mopion, molion, milarin, miliaria, sagirlon, sagilaria [various sorts of clowns and buffoons]—lo, this is prohibited [only] on the count of not sitting in the seat**

of the scornful, as it is said, "Happy is the one who has not walked in the counsel of the wicked . . . nor sat in the seat of the scornful, [but his delight is in the Torah of the Lord]" (Ps. 1:1–2) [T. A.Z. 2:5].

[D] And all of these sorts of performances bring a person to neglect learning of the Torah, as it is said, ". . . but his delight is in the Torah of the Lord."

[E] "He who goes up into the theater—it is prohibited on the count of idolatry," the words of R. Meir.

[F] And sages say, "[If one goes up] when they are 'manuring' [engaging in idolatrous worship through orgies], it is forbidden on the count of idolatry. But if not, it is still forbidden on the count of not sitting in the seat of the scornful, [but on that count] alone."

[G] **He who goes up into an amphitheater, if it is on account of the service of the state's requirements, lo, this is permitted. But if he takes account [of what is happening therein], lo, this is forbidden.**

[H] **He who sits in a stadium, lo, this one [witnessing the fight of gladiators] is guilty of bloodshed.**

[I] **R. Nathan permits on two counts, first, because the Israelite cries out in favor of saving the life [of the loser], and because he may give evidence in behalf of the wife [whose husband is killed in the struggle], so that she may remarry [T. A.Z. 2:7].**

[**II**.A] [If] one has transgressed [and helped a gentile] build [a basilica and the like, as to the disposition of the proceeds]:

[B] R. Eleazar said, "It is permitted [to make use of the proceeds]."

[C] Said R. Mana, "This ruling is hardly reasonable, that we should not prohibit [benefit from the salary].

[D] "For [the gentile] designates each vaulting [for use for setting up an idol, so it is as if the Israelite has assisted in setting up the pedestal for an idol, no matter what part of the work he actually does]."

The reasoning of **I**.A–D is acute. The purpose is to link the available tradition, cited at C, to the Mishnah pericope. This is done through reasoning that 1:7A[3] does not prohibit matters on grounds of idolatry but nonetheless deems them to be forbidden for other reasons (cf. Pené Moshe). So what is not a danger to the public will be prohibited on a separate count, and this is, as specified at C, on the count of neglect of the Torah. Since the obvious requirement of the exegesis of the Mishnah does not lead to the materials of C, G–I, it appears that these materials are ready at hand. Then the redactor wishes to find a route from the Mishnah to those materials (= Tosefta). The alternative is to see B as an interpolation. Then we should read A and C ff. as essentially independent of one another. The whole is simply a composite of unrelated, available entries. Once more, lower criticism, when systematically carried out, will improve our understanding of the fundamental composition of the Talmud before us. For our present, preliminary account we had best deem B integral and retain the original approach to the whole. Unit **II** presents no surprises.

1:8

[A] *They do not sell them produce as yet unplucked.*

[B] *But one may sell it once it has been harvested.*

[C] *R. Judah says, "One may sell it to him with the stipulation that he will harvest it."*

[**I**.A] R. Bun bar Ḥiyya raised the question, "[In regard to Judah's stipulation that the gentile will harvest the crop, in which case it is permitted to sell him a crop which has not been harvested,] is there also a dispute with regard to [the sale to a gentile] of a large beast? [Will he take the same position, namely, that] one may sell to a gentile a large beast on condition that he slaughter it[, and not use it for labor on the Sabbath]?"

[B] Indeed we find a Tannaitic teaching to that effect:

[C] R. Judah says, "One sells [to a gentile a large beast] on condition that he slaughter it."

The same reasoning used here applies at 1:6, as is made explicit.

1:9

[A] *"They do not rent [to gentiles] houses in the land of Israel,*

[B] *"and, it goes without saying, fields.*

[C] *"But in Syria they rent them houses, but not fields.*

[D] *"And abroad they sell them houses and rent them fields," the words of R. Meir.*

[E] *R. Yosé says, "Even in the land of Israel they rent them houses[, but not fields];*

[F] *"in Syria they sell them houses and rent them fields;*

[G] *"and abroad they sell them both the one and the other."*

[**I**.A] R. Zeira in the name of R. Yosé ben Ḥaninah, R. Abba, R. Ḥiyya in the name of R. Yoḥanan:

[B] " 'You will show no mercy to them [TḤNM]' (Deut 7:2).—You will show them no grace.

[C] " 'You will show no mercy to them.'—You will give them no unrequited gift [MTNT ḤNM].

[D] " 'You will show no mercy to them.'—You will give them no place to settle [MQWM HṆYH] in the Holy Land."

[E] Now has it not been taught in a Tannaitic teaching: *R. Yosé says, "Even in the Land of Israel they rent them houses"?*

[F] As to a house, it is uncommon to profit from it, while it is quite common to profit from a field.

[G] R. Yosé b. R. Bun gave instructions that it is forbidden to rent them a burial place in the land of Israel, on the count of not giving them a place to settle in the Holy Land.

[H] "You will show no mercy to them."—You will give them no unrequited gift.

[I] Now has it not been taught in a Tannaitic tradition [that Gamaliel gave such a gift]:

[J] MʿSH B: **Rabban Gamaliel was going along the road [from Akko to Kezib]. He found a loaf of cheap bread on the road. He said to Ṭabi, his slave, "Take the loaf."**

He saw a gentile coming toward him. He said to him, "Mabgai, Take this loaf of bread."

R. Ilai ran after [Mabgai] and said to him, "What is your name?"

He said to him, "Mabgai."

"And where do you come from?"

"From one of the [nearby] station-keeper's villages."

"Now did Rabban Gamaliel ever in your whole life meet you?"

He said to him, "No."

[On the basis of this event we learn that] Rabban Gamaliel divined by the Holy Spirit.

And from what he said we learn three things.

We learn that the leaven of a gentile is permitted immediately after Passover [cf. M. Pes. 2:2].

And they do not pass by food [but pick it up].

And they follow the status of the majority of those who travel the roads [in a given place, in this instance, gentiles] [T. Pes. 2:15].

[K] R. Jacob bar Zabedai in the name of R. Abbahu: "That rule [about not walking past food, but stopping and picking it up] was valid in the past, but now they do pass by foodstuffs because of the possibility of witchcraft."

[L] **When he was leaving Kezib, someone came along and besought from him [absolution of] his vow. He said to the one who was with him, "Have we drunk so much as a quarter-log of Italian wine?"**

He said to him, "Yes." He said to the one who asked the question, "Walk along with us until the effect of our wine has worn off."

Once they got to the Ladder of Tyre, he got off his ass and wrapped himself in his cloak and sat down and declared his vow to be absolved.

From these statements of his we learn that a quarter-log of wine causes drunkenness;

that traveling wears down the effects of wine;

that they do not grant absolution from vows or give decisions when they are drunk;

and that they do not absolve vows either while riding on an ass or while walking or while standing, but only sitting down and wrapped in a cloak [T. Pes. 2:16].

[M] Said R. Yoḥanan, "Thus he opened the discourse for him: 'There is one whose rash words are like sword thrusts [but the tongue of the wise brings healing]' (Prov. 12:18).

[N] "This may be compared to one who has taken a vow not to eat bread. Woe to him if he eats, woe to him if he does not eat. If he eats, he violates his vow. If he does not eat, he sins against his soul. What should he do? Let him go to sages and beseech absolution from his vow, as it is written, 'But the tongue of the wise brings healing.' "

[**II**.A] "You will show no mercy to them."—You will show them no grace.

[B] Now has it not been taught MʿŚH B: Rabban Gamaliel was strolling about the temple mount, and he noticed a certain gentile woman and said a blessing over her [because of her beauty].

[C] Now was it Rabban Gamaliel's usual habit to stare at pretty women?

[D] But it was a crooked path [so that he could not avoid seeing her], like a narrow alley, in which he looked at her. [This was] not for his own enjoyment, but nonetheless he said a blessing over her.

[E] Now is it not so that R. Zeira in the name of R. [40b] Yosé ben Ḥanina, R. Ba R. Ḥiyya in the name of R. Yoḥanan said: " 'You will show no mercy to them.'—You will show them no grace."

[F] What did he say?

[G] He did not say "*Abaskantah!* [May no harm befall you!]" He said only, "Blessed is he in whose world are such beautiful creatures."

[H] For thus even if one saw only an ass that is pretty, a camel that is pretty, or a horse that is pretty, one says, "Blessed is he who has such beautiful creatures in his world."

[**III**.A] R. Simeon, R. Abbahu in the name of R. Yosé bar Ḥanina, "An Israelite hairdresser should not dress the hair of a gentile woman, on the count of 'You will show them no grace.'

[B] "And an Israelite should not serve as a best man for a gentile, on the count of 'You shall not intermarry with them' (Deut. 7:3)."

[C] R. Isaac bar Goptah asked in session before R. Mana, "[If] it is forbidden to go to a gentile's banquet party, is it not an argument *a fortiori* that it should be forbidden to serve as his best man?"

[D] He said to him, "The purpose is to apply a negative commandment to those who serve as best men for gentiles."

[**IV**.A] R. Simon had some vine growths [in his fields] in the Royal Mountains. He asked R. Yoḥanan [about whether it is permitted to rent the plants to a gentile]. He replied, "Let them lie uncultivated, but never rent them out to a gentile."

[B] He asked R. Joshua [b. Levi] about the law governing renting them out to a gentile, and R. Joshua permitted him to rent them out in a place in which Israelites are not commonly located, for example, in Syria.

[C] Now what is the law as to Syria itself?

[D] We may infer it from the following teaching:

[E] R. Haggai went down to Ḥamaṣ. Members of the household of Ashtor came and asked him, "Since Israelites are not numerous in that place, and we rent out land to gentiles, what is the law as to our having to separate tithes in their behalf [from the produce produced by them]?"

[F] He sent and asked R. Zeira. R. Zeira asked R. Ami. He said to him, "Rabbi, what is the law as to their having to separate tithes?"

[G] He said to him, "It is not necessary to separate tithes in their behalf."

[H] From whom do you derive the ruling that it is permitted to rent the land to him? It is in accord with R. Yosé.

[I] And further, from the following teaching, which R. Ḥaninah son of R. Abbahu said in the name of R. Abbahu, "A case came before father, and he sent and asked R. Ḥiyya, R. Yasa, and R. Ami, and they gave instruction to him [to permit] renting fields to them, in accord with the opinion of R. Yosé" [M.

A.Z. 1:9F]. Now as to the rule governing setting aside tithes, it is not required to set aside tithes in their behalf.

What is striking in this protracted pericope, **I–II**, is how the Talmud reveals the beams of its jerry-built construction. There is no serious interest in the Mishnah pericope at all. What we have is a scriptural exegesis, followed by diverse materials pertinent to the exegesis, the whole (despite **I**.E) relevant only in the most general way to the Mishnah pericope's theme. That materials are inserted whole and without significant editorial interference is shown at **I**.J–L, with the appended materials, M–N, all of them relevant to J–L, and none of them remotely pertinent to the Mishnah pericope. The mass is connected only because, in the story about Gamaliel, it is told that he gave a gift to a gentile, which, **I**.C/H say, is not to be done. Yet that the formation and inclusion of the entire construction are not random is shown at **II**, which takes up precisely the same discourse, weaving a story about Gamaliel with the established exegetical framework just as is done at **I**. Only at **IV** do we reach the Mishnah pericope before us. There it is to show the relationship of tithing grain grown by gentiles in Syria and renting land to them. Yosé permits renting land to them, and, it is deemed to follow, Israelites are not responsible for that land. Then the Israelite owner need not tithe in behalf of the gentile sharecropper or renter. So, in Yosé's mind, if he may rent the land, he bears no responsibility for the disposition of the crops.

1:10

[A] *Even in the situation concerning which they have ruled [that they may] rent,*

[B] *it is not for use as a residence that they ruled that it is permitted, because he brings an idol into it,*

[C] *as it is said, "You shall not bring an abomination into your house" (Deut. 7:26).*

[D] *And in no place may one rent him a bathhouse, since it would be called by his [the Israelite's] name[, and its use on the Sabbath will be attributed to the Israelite].*

[**I**.A] Lo, in a place in which it is customary to sell [houses to a gentile, e.g., abroad, in accord with the view of Meir, in Syria, in accord with the view of Yosé], one sells him even a residence, or rents him even a residence.

[B] R. Aḥa, R. Tanḥum bar Ḥiyya in the name of R. Eleazer b. R. Yosé, "And even a small stall, for example, like the tannery in Sidon.

[C] "It is [thus] not the end of the matter that one may rent out the entire house but even a single room."

[**II**.A] *[R. Judah says "If there are] two courtyards, one within the other, the inner courtyard is subject to the law [of tithes and renders liable to tithes produce brought within it], and the outer courtyard is exempt from the law" [M. Ma. 3:5G–I].*

[B] If it was a single courtyard and divided into two and made into one [what is the law? This question is not answered].

[**III**.A] [In the light of M. 1:10D,] R. Abin in the name of the rabbis over there: "That is to say, a field that is situated by the road is it prohibited to rent out to gentiles, because it bears the name of an Israelite, and [gentiles] will work the field on the Sabbath or on festivals."

The Talmud's treatment of the Mishnah pericope at **I** and **III** provides a close and persuasive secondary exegesis. If one may actually sell a field, one may also sell a residence, and the operative consideration of M. 1:10B does not apply. **III** applies the reasoning of M. 1:10D to a parallel case. The insertion of **II** presumably is provoked by the reference of **I**.B, C, to individual rooms, but the issue of **II** is wildly irrelevant to what is under discussion here.

2 Yerushalmi Abodah Zarah Chapter Two

2:1

[A] *They do not leave cattle in gentiles' inns,*

[B] *because they are suspect in regard to bestiality.*

[C] *And a woman should not be alone with them,*

[D] *because they are suspect in regard to fornication.*

[E] *And a man should not be alone with them,*

[F] *because they are suspect in regard to bloodshed.*

[G] *An Israelite girl should not serve as a midwife to a gentile woman,*

[H] *[Editio princeps omits: because she serves to bring forth a child for the service of idolatry.]*

[I] *But a gentile woman may serve as a midwife to an Israelite girl.*

[J] *An Israelite girl should not give suck to the child of a gentile woman.*

[K] *But a gentile woman may give suck to the child of an Israelite girl,*

[L] *when it is by [her] permission.*

[**I**.A] [40c] [Since, at M. Par. 2:1C–D, Eliezer declares that a red heifer for burning for ashes for purification water may not be purchased from gentiles, while the sages permit doing so, and since the present pericope assumes gentiles routinely practice bestiality,] R. Zeira, R. Abbahu in the name of R. Yosé b. R. Ḥaninah, R. Ba, R. Johah [declare]: "Interpret the Mishnah to accord with the position of R. Eliezer.

[B] "For *R. Eliezer* said, '*[The red heifer for burning for ashes for purification water] is not to be purchased from gentiles.*' "

[C] R. Jonah raised the following inquiry: "Now why do we not interpret the Mishnah pericope to represent the opinion of all parties [and not merely Eliezer, for a distinction is possible here which is not operative at M. Par. 2:1].

[D] "This then would accord with the position outlined by R. Eleazar in the name of Rab: 'And even in accord with the opinion of him who said that it is permitted to sell them [beasts], it is still prohibited to house them [with gentiles, or to designate them as the property of gentiles].' "

[E] [If furthermore] one has violated the law and done so [purchased the beast], it is in accord with the opinion of all authorities [that it then is permitted to make use of the beast, and we do not take account of the possibility that the gentile has committed an act of bestiality with the beast].

[F] [Now that we have raised the issue of whether we distinguish between the state prevailing at the outset and that which governs once an act has been permitted *(post facto)*, we may find evidence that we do indeed make such a distinction, in line with that which] R. Jeremiah said, "Let us infer the answer from the following:

[G] *"The woman who was taken prisoner by gentiles—[if it was for an offense concerning property, she is permitted to return to her husband"* (M. Ket. 2:9A–B). Now since at M. 2:1C–D the rule is that a woman should not be alone with gentiles, and since, if she should be alone with them, under the stated circumstance we say she may return to her husband, it follows that the Mishnah rule applies to the situation prevailing at the outset. But if, *post facto,* such a deed should be done, we do not rule stringently, but we permit the woman to go back to her husband under the stated circumstance. We thus make a distinction between the rule pertinent at the outset and that applying *post facto.* Likewise in the case of the beast: all parties can agree that, to begin with a beast should not be designated for gentile use, Eliezer as much as the sages. But they then can disagree on whether, if the beast *was* so designated, it may be used for the red heifer. It follows that Eliezer can accept the rule of M. A.Z. 2:1A–B]."

[H] Said R. Yosé, "There is a distinction to be made between the case of the woman[, who after the fact may be permitted to return to her husband, and the beast subject to bestiality]. For a woman will usually cry out [when she is raped, and the gentile will hesitate to rape her, lest the woman lose all value for ransom]."

[I] But take note of this: what if the woman was a deaf-mute? [She still may return to her husband, so H is invalid!]

[J] For her [too] it would be usual to give signs of protest.

[K] What is there left to say [to the one who wishes to make the distinction between a rule applying prior to a deed and that applying once the deed has been done? For the proposed distinction now cannot be shown valid through the evidence concerning a parallel case]. One indeed must interpret the Mishnah rule as the opinion of R. Eliezer [and not of the sages *vis-à-vis* Eliezer].

[L] For *R. Eliezer says, "[The red heifer] may not be purchased from gentiles."*

[M] [The disciples] wished to propose [that the present rule may accord with Eliezer and sages, because at issue in connection with the red heifer is another consideration entirely, so there is no reason to assume sages *vis-à-vis* Eliezer will not have agreed in the present instance].

[N] Now the disagreement between R. Eliezer and the sages in connection with the red heifer is concerning [whether we apply in that instance] a stricter rule [than we apply in other aspects of the law, because the rules governing the red heifer in general are far more strict than those applying to animals for other sacrifices]; [they constitute a] distinction applicable to the red heifer. [So the sages and Eliezer differ solely in regard to the red heifer.]

[O] From that verse adduced in evidence by the rabbis to counter R. Eliezer's position, which is, "All the flocks of Kedar shall be gathered to you, the rams of Nebaioth shall minister to you; they shall come up with acceptance on my altar, and I will glorify my glorious house," (Is. 60:7) [meaning that, so far as the sages are concerned, all sorts of beasts are acceptable,] one must conclude that also with regard to all sorts of [offerings, and not only the animal for use as the red heifer], did R. Eliezer differ [from sages. Thus N is rejected.]

[P] [In regard to the citation of the verse in Isaiah, referring to the age to come,] R. Hoshaiah raised the question: "Do people draw evidence from a saying concerning that which will come about in the future in a matter of [practice pertaining] in matters applying in the past [when the temple stood]?"

[Q] [In this same regard,] R. Abin raised the question: "Do people draw evidence from a saying concerning an age in which the impulse to do evil shall be null in a matter of [practice pertaining in] an age in which the impulse to do evil is yet powerful?"

[R] [In explanation of his position at P, regarding the interpretation of Eliezer's position in the light of Is. 60:7, Hoshaiah will now attempt to indicate that Eliezer too can accord with the cited verse.] R. Hoshaiah said, "And [why] do we not interpret the matter as the opinion of all parties? For [the cited verse is to be read] in accord with that which R. Huna stated in the name of Rab: 'And they weighed out as my wages thirty sheqels of silver' (Zech. 11:12)—these are the thirty commandments that the children of Noah are destined to accept upon themselves[, and all the more so will the children of Noah no longer practice bestiality, a position Eliezer also will accept].' "

[S] But the rabbis state [in interpreting the cited verse]: "These [thirty pieces of silver, to which Zechariah makes reference,] are the thirty righteous men, without whom the world cannot endure."

[T] For R. Naḥman said in the name of R. Mana, "The world cannot endure without thirty righteous men, of the sort of Abraham, our father.

[U] "And what is the scriptural evidence for that statement? 'And Abraham will surely be' (Gen. 18:18) [HYH YHYH]. Now the numerical value of the letters for the word, *will be* [YHYH] is thirty [Y = 10, H = 5]."

[V] [On the subject of these thirty righteous men, it is to be said:] There are times when the majority of them are in Babylonia and the minority of them are in the land of Israel. There are times when the majority of them are in the land of Israel and the minority of them are in Babylonia. It is a good sign for the world at the time when the majority of them are in the land.

[W] [On the subject of the commandments pertinent to the children of Noah, it is to be said:] R. Hiyya bar Luliani in the name of R. Hoshaiah: "All of the commandments[, not just thirty,] are the children of Noah destined to accept upon themselves.

[X] "What is the scriptural evidence for that statement? 'Yea, at that time I will change the speech of the peoples to a pure speech [that all of them may call on the name of the Lord and serve him with one accord]' (Zeph. 3:9).

[Y] "But in the end they are destined to retract. And what is the scriptural evidence for that statement? '[The rulers take counsel together against the Lord and his anointed, saying,] Let us burst their bonds asunder, and cast their cords from us' (Ps. 2:2). This refers to the commandment of wearing phylacteries. This refers to the commandment of wearing show-fringes [on one's garment]."

[**II**.A] R. Isaac and R. Ami were in session. They raised the question, "And lo, it is written, 'They sacrificed to the Lord on that day, from the spoil [which they had brought]' (2 Chron. 15:11). [Now this verse shows that the people did not distinguish among the beasts, or scruple as to which animal may have been a victim of bestiality. This would represent an objection to the position of Eliezer at M. Par. 2:1, that we do take account of the prior treatment of the beast.]"

[B] Now we have interpreted this verse [in a different way, as will be seen in a moment, from the discussion involving Eliezer], but we do not know whether it was the associates who interpreted the verse or whether it was R. Ami who interpreted the verse [in the following manner].

[C] It was from the spoil that they had in their hand at the outset that they made offerings [and not from that which came from gentiles, so there was no reason to scruple about bestiality].

[D] Now has it not been written, "And the men of Beth-Shemesh offered burnt offerings and sacrificed sacrifices on that day to the Lord" (1 Sam. 6:15). [Now what they sacrificed were] the cows [sent out by the lords of the Philistines to bring the ark of the Lord back to Israel, and this would be evidence against the position of Eliezer that we take account of the possibility that gentiles have committed an act of bestiality with the animals. Clearly, in this case, the men of Beth-Shemesh did not scruple on that account.]

[E] Now do we learn the law from what was done by the lords of the Philistines?! [In fact this was a special case, involving a miracle.]

[F] And was it not this which R. Abbahu said in the name of R. Yosé bar Ḥaninah, "And even cows did they offer up: 'They offered the cows as a burnt offering to the Lord' " (1 Sam. 6:14).

[G] And has it not been written [as evidence that Israelites sacrifice beasts belonging to gentiles, without scruple as to a prior act of bestiality committed with such beasts]: "Saul said 'They have brought them from the Amalekites' " (1 Sam. 15:15).

[H] The law is not to be learned from the deeds of Saul.

[I] And this is in line with that which R. Simeon b. Laqish said: "Saul was 'a block of a sycamore tree' [utterly barren of thought, ignorant]."

[J] And has it not been written, "[And Araunah said, 'Why has my lord, the king, come to his servant?' David said, 'To buy the threshing floor of you, in order to build an altar. . . .' Then Araunah said to David, 'Let my lord, the king, take and offer up what seems good. . . .'] So David bought the threshing floor [and the oxen for fifty shekels of silver]" (2 Sam. 24:21–24). [This would prove that David offered up animals purchased from a gentile.]

[K] He bought [the threshing floor and the animals], but he did not [actually] offer up [the animals].

[L] Now is it not written [in that same context], "And Araunah said to the king, 'The Lord your God accept you' " (2 Sam. 24:23) [which would indicate that the animals indeed were sacrificed]?

[M] [The meaning is,] May he accept your prayer.

[N] "Neither shall you offer as the bread of your God any such animals gotten from a foreigner. [Since there is a blemish in them, because of their mutilation, they will not be accepted for you]" (Lev. 22:25).

[O] "Of any such animals [as are specified at Lev. 22:17ff., e.g., an animal whose testicles are bruised or crushed or torn], you shall not make an offering, but you may purchase beasts [from gentiles] without blemish and offer them [in line with the sages *vis-à-vis* Eliezer].

[P] And how does R. Eliezer interpret this same verse? "You purchase [a beast] with money and offer it up" [that is, a gentile may contribute funds for an offering].

[Q] And yet has it not been taught above, it is not in accord with R. Eliezer [that one may purchase a beast from a gentile]!

[**III**.A] *They do not leave cattle in gentiles' inns* [M. 2:1A], **even male cattle with men, and female cattle with women[, because a male may bring a male beast over him, and a female may do the same with a female beast], and it goes without saying, males with women, and females with men [T. A.Z. 3:2A–D].**

[B] **Male cattle with men**—on what grounds do you scruple?

[C] His girlfriend may come and not find him and will then engage in sexual relations with [the beast].

[D] **Female cattle with women**—on what grounds do you scruple?

[E] Her lover may come and not find her and will then have sexual relations with the female beast instead.

[F] R. Haggai in the name of R. Zeira: "It is not the end of the matter [that one may not leave] a beast belonging to an Israelite with a gentile. But even a beast belonging to a gentile with one belonging to an Israelite one may not leave along with one belonging to another gentile friend of his, so as not to provide him with the occasion for transgression."

[G] If that is the case, then even [if] one has hired a gentile's beast, it is really not proper to return and leave it with him, so as not to provide him with the occasion for transgression.

[H] [No, that is no consideration, for a gentile] is suspect of having sexual relations with the beast belonging to his neighbor, but he is not suspect of having sexual relations with a beast of his own, for, since he knows that if he has sexual relations with the beast, he renders the beast barren, he will refrain from having sexual relations with it.

[**IV**.A] **But they leave cattle in Samaritans' inns [even male cattle with women and female cattle with men and female cattle with women. And they hand over cattle to Samaritans' shep-**

herds, and they hand over a child to him to teach him reading, etc. (T. A.Z. 3:1)].

[B] It follows from this statement that Samaritans are not suspect with regard to violating the law against fornication.

[C] And it has been taught in a Tannaitic tradition to the same effect:

[D] *A woman may remain alone with two men* [M. Qid. 4:12a], **even if both of them are Samaritans, even if both of them are slaves, even if one of them is a Samaritan and one a slave[, except for a minor. For she is shameless about having sexual relations in his presence, T. Qid, 5:9], As to his sister and his sister-in-law and all those women in a prohibited relationship to him who are listed in the Torah, they should not be alone with him except before two witnesses [T. Qid. 5:10].**

[**V**.A] It has been taught in a Tannaitic tradition: **They do not sell them either a sword or the paraphernalia for a sword, and they do not polish a sword for them [T. A.Z. 2:4A–B].**

[B] Interpret this rule to apply to a city which is made up wholly of gentiles.

[**VI**.A] [*And a woman should not be alone with them, because (gentiles) are suspect in regard to fornication* (M. A.Z. 2:1C–D):] And do not women fall within the category of those who are murdered [as is said with reference to a man, *because they are suspect in regard to bloodshed*]?

[B] Said R. Ami, "Interpret the Mishnah rule to apply to a case of a strong woman [who is not afraid of people, because she can defend herself]."

[C] Said R. Abin, "And you may even propose [a quite different reason that a woman need not be concerned about bloodshed]: A woman can hide her status and claim, 'I am a gentile,' but a man cannot hide his status and claim, 'I am a gentile.' "

[D] It has been taught in a Tannaitic tradition:

[E] **[When] an Israelite goes along with a gentile, he puts him at his right hand[, and he does not put him at his left hand].**

[F] **R. Ishmael son of R. Yosé [b. R. Yoḥanan b. Beroqah] says, "[And he goes] with a sword in his right hand, with a staff in his left hand."**

[G] **[If] there are two going up on an ascent or going down on a ramp, the Israelite goes up ahead, and the gentile behind. And he may not bow before him, lest he break his skull. And he should leave a good distance for him.**

[H] **[If] they asked him, "Where are you going," he indicates to him a way other than the one he has in mind, just as Jacob said to Esau, "Let my lord pass on before his servant . . . until I come to my lord in Seir. But Jacob journeyed to Succoth" (Gen. 33:14, 17) [T. A.Z. 3:4F–M].**

[I] Said R. Huna, "We do not find that Jacob our patriarch [actually] went to Seir."

[J] Said R. Yudan son of Rab, "He was destined to go there."

[K] He said to him, " 'Saviors shall go up to Mount Zion to rule Mount Esau; and the kingdom shall be the Lord's' " (Obadiah 1:21).

[**VII**.A] *An Israelite girl should not serve as a midwife to a gentile woman* [M. A.Z. 2:1G] because she serves to bring forth a child for the service of idolatry.

[B] *But a gentile girl may serve as a midwife to an Israelite woman* [M. A.Z. 2:1I].

[C] And it has been taught in a Tannaitic source to the same effect:

[D] **She serves as a midwife on the outside [with others watching her], but not inside [all by herself]. She should not put her hand inside [the womb], so that she may not crush the fetus in her womb. And she should not give her a cup of bitters to drink [T. A.Z. 3:4C].**

[E] [If a gentile woman] was expert [however], let her come [and serve as a midwife].

[F] This is in accord with that which R. Jacob bar Aḥa said in the name of R. Yoḥanan, "If [a gentile] was deemed an expert physician, it is permitted [to accept healing from him]."

[G] Here too, if the woman was an expert, it is permitted [to accept her ministrations].

[**VIII**.A] *An Israelite girl should not give suck to the child of a gentile woman* [M. A.Z. 2:1J] because she gives him life.

[B] Said R. Yosé, "Along these same lines the rule is that it is forbidden to teach him a craft [since that gives him a livelihood]."

[C] This is [illustrated by the story] that there were two families of craftsmen in Giero, one glass cutters, the other sauce makers. The glass cutters did not teach their craft to gentiles, and they flourished. The sauce makers did teach their craft to gentiles, and they became barren.

[**IX**.A] *But a gentile woman may give suck to the child of an Israelite girl* [M. A.Z. 2:1K].

[B] This is in accord with the following verse of Scripture: "Kings shall be your foster fathers, and their queens your nursing mothers" (Is. 49:23).

[C] It has been taught in a Tannaitic tradition: A baby may continue sucking from a gentile woman or from an unclean beast, and they bring him milk from any source without scruple as to uncleanness.

Units **I** and **II** ignore the Mishnah's interests and pursue their own, which concern the use of gentiles' beasts in the cult. The route to this topic is in the inquiry into the position of sages *vis-à-vis* Eliezer at M. Par. 2:1. The sages who differ from Eliezer at the cited passage should not concur with the present rule, thus **I**.A–B. From that point the effort is made to harmonize the sages and Eliezer, by showing that the sages *vis-à-vis* Eliezer can concur with the rule before us, while still differing from Eliezer in the matter of the red heifer. The effort at harmonization depends upon the familiar distinction between rulings that are *propter hoc* and those that are *post facto*. Once the disciplined exegesis along the stated lines is worked out, a rather less coherent discourse begins (**I**.O ff). The whole of unit **II** proceeds essentially indifferent to the Mishnah, with its sequence of proof-texts to show that beasts for sacrifice may (or may not) be purchased from gentiles. A sequence of proofs drawn from precedents in Israelite history is laid forth. Only the interpretation of Q poses problems. For the variety of possibilities, see Pené Moshe. At unit **III**, then, we reach the detailed exegesis of what the Mishnah pericope actually says, taking the route of the analysis not of the Mishnah but of the Tosefta's complement to the Mishnah. Units **IV** and **V** likewise pursue the exegesis of relevant passages of the Tosefta. When we come to **VI**, we find a systematic exercise in the explanation of the Mishnah's rules, and this goes on through **VII**, **VIII**, and **IX**. These materials are clear and pose no problems.

2:2

[A] *They accept from them healing for property,*

[B] *but not healing for a person.*

[C] *"And they do not allow them to cut hair under any circumstances," the words of R. Meir.*

[D] *And sages say, "In the public domain it is permitted,*

[E] *"but not if they are alone."*

[**I**.A] [40d] R. Jacob bar Zabedi in the name of R. Abbahu: "*Healing for property* refers to [using a veterinarian for healing of his] beast, *healing for a person* refers to [using a physician for healing for] his own body."

[B] R. Ba in the name of R. Judah: "If he was one who had inflamed a wound [with the medicine he prescribed for it, rather than healing the wound], then [for all time] it is prohibited [to make use of his services]."

[C] That ruling is illustrated in the following: R. Ami went up with R. Yudan the patriarch to the hot springs of Gerar. He injured his finger and put on it a plaster [which he got from a gentile physician]. He saw that [the wound] began to sink and deepen [relative to the surrounding flesh]. So he removed [the plaster].

[D] Now did he not take account of that which R. Jacob bar Aḥa said in the name of R. Yoḥanan: "If he was an experienced physician, it is permitted [to rely on his advice]"?

[E] And are the two cases not parallel?

[F] [Surely they are.] There, if he was one who had inflamed a wound, it will be prohibited [to make use of his services], while here, if he was one who had inflamed a wound, will it [nonetheless] be permitted [to make use of his services]? [Obviously not.]

[**II**.A] What is the rule as to accepting bluing [for the eyes] from [gentiles]?

[B] Rab said, "Whoever wants to go blind may go blind [by accepting eye-bluing from gentiles. But there is no issue of danger to life]."

[C] Levi said, "Whoever wants to die will die[, and so, to avoid danger to life, one may not accept eye-bluing from gentiles]."

[D] Rab did not practice eye-bluing [so he did not know the dangers involved, and hence minimized the possibility of poisoning through the eyes].

[E] Levi practiced eye-bluing[, so he realized the dangers and hence prohibited using gentiles for the practice].

[F] Said R. Ba, "Now lo, we see them tasting the bluing [that they put in the eyes, and that shows that there is no poison in the bluing]."

[G] I should say that he tastes the bluing in order to see whether it is good. When it is not good, he keeps it and applies it [and so blinds the Israelite or poisons him].

[H] An opium drink [prepared by a gentile] is dangerous.

[I] *Theriak* [a drug against snake-bite]—

[J] R. Simon said, "It is forbidden [to accept from gentiles]."

[K] R. Yoḥanan said, "It is permitted."

[**III**.A] Associates in the name of R. Ba bar Zabeda: "Any [wound] that is located from the lips and inward do they heal on the Sabbath [since such a wound involves danger to life]."

[B] R. Zeira objected, "Lo, we have learned in the Mishnah: *He who is suffering from his teeth [nonetheless, on the Sabbath] may not suck vinegar through them* [M. Shab. 14:4]. Now are not the teeth interior to the lips? [So why is it not permitted to apply healing on the Sabbath?]"

[C] R. Zeira did not rule as has been stated, but R. Zeira in the name of R. Abba bar Zabeda: "Whatever [wound] is located from the throat and inward do they heal on the Sabbath[, since such a wound involves danger to life]."

[D] R. Zeira, R. Ba bar Zutra, R. Ḥaninah in the name of Rabbi: "They raise up the bone of the head on the Sabbath."

[E] R. Ḥiyya bar Madayya, R. Jonah, R. Zeira, R. Ba bar Zutra, R. Ḥaninah in the name of Rabbi: "They remove swollen glands of the throat on the Sabbath."

[F] R. Abbahu in the name of R. Yoḥanan: "An eye that became inflamed do they treat on the Sabbath."

[G] There [in Babylonia] they say in the name of R. Yoḥanan, "[Injuries] to hands and feet are a danger [to life]."

[H] R. Abbahu in the name of R. Yoḥanan: "Reddening [of a wound] is a danger [to life, and must be treated on the Sabbath]."

[I] Said R. Abin, "They remove the stinger of a scorpion on the Sabbath."

[J] Rab said, "Wine may be placed outside of the eyes [on the Sabbath], but may not be placed inside of the eyes."

[K] Samuel said this: "It is prohibited to put tasteless spit into the eye on the Sabbath."

[L] From this case you learn the rule as to treating scabs [of the eye].

[M] Rabbis of Caesarea say this: "[A wound] in the shape of a frog is a danger [to life]."

[N] R. Hezekiah said in the name of rabbis of Caesarea, "A wound from a spider's bite is a danger [to life and should be treated on the Sabbath]."

[O] R. Samuel bar R. Isaac: "A burn is a danger [to life and should be treated on the Sabbath]."

[P] Said R. Jeremiah, "On the Passover they apply to it leavened [food, for healing, even though ordinarily one may not utilize leavened food on Passover]."

[Q] [If such leaven] should be absorbed, it is permitted [on Passover, as stated above].

[R] Said R. Yosé, "The Mishnah itself has made the same point: *[On the Sabbath one may handle] a sewing needle to take out a thorn* [M. Shab. 17:2G]. Now if you do not concur, then you must explain the difference between removing a thorn and removing pus."

[S] As to an eye that grew dim, they asked R. Jeremiah. He said to them, "Lo, R. Ba is before you."

They asked R. Ba and he permitted them [to apply healing in such a case].

[Jeremiah] said to them, "Also I permit [applying healing in such a case]."

[T] R. Abbahu in the name of R. Yoḥanan: "Scurvy is a danger to life [and may be healed on the Sabbath]."

[U] R. Yoḥanan had [scurvy], and he was receiving treatment from [the daughter of] Domitian in Tiberias. On Friday he went to her. He said to her, "Do I need to be treated tomorrow [on the Sabbath]?"

She said to him, "No. But if you should need something, put on seeds of date palms (and some say, seeds of Nicolaos dates), split in half and roasted, and pounded together with barley husks and a child's dried excrement, and apply that mixture. But do not reveal to anyone [this potion which I have prescribed for you]."

The next day he went up and expounded [this very prescription] in the study house. She heard about it and choked on a bone (and some say, she converted to Judaism).

[V] From this story you learn three lessons:

[W] [1] You learn that scurvy is a danger [to life and may be treated on the Sabbath] [T].

[X] [2] You learn that any wound that is located from the lips and within do they heal on the Sabbath [A].

[Y] [3] You learn that which R. Jacob bar Aḥa said in the name of R. Yoḥanan: "If [a gentile] was an experienced physician, it is permitted [to accept healing from him or her]" [I.D].

[Z] R. Joshua b. Levi had colic. R. Ḥaninah and R. Jonathan instructed him to grind cress on the Sabbath and put old wine in it and drink it, so that he not be in danger [as to his life].

[AA] [Joshua b. Levi] had a grandson, who swallowed [something dangerous]. Someone came along and whispered over him [and the child was healed]. When he [the magician] went out, [Joshua] said to him, "What did you say over him?"

He said to him such and such a word.

He said to him, "What will be [the child's fate]! If he had died but had not heard [these words], it would have been [better] for him."

[BB] [But why should the healing have worked?] It was as an error done by a ruler.

[CC] R. Jacob in the name of R. Yoḥanan: "With all sorts of things do they effect healing, except for an idol, fornication, or committing murder[, which explains AA]."

[DD] R. Pinḥas raised the question, "Certainly the law applies when he said to him, 'Bring me leaves from an idol,' and he brought them to him. But if he said to him, 'Bring me leaves,' without further specification, and he brought them from an idol [what is the rule]?"

[EE] Let us infer the answer to the question from this:

[FF] R. Aḥa had chills and fever. [They brought him] a medicinal drink prepared from the phallus of Dionysian revelers [thus Jastrow, I 400 B]. But he would not drink it. They brought it to R. Jonah, and he did drink it. Said R. Mana, "Now if R. Jonah, the patriarch, had known what it was, he would never have drunk it."

[GG] Said R. Huna, "That is to say, 'They do not accept healing from something that derives from an act of fornication.' "

[HH] The Sabbath has been removed from the category [of that which may not be violated, even at the cost of death, since, as we have seen, many sorts of healings may be administered on the Sabbath in order to save life]. But a betrothed girl has not been removed from the category [of that which may not be violated at the cost of death. So one must die but not violate a betrothed girl, just as GG has stated].

[II] *The Sabbath has been removed from the category*—it is not as regards accepting healing [on that day], and, similarly, *a betrothed girl has not been removed from the category*—is it not as regards bringing about healing [in order to save a life]? [That surely is the case. One may not save a life by violating a betrothed girl, as JJ–VV will now explain.].

[JJ] And it is not the end of the matter that [if the ailing person said to one,] "Bring me a married woman [so that I may have sexual relations with her and so be healed," that one may not do so], but even if [the ailing person said it was only] to hear the voice [of a married woman, one may not permit him to hear the woman's voice].

[KK] This teaching accords with the following:

[LL] In the days of R. Eleazar, a man so loved a woman that he was in danger of dying [from unconsummated desire]. They came and asked R. Eleazar, "What is the law governing her 'passing before him' so that he may live?"

[MM] He answered them, "Let him die but [let matters not be done] in such a way."

[NN] "What is the law as to his merely hearing her voice, so that he may live?"

[OO] "Let him die, but [let matters not be done] in such a way."

[PP] Now what was the character of this girl [who was to be kept away from the man pining for her]?

[QQ] R. Jacob bar Idi and R. Isaac bar Naḥman—one maintained that she was a married woman, and the other maintained that she was unmarried.

[RR] Now so far as the opinion of the one who maintained that she was a married woman, there are no problems. But as to the one who maintained that she was unmarried[, why should she not have married the man]?

[SS] Now, lo, Bar Koha Nigra so loved a woman in the days of R. Eleazar, that he was in danger of dying [from unconsummated desire]. [Read: And R. Eleazar permitted him to marry her.]

[TT] In the former case [LL–OO, we deal] with a married woman, in the latter [SS] with an unmarried woman.

[UU] Now even if you maintain that both cases deal with an unmarried woman [delete: or in both cases we deal with a married woman], interpret the case to apply to one who formed a desire for the woman while she was still married [in which case even after the divorce he may not marry her].

[VV] There are some who would explain [the rabbi's prohibiting the man to marry the unmarried woman] because she was a woman of high station, and she would not have accepted the judgment of [the rabbi to marry the love-stricken suitor], so whatever [the suitor] might do would be done subject to the prohibition of the rabbi. On that account he did not permit [the marriage].

[**IV**.A] "The [Mishnah pericope cited below]," said R. Ḥaninah, "means that one may not attain healing through bloodshed.

[B] "For we have learned in the following Mishnah passage:

[C] "*[The woman who is in hard labor—they chop up the child in her womb and remove it limb by limb, because her life takes precedence over its life.] [If] the greater part [of the child] had gone forth, they do not touch it, for they do not set aside one life on account of another life* [M. Oh. 7:6].

[D] "They take account of the possibility that he might die, *and they do not set aside one life on account of another life.*"

[E] It is not the end of the matter that [if] someone said to a person, "Kill so-and-so," [he should not do so, even to save the life of the other,] but even if he said, "Do violence to so-and-so," [one should not do so.] [Now this stated rule applies in the case of] one gentile against another, or a gentile against an Israelite [in which case, the perpetrator is liable]. But in the case of an Israelite against a gentile, [the perpetrator] is exempt.

[F] R. Ḥisda raised the question: "What is the law as to saving an adult at the sacrifice of the life of a child?"

[G] Responded R. Jeremiah, "And has it not been taught in the Mishnah: *[If] its greater part has gone forth, they do not touch it, for they do not set aside one life on account of another life!*"

[H] [Still, that evidence may not be probative, for] R. Yosé bar R. Bun in the name of R. Levi: "That case is different, for it is not known who will be responsible for the death of whom."

[I] MʿŚH B: A snake bit Eleazar b. Dama. He came to Jacob of Kefar Sama for healing. Said to [Ben Dama] R. Ishmael, "You have no right to do so, Ben Dama."

He said to him, "I shall bring proof that it is permitted for him to heal me."

But he did not suffice to bring proof before he dropped dead.

Said to him R. Ishmael, "Happy are you, [41a] O Ben Dama, for you left this world in peace and did not break through the fence of the sages, and so in dying you have carried out that which has been said: 'A serpent will bite him who breaks through a wall' " [Qoh. 10:8].

[J] And did not a snake already bite him?

[K] But a snake will not bite him in the age to come.

[L] And what did he have to say [in reply to the prohibition to go to Jacob]?

[M] "You shall therefore keep my statutes and my ordinances, by doing which a man shall live" (Lev. 18:5).

[V.A] **He who gives a haircut to a gentile clips until he reaches the forelock. Once he reaches the forelock, lo, this one removes his hands [and does not cut it off] [T. A.Z. 3:6A].**

[B] **[An Israelite] who is getting a haircut from a gentile watches him in the mirror. [If it is] from a Samaritan, he does not watch in the mirror [T. A.Z. 3:5A–B].**

[C] **They permitted the household of Rabbi [Tosefta: Rabban Gamaliel] to look [at themselves in the mirror], because they are subject to the government [T. A.Z. 3:5C–D].**

[D] Three matters did they permit to the household of Rabbi [which ordinarily are prohibited to Israelites]:

[E] [1] They may look at themselves in a mirror.

[F] [2] They may get a haircut in the gentile manner.

[G] [3] And they may teach Greek to their children, because they are subject to the government.

[H] A certain person [who was destined to] convert [to Judaism] was a barber and also an astrologer. Now he saw through his astrological learning that Jews were going to shed his blood [and he assumed that this meant Jews would kill him, though the vision referred to the rite of circumcision that would take place] upon his conversion. Consequently, when a Jew would want to get a haircut from him, he would kill him.

[I] How many did he kill? R. Eleazar bar Yosé said, "Eighty." R. Yosé b. R. Bun said, "Three hundred."

[J] But in the end, [the Jews] prayed for him, and he returned to his senses.

[K] It has been taught in a Tannaitic source: A gentile who sells scrolls, phylacteries, and *mezuzot*—they do not purchase [such objects] from him [cf. M. Git. 4:6].

[L] And has it not been taught: MᶜŚH B: A gentile in Sidon was selling scrolls, phylacteries, and *mezuzot*. The case came before sages, who ruled, "It is permitted to purchase from him."

[M] R. Samuel bar Nathan in the name of R. Ḥama bar Ḥanina: "It was [the case of a] proselyte who returned to his former ways [Pené Moshe: out of fear of gentiles. But he knew that the objects had to be prepared for their own purpose, and he prepared them correctly]."

M. 2:2A refers to use of a gentile veterinarian, B to a physician, and C–E are clear as stated. The first two units deal with the stated theme of the Mishnah pericope, specifying the sorts of healing one may accept from a gentile. Unit **III** is relevant only in a general way, and speaks of healing on the Sabbath. The point shared with the present setting is interest in what is a danger to life. One may not endanger his life, and therefore he may not accept healing from a gentile, but, for that same reason, he may practice healing on the Sabbath. Now the second of these two points is worked out at great length. The impression of the irrelevance of the matter to the Mishnah in fact is removed at W–Y, which link both themes. The important point, Y, is what ties the whole to the Mishnah pericope. There may be need to improve the handling of BB. CC–XX then go forward along the same lines, namely, saving life at nearly all costs, as Yoḥanan maintains should be done. Now the emphasis shifts to things one must not do in order to save a life, thus complementary to the matter of the Sabbath, but wholly remote from the matter of accepting healing from a gentile. Unit **IV** goes on with this same matter but is essentially distinct from the concluding materials of **III**. It is only at unit **V** that we reach materials somewhat pertinent to the Mishnah's rules. But as soon as these materials are introduced (**V**.A, B), they go off once more on a tangent, this time the matter of special rights enjoyed by Rabbi's household. In all the Talmud does not give the impression of having been constructed to serve in particular the Mishnah pericope before us.

2:3

[A] *These things belonging to gentiles are prohibited, and the prohibition affecting them extends to deriving any benefit from them at all:*

[B] *[1] wine, [2] vinegar of gentiles which to begin with was wine, [3] a Hadrianic pot, and [4] hides pierced at the heart.*

[C] *Rabban Simeon b. Gamaliel says, "When the tear in the hide is round, it is prohibited. [If it is] straight, it is permitted."*

[D] *"Meat that is being brought in to an idol is permitted.*

[E] *"But that which comes out is prohibited,*

[F] *"because it is like 'sacrifices of the dead' " (Ps. 106:28), the words of R. Aqiba.*

[G] *Those who are going to an idolatrous pilgrimage—it is prohibited to do business with them.*

[H] *Those that are coming back—they are permitted.*

[**I**.A] R. Isaac bar Naḥman in the name of R. Joshua b. Levi would say, "[If wine was] sweet, bitter, or strong, the [prohibition of wine that has been left] uncovered does not [apply, because that prohibition is based on the possibility that a snake has drunk from the open keg and imparted its venom to the wine in the keg, and snakes will not drink from these three sorts of wine]."

[B] R. Simon in the name of R. Joshua b. Levi [said], "Strong, bitter, and sweet wine is not subject [to prohibition on the count of wine that has been left] uncovered or [to prohibition on the count of wine that has been used] for idolatrous purposes[, because gentiles will not use wine of such character for libations]."

[C] R. Simon explains the character of these three types of wine: "Strong is spiced wine, bitter is absinthiatum, and what is sweet? It is boiled wine."

[D] R. Joshua b. Zeidel possessed boiled wine that had been set aside [for a time] in the domain of a gentile. He asked R. Yannai b. R. Ishmael [whether or not he might make use of this wine, since it was boiled and so, in line with Simon's view of Joshua b. Levi's opinion, not likely to have been utilized for a libation].

He said to him, "Thus did R. Simeon b. Laqish say: 'Sweet wine is not subject [to prohibition on the count of wine that has been left] uncovered or [to prohibition on the count of wine which has been used] for idolatrous purposes.' " [The status of boiled wine would appear, then, to be different, since it is omitted from the cited list, and so boiled wine would be prohibited under the stated circumstances.]

[E] R. Yannai b. R. Ishmael fell sick. R. Zira, R. Joshua, R. Bun bar Kahana, and R. Ḥananiah, associates of the rabbis, went up to visit him. They found R. Joshua bar Zeidel sitting there. They said, "Lo, here is the master of the tradition, and here also is the master about whom the story is told [that is, here are both Yannai and Joshua b. Zeidel]. Let us then phrase the question [once again]."

[F] He [Yannai] said to them, "Thus did R. Simeon b. Laqish say: 'Sweet wine is not subject [to prohibition on the count of wine that has been left] uncovered or [to prohibition on the count of wine that has been used] for idolatrous purposes.' "

[G] He said to him, "Perhaps the saying of R. Simeon b. Laqish [serves merely to state] thus and so [that is, what is reasonable but not an applied law]."

[H] [Yannai] said to them, "It was for a concrete precedent, and they relied [for a practical ruling] on it."

[I] After they left, R. Ila [met] R. Bun bar Kahana. He said to him, "If it were not that you prefer traditions [in the name of Amoraic authorities, you might have taken note of an earlier Tannaitic ruling, for] is it not a Mishnah tradition?

[J] "[For] R. Ḥiyya taught, 'As to boiled wine belonging to a gentile, why is it prohibited? It is because, to begin with, it was wine [and useful for a libation, even though its character now has changed].' "

[K] R. Yosé said, "The Mishnah itself has [explicitly] said the same: [Prohibited are] *wine and vinegar that to begin with was wine*" [M. A.Z. 2:3B].

[L] R. Ami had guests. He said to them, "If it were not that my boiled wine had been left uncovered, I should have been able to give you something to drink."

[M] Said to him R. Bibi, "Bring it along, and we shall drink it [since, if it was left uncovered, being boiled wine, it is not prohibited anyhow]."

[N] He said, "Someone who wants to die—let him go and die in his own house [and not in my house]!"

[O] Bar Yudenah had spiced wine [that had been left] uncovered. He asked rabbis, and they declared it prohibited. Now did not R. Isaac bar Naḥman say in the name of R. Joshua b. Levi, "[If wine was] sweet, bitter, or strong, the [prohibition of wine that has been left] uncovered does not [apply? And spiced wine falls within the stated rule, as at C.]"

[P] Rabbis of Caesarea in the name of R. Yudah bar Titus [!] [interpreted the rule governing spiced wine to apply to a heavily spiced wine, in which] one pounded one [spice] into three parts [so that the wine was thickened by the pulverized spices. If P responds to O, the meaning is that the wine was not really spiced.]

[Q] They asked in session before R. Abbahu, "Boiled wine that was left uncovered—what is the law?"

[R] He said to them, "[Concerning the same problem in connection with] *Qarina* wine [a very sweet sort] did I have to ask R. Yoḥanan, and do you now ask me about this kind?"

[S] They asked R. Isaac, and he declared it prohibited to them. At that point R. Abbahu recalled that R. Yoḥanan [also] had ruled that it was prohibited.

[T] The water tank of Bar Netizah was left uncovered. He asked R. Bar bar Mamal [whether or not he might still make use of the contents]. He said to him, "If [someone] was going in and coming in, it is permitted [on grounds that a person would frighten away a snake]."

[U] R. Jacob bar Aḥa, R. Ami in the name of R. Eleazar: "If [someone] was sleeping [in the room, the contents of the vat are] permitted."

[V] R. Ḥaninah, R. Joshua b. Levi—one said, "[If] someone was sleeping [in the room, the contents of the vat are] permitted." And one said, "[If someone was] sleeping [in the room, the contents of the vat are] prohibited."

[W] It is reasonable to suppose that it is R. Ḥaninah who said, "[If someone] was sleeping [in the room,] the [contents of the vat are] permitted," because in all instances, R. Eleazar relied upon the rulings of R. Ḥaninah[, and R. Eleazar said that if someone was sleeping in the room, the contents of the vat are permitted, U].

[X] R. Yosé b. Saul told the story of the following case: There was an incident involving a certain woman, who loved to perform the religious commandments [such as feeding the hungry], while her husband hated to perform them. Now a poor man came along, so she gave him food, and he ate. When she sensed that her husband was coming back, she took the poor man away and hid him in the attic. She set food before her husband, and he ate and then fell asleep. A snake came along and supped from the same dish. When her husband woke up from his sleep, he wanted to eat. The man in the attic began to chatter [so warning the husband not to eat the food].

[Y] Now does the law not state, "If someone was sleeping [in the same room as the food], [the food] is permitted"? [So why should the man have refrained from eating the food anyhow?]

[Z] [The serpent] was wrapped around [the bowl, so there was every reason to believe that the serpent had eaten some of the food].

[AA] And is not [the wife] prohibited [to the husband] by reason of having been alone [with the poor man]? "Because they are adulteresses, and blood is upon their hands" (Ez. 23:45) [—meaning if she is guilty of the one, she will be guilty of the other]. Because [the poor man] was not suspect in regard to shedding blood [as he would have been had he permitted the husband to eat the poisoned food], so he was not suspect in regard to fornication.

[BB] MʿŚH B: Now there was a certain pious man, who [nonetheless] ridiculed [the rules governing leaving liquids] uncovered. [Because he drank polluted liquid,] he was smitten with a fever. People saw him sitting and expounding [the law] on the Day of Atonement with a flask of water in his hand [on account of his fever.].

[CC] MʿŚH B: A butcher in Sepphoris fed Israelites carrion and *ṭerefah*-meat. One time at the eve of the Day of Atonement toward dusk he drank a great deal of wine and got drunk. He climbed up to the roof of his house and fell down and died. Dogs began licking at his blood.

They came and asked R. Ḥaninah, "What is the law as to carrying in his corpse [out of the public domain] on account of [the dogs]?"

He said to them, "It is written, 'You shall be men consecrated to me; therefore you shall not eat any flesh that is torn by beasts in the field; you shall cast it to the dogs' (Ex. 22:31). This man stole from the dogs and fed Israelites carrion and *ṭerefah*-meat. Leave him be. [The dogs] are eating what belongs to them anyhow."

[DD] A man had an open keg. On the eve of the Great Fast [the Day of Atonement] he went, planning to empty out [the contents of the keg]. His friend said to him, "I shall come and drink what is in the keg."

He said to him, "It has been left uncovered."

He said to him, "The Master of the Day will preserve [me, since it is a religious duty to eat and drink on the eve of the Day of Atonement]."

He did not give thought to drinking [all] the wine in the keg. He had tasted only a little bit when he grew weak [because of the poison in the wine].

[EE] R. Jeremiah in the name of R. Ḥiyya bar Ba: "All poisons cause sores. But the poison of a snake kills."

[FF] R. Ḥiyya said, "They do not accept questions concerning liquids that have been left uncovered."

[GG] R. Jeremiah asked R. Zeira a question [concerning liquids that had been left uncovered].

[HH] Now does the master of the tradition ask a question concerning that same tradition [which is attributed to him]?

[II] He was dozing off [and did not pay attention].

[JJ] R. Zeira was sitting and eating in the evening. The lamp went out. He put out his hand on the lamp and kindled a light and found an adder as thin as a hair wrapped around the lamp. He said to it, "Wicked one! I should never have been careful to watch out for you."

[KK] Said R. Ami, "We have to scruple concerning things about which people in general are scrupulous. Thus: It is forbidden to put small coins into your mouth, bread under your arm [because of the perspiration], a cooked dish under a bed, to stick a knife into an *etrog*, or a knife into a radish."

[LL] Said R. Yosé b. R. Bun, "Any form of sweat that exudes from a person is a poison, except for the sweat of the face."

[MM] Said R. Yannai, "[If people want to endanger themselves for some small benefit, say to them,] 'If he plucks [gains anything], he plucks a piece of coal, if he loses, he loses a pearl [his life, thus risking his life for a trifle]."

[NN] As to R. Jonathan, when someone would ask him a question [involving a liquid left uncovered], he would reply to him, "Am I a pledge for your life [if you want to risk it]?"

[OO] Said R. [41b] Simeon b. Laqish [to someone who asked about drinking that which had been left uncovered], "If you sold yourself to Lyddians [who eat human flesh, for which they pay a high price], you would then sell yourself for a good price. But here [are you ready to sell yourself] for a paltry sum!"

[**II**.A] R. Asi, R. Yoḥanan in the name of Ben Beterah: "Libation wine that fell into a winepress—one may sell the whole of [the contents of the press] to a gentile, [deriving benefit from the entire proceeds] except for the value of the libation wine that is in [the press]."

[B] R. Asi in the name of R. Yoḥanan: "Ordinary wine belonging to a gentile is forbidden but does not impart uncleanness [as does libation wine = E–I].

[C] "[If an Israelite] deposited [wine] with [a gentile], it is prohibited for consumption, but permitted [so far as the Israelite's] deriving benefit [from the sale of the wine]."

[D] R. Zeira asked in session before R. Yasa, "What is the law governing the case in which [the gentile] sets aside a given corner for that wine [in the house of a gentile]?"

[E] [He said to him, "In this case that one may derive benefit from the wine, even though he may not drink it himself,] if he deposited the wine with a gentile."

[F] R. Abbahu came [and taught a ruling] in the name of R. Yoḥanan:

[G] "There are three types of wine [so far as the prohibition of gentiles' wine on the count of libation to idolatry is concerned]:

[H] "[There is wine] that [an Israelite] assuredly saw a gentile offer up as a libation to an idol. This sort of wine imparts uncleanness of a severe sort, like a dead creeping thing.

[I] "[There is] ordinary wine [of a gentile]. It is prohibited [for Israelite use or benefit]. But it does not impart uncleanness.

[J] "[If an Israelite] deposited [wine] with [a gentile], sealed by a single seal, it is prohibited for drinking, but permitted for [other sorts of] gain [e.g., sale]."

[K] Said R. Jeremiah before R. Zeira, "Notice then what he has said. He has said [that the stated rule applies] only in the case in which a seal [has been used to protect the keg of wine]. Lo, [if he should leave the wine] without a seal, it is prohibited both as to drinking and as to other forms of benefit." [This then rejects the view of C.]

[L] R. Eleazar gave instruction: "It is in the case of [the gentile's] setting aside [a particular corner for the location of an Israelite's keg of wine that it is permitted to derive benefit from that keg of wine, but not in a case in which the Israelite deposits the keg of wine with a gentile without placing on it any sort of seal]. And R. Zeira was [merely] examining that tradition."

[**III**.A] There we repeat the following tradition: *"[He who leaves his tithed product] in the keeping of a gentile—[the produce is deemed to be] like [the gentile's] produce. R. Simeon says, "It is deemed to be demai"* **[M. Dem. 3:4G–I].**

[B] R. Ḥananiah asked before R. Mani, "Is the meaning of 'the produce is deemed to be like the gentile's produce' to be taken literally and [so Simeon's opponent's] reasoning is that they are in fact free of tithes entirely? But what of totally untithed produce deriving from some other source [that one deposited with a gentile]? [Shall we then say that that sort of totally untithed produce, deposited with a gentile, also will be wholly exempt from tithing?]"

[C] He said to him, "And that is so for all that is in [the keeping of a gentile, whatever its status. It is deemed free of the obligation to tithing]."

[D] But it was not of any value at all that R. Ḥaninah raised questions concerning this tradition[, for we rule that only if one deposited unconsecrated food that had been suitably tithed do we rule the produce deposited with a gentile is deemed free of the requirement to tithe].

[**IV**.A] [If an Israelite] deposited [his keg of wine] with a [gentile] when the keg was sealed [but not in a specified and designated corner of the gentile's house]—

[B] Ḥananiah and R. Mana—one said [the wine] is forbidden, and one said [the wine is] permitted.

[C] Concerning what do they differ? It is concerning deriving benefit [from the wine], but so far as drinking the wine [all parties of course concur] that that is prohibited.

[D] Rab said, "When protected by only a single seal, milk, meat, wine, and blue wool [in a gentile's domain] are prohibited. Asafetida, fish sauce, bread, and cheese are permitted.

"A piece of fish on which is no seal [is forbidden]."

[E] Said R. Yudan, "The reasoning of Rab [is this:] Whatever may be prohibited by reason of its own traits will be prohibited if protected by only a single seal. [Whatever is prohibited] only because it is mixed [with other objects] is permitted when protected by only a single seal. [For instance, cheese is prohibited because it may contain unclean milk.]"

[**V**.A] R. Jacob bar Aḥa, R. Simeon bar Ba, R. Eleazar in the name of R. Ḥaninah, R. Ba, R. Ḥiyya in the name of R. Yoḥanan, R. Zeira in the name of R. Joshua b. Levi: "Everything is permitted [that has been in a gentile's domain so long as it is protected by even] a single seal, except for wine and a Hadrianic pot."

[B] R. Zeira in the name of R. Jeremiah, "The law is in accord with the position of R. Meir in the following Tannaitic tradition: 'A Hadrianic pot is prohibited, and the prohibition concerning it extends even to deriving benefit from proceeds received in selling it,' the words of R. Meir. And the sages say, 'The prohibition concerning it does not extend even to deriving benefit from proceeds received in selling it.' "

[C] R. Jeremiah asked before R. Zeira, "As to a garment [made from yarn dyed with shells of fruit subject to the ʿ*orlah*-taboo, which prohibits deriving benefit from fruit of a tree during the first three years of its growth]—what is the law [as to using such a garment to support a bed, e.g., to place the garment underneath the leg of a bed]?"

[D] And [R. Zeira] refused to accept [the case as parallel to the one involving Meir and the sages].

[E] He said to him, "Even in accord with the view of the one who ruled in that case that it is permitted, in this case he will maintain that it is forbidden [to derive benefit from the sale of a Hadrianic pot]. For there [in the case of the Hadrianic pot], the prohibition affecting the pot is not readily discerned [since the wine is absorbed in the clay]. But here it is readily discerned [that the man has dyed the yarn]."

[F] What is the law as to setting such a pot under a bed and supporting the leg of a bed with it?

[G] R. Eleazar said it is permitted to do so, and R. Yoḥanan said it is prohibited to do so.

[**VI**.A] *Hides pierced at the heart [M. A.Z. 2:3B(4)]:*

[B] R. Jeremiah in the name of Rab: "The law is in accord with the position of Rabban Simeon b. Gamaliel."

[C] How does one make such a hide?

[D] He tears the hide while the animal is yet alive and takes out the heart for an idol.

[E] How does he know [that the hole was made while the animal was yet alive]?

[F] R. Huna said, "If someone tears at the hide while the animal is still alive, the hole rebounds and becomes rounded. [If he should do so] after the animal is slaughtered, [the tear will be] elongated."

[G] Said R. Yosé, "And you should infer from this ruling [that, by doing a deed for idolatrous purposes, the man has prohibited Israelite use of the hide], that if one slaughtered [only] one organ of the animal[, he has prohibited the beast for Israelite use], even though you have in general maintained that something that is alive may not be prohibited by reason of idolatry, here it is forbidden."

[**VII**.A] *Meat that is being brought into an idol is permitted [M. 2:3D].*

[B] R. Ba, R. Ḥiyya in the name of R. Yoḥanan said, "This ruling is stated to exclude the position of R. Eliezer.

[C] "For R. Eliezer says, 'The [mere] intention of a gentile [to make use of meat] for idolatry [is sufficient to prohibit Israelite use of that meat].' " [We see, A, that that position is not valid.]

[**VIII**.A] *But that which comes out is prohibited [M. 2:3E].*

[B] R. Abina in the name of R. Jeremiah, "This is the case if one has brought the meat further in than the bars [enclosures into the sanctum], but if he did not bring it within the bars, also that which comes out is permitted."

[C] That is the rule in the case of a temple that has bars.

[D] But in the case of a temple that does not have bars, the entire building is deemed equivalent to bars. [The whole is an inner sanctum.]

[**IX**.A] *Those who are going to a "tarput" [idolatrous pilgrimage]—it is prohibited to do business with them [M. A.Z. 2:3G].*

[B] R. Ḥiyya in the name of R. Yoḥanan, "It is a case of a *TWRYBS* [a pedestal for a mountain]: They bring a large idol to a small idol."

[C] Some read [in the Mishnah] the word TRPWT [rather than TWRBWT].

[D] The one who reads the word TRPWT derives it from *terapim*, and the one who reads it TRBWT derives it from TWRYBS [a pedestal for a mountain].

[**X**.A] *But those that are coming back—they are permitted [M. A.Z. 2:3H].*

[B] R. Abina in the name of R. Jeremiah, "This is the rule in a case in which, when they are coming back, they are not as they were when they went [in large groups]. But if, when they were coming back, they are as they were when they went, they too are prohibited."

The wine is prohibited because it is assumed under all circumstances to have been used for a libation. One may not use the wine or sell it and use the proceeds. Vinegar is prohibited on the same count. Earthenware is assumed to have absorbed wine. The heart is removed while the animal is yet alive and offered to the idol, with the result that what remains—like wine remaining in a jug after some of the jug's wine has been poured out as a libation—also is prohibited. C glosses B[4]. D–F and G–H make the same distinction between what has been subjected to the idolatrous worship and what has not. But the practical result is different. Meat that may be offered is not yet offered, thus Aqiba. People going to the idol's temple, on the other hand, are under the spell of their liturgy, which is not the case when they have completed it.

The relevance of unit **I** to the Mishnah pericope is tenuous, since the principal interest of the unit is in rules governing liquids that have been left uncovered. The point of contact with the Mishnah is at **I**.B, and there alone. That is, the same rule that governs liquids that have been left uncovered, in the opinion of some, also governs liquids that may have been used for idolatry. What snakes will not drink idolators will not use for a libation. That that point of contact is subordinate, a mere pretext for including in the present location the whole vast construction, is clear from the character of what follows, which deals solely with uncovered liquids. People who raise such questions concerning whether or not one may drink wine left uncovered are risking their lives for very little. Hence, in the end, the concern of the whole is shown to be paltry, since there is little to be gained from permitting something that is so full of danger to life. The opening sections of unit **I**, A–K, do focus upon what is relevant to the Mishnah, and this is made explicit, in particular, by K, which stands separate from its context. At L the sequence of materials, running on to the end, commences on not drinking wine that has been left uncovered. Essentially, on the stated theme all the Talmud has to offer is this sequence of sayings and stories, strung together with little, if any, analysis. L–N announce the basic viewpoint of all that will follow; then come O–P, Q–S, T + U–W. There follows a sequence of stories, not all of them relevant in more than general theme: X–AA, BB, CC (totally irrelevant), DD, a set of simple sayings, EE, FF–II, then further stories and sayings mixed together, JJ, KK, LL, MM–OO. In fact, at best the materials use the Mishnah as a mere pretext for a discussion of an essentially distinct topic.

Unit **II** brings us no closer than does unit **I** to a close reading of the Mishnah pericope. Its interest lies in the condition in which Israelite wine left in gentile hands may be profitably sold by the Israelite, and that in which Israelite wine may provide no benefit whatsoever to the Israelite owner. This concern runs through **IV** and **V** as well. There are two separate conditions. First, the gentile sets aside a particular place in his house for the storage of the Israelite wine. Second, the Israelite protects his wine with a seal, which would then have to be broken for the wine to be used and contaminated by idolatry. The dialectic of argument is somewhat complicated, since available materials are cited without significant revision for the present purpose rather than being restated for analysis. Thus F–J are inserted whole, because the information they supply is required for understanding B and the question phrased at D–E. K resumes the discussion broken off by the intrusion of F–J's unit.

Unit **III** is inserted whole; it interrupts the flow of thought. The reason for the insertion of **III** is not difficult to discern, however, since it carries forward the common theme of depositing Israelite produce in gentile hands. We need not be detained to spell out the passage, since it recurs in its own appropriate setting.

At **IV** we resume the theme of **II**. But the substance of this unit is simply a sequence of unconnected rules on eating or drinking produce subject to gentile preparation. From unit **V** we undertake a fairly systematic analysis of the Mishnah pericope's statements, beginning at M. 2:3B[3]. The Talmud's discussion of the Hadrianic pot, assumed to have absorbed prohibited wine kept within it, is interesting because of the introduction of what is alleged to be a parallel case. We note that at B Zeira maintains that the law follows Meir, who prohibits even deriving benefit indirectly. Jeremiah challenges this view by adducing a parallel case, in which important authorities will permit indirectly deriving benefit from a prohibited substance, even though, all will of course concur, an Israelite may not directly benefit from that substance. This is spelled out at C. As is its way, this Talmud does not fully articulate and amplify the issue. At E Zeira distinguishes the two cases, and so the matter is dropped. Then, at the end of **V**, we are given two Amoraic opinions on the matter at hand. The next five units, **VI–X**, follow essentially a single pattern, citing and then glossing a phrase of the Mishnah pericope.

2:4

[A] *"Skins of gentiles and their jars, with Israelite wine collected in them—*

[B] *"they are prohibited, and the prohibition affecting them extends to deriving benefit from them at all," the words of R. Meir.*

[C] *And sages say, "The prohibition affecting them does not extend to deriving benefit from them."*

[I.A] **Skins belonging to gentiles, that are scraped, lo, these are permitted.**

[B] **Those that [are sealed or] covered with pitch, lo, these are prohibited.**

[C] **[If] a gentile works it and pitches it, while an Israelite supervises him,**

[D] **[an Israelite] may collect wine or oil in it without scruple [T. 4:10C–F].**

[E] And [should one not] scruple to [take account of the] possibility that [the gentile] has made a libation [while working the skin]?

[F] Said R. Ba, "It is not common [for a gentile] to make a libation of something that is repulsive."

[G] If so, then even if an Israelite is not supervising him [it should be permitted to make use of the hides worked by a gentile].

[H] I reply, [We take account of the] possibility [that] the gentile has exchanged [the hides on which he was working, not subject to a libation, for hides on which he was not then working, which are subject to a libation].

[I] And jars belonging to gentiles—

[J] new ones are permitted, even though they are covered with pitch.

[K] Old ones are forbidden, even though they are not covered with pitch.

[L] Now lo, here you say that the [jars] that are pitched are permitted [J], while earlier you ruled that the [skins] that are pitched are prohibited [B].

[M] Said R. Abbahu, "I observed their [gentiles'] pitching of jars, and they do not put into them any sort of vinegar when they pitch them[, and that is why the rule of I–J permits such jars]."

[N] R. Jacob bar Aḥa in the name of rabbis: "Wine that is prohibited for [Israelites'] drinking but permitted for [sale for their] benefit, [which] was put into jars—the jars [thereafter] enter the status of the wine. [The consequence is that if] one emptied the jars and put other wine into the same jars, the [new] wine in the jars enters the status of the jars. [If one then again] emptied [out that wine] and put in yet another wine, the wine [now put into the jars] is prohibited, but the jars [now become] permitted."

[**II**.A] And why [at M. 2:4C do the sages say that wine collected in skins of gentiles is] prohibited for drinking, yet permitted for other sorts of benefit?

[B] Since R. Meir said, *"It is prohibited for drinking, and the prohibition extends to deriving benefit from them at all"* [M. A.Z. 2:4B, it was deemed sufficient to take one step only in the direction of liberalization, so permitting deriving benefit, while granting Meir's strict rule as to drinking the wine].

[**III**.A] Said R. Ba, "When R. Aqiba went to Sepphoris, they came and asked him, 'Jars belonging to gentiles—in what manner are they to be cleansed [of their uncleanness]?'

[B] "He said, 'On the basis of this [rule of I–J] I taught concerning [those jars]: Now if when they are not pitched at all, you teach that they are permitted, when they have been pitched, but when the pitch has been scaled off, is it not an argument *a fortiori* [that they should be deemed clean and permitted for Israelite use, since the pitch is now no longer present]. And when I came to my colleagues, they said, '[That is no argument, for] because of the pitch [the pots] absorb [the wine that has been put into them, so scaling is not enough].' "

[C] [If] a gentile has collected water in [jars], an Israelite [who wishes to make use of the same jars] puts water into them and then goes and puts wine into them and need not scruple.

[D] [If] a gentile collected brine or fish-brine in them, an Israelite may then put wine into those same jars.

[E] [If] a gentile collected wine in them, an Israelite may put into them brine or fish-brine and then go and put wine into them, and he need not scruple.

[F] R. Yoḥanan went out to receive R. Yudan the Patriarch in Acre. They came and asked him, " As to jars, what is the mode of cleaning them?"

[G] He said, "On the basis of [the aforestated rule, D–E], I taught them: Now if, when a gentile has gathered into them brine or fish brine, an Israelite may put wine in them. . . ." [The sentence is not completed. The authorities now cited, I–J, will propose ways in which one may complete this account of Yoḥanan's reasoning.]

[H] R. Yasa in the name of R. Yoḥanan: ". . . if one puts them into the fire, is it not an argument *a fortiori* [that they should be cleaned in such a manner]?"

[I] R. Ḥiyya in the name of R. Yoḥanan, ". . . if one scales off their pitch, is it not an argument *a fortiori* [that that should be the proper way to clean them]?"

[J] [But will the jars] stand up [in the fire]?

[K] [If] they stand up, they stand up [and if not, they will be useless anyhow].

[L] Jars [belonging to a gentile] that are not pitched—

[M] R. Assi said, "They are forbidden."

[N] R. Ammi said, "They are permitted."

[O] R. Jacob b. Aḥa said, "R. Assi [in ruling that they are prohibited] raises the question, 'Can we rule that a sherd does not absorb [wine? Lo, we see that it does absorb wine. That is why they will be forbidden]."

[P] R. Ba said, "R. Sheshet asked, 'Do we maintain that the chamber pot does not absorb [urine]? [It certainly does absorb urine.]"

[Q] R. Jacob bar Aḥa, R. Simeon bar Aḥa in the name of R. Ḥaninah: "Jugs belonging to gentiles [that one wishes to use for Israelite purposes]—one fills them with water [and leaves it in them] for three days of twenty-four hours each."

[R] R. Jacob bar Aḥa said, "R. Assi raised the question: [41c] 'Do we actually do so?' "

[S] R. Yosé of Milḥayya brought a case before R. Mana. He said to him, "Is this *post facto* [that someone already has put wine into the jugs after leaving them filled with water for three days]?"

[T] [Supply: He said to him, "Yes."]

[U] He said to him, "[If so,] it is permitted."

[V] "But if it had been at the outset [and the deed had not yet been done]?"

[W] He said to him, "[Under such circumstances, it is] forbidden."

[X] R. Jeremiah went to Gobelanah. He gave instructions concerning certain large cups, [that, in order to clean them] one fills them with water [and leaves it standing in them] for three days of twenty-four hours each.

[Y] A skin of an Aramaean split open, and an Israelite saved [the wine] in his. The case came before rabbis [concerning the further use of the Israelite's skin]. They ruled, "One fills it with water [and leaves it standing therein] for three days of twenty-four hours each."

[Z] R. Yasa went to Tyre. He saw them putting pitch into small skins, and Israelites were buying them. He said to them, "Who permitted you to do this?" They went and asked R. Isaac and R. Mani, who declared the practice to be forbidden.

The first unit takes up the task of analyzing further relevant legal formulations (A–D, I–K) and comparing their laws. Skins and jars are subject to contrasting rules, as L points out. The Talmud's interest in connection with both formulations is to explain the basis of the rule and to test the explanation, thus E–H and L–M. Abbahu, at M, explains the difference: it has to do with how the items are prepared for use. N is tacked on. Unit **II** carries forward the analysis of the Mishnah's materials. At **III** we have two parallel constructions, in which available materials are used to develop secondary rules. Aqiba is made to refer to the rule analyzed at I–J in framing an answer to a question, **III**.B, and the same procedure is repeated at **III**.F. Unit **III** proceeds to present a repertoire of other rulings on the status of jars, pitched and otherwise, belonging to gentiles, as well as relevant cases. The entire construction is acutely relevant to the interests and principles of the Mishnah's rule.

2:5

[A] *"Grape pits and grape skins belonging to gentiles are prohibited, and the prohibition affecting them extends to deriving any benefit from them at all," the words of R. Meir.*

[B] *And the sages say, "[If] they are moist, they are forbidden. If they are dry, they are permitted."*

[**I**.A] [Interpreting the position of sages, M. 2:5B,] R. Sheshet in the name of Rab: "*If they are moist, they are forbidden* even for deriving benefit from them. *If they are dry, they are permitted* even for eating."

[**II**.A] Now do we not learn in the Mishnah: *[Wine] does not become libation wine until it descends into the vat [M. A.Z. 4:8]* [so why should the moist grape pits and skins belonging to gentiles be prohibited at all]?

[B] R. Ba in the name of R. Judah: "The Mishnah speaks of a case in which [a gentile] dips [the wine] out of the vat [after the grapes have been trodden]."

[**III**.A] There we have learned in the Mishnah: *And so with new olive peat. But with respect to year-old olive peat, the oven is clean. [And if it is known that liquids exude from the old olive peat, even after three years the oven is made unclean (M. Kel. 9:5).]*

[B] **What is new peat? That which is within twelve months of its preparation. And old? After it is twelve months old [T. B.Q. 6:18].**

These materials look like notes that have not been subjected to analysis and development. Unit **I** glosses the Mishnah's language and demands, but does not receive, contrary argument. Unit **II** asks a most fundamental question, which is not amply answered. Unit **III** cites a law parallel only in its operative distinction to that of the sages (M. 2:5B). Interestingly, when the Talmud cites the Mishnah's rule (**III**.A) it carries in the wake of that citation relevant Toseftan materials (**III**.B). Once more we see an instance in which the process of glossing the Mishnah has led to the accretion to the Mishnah of materials to be added, whether relevant or not, when the pericope of the Mishnah is cited to which the extraneous Toseftan materials are tied.

2:6

[A] *"Fish brine and Bithynian cheese belonging to gentiles are prohibited, and the prohibition of them extends to deriving any benefit from them at all," the words of R. Meir.*

[B] *And the sages say, "The prohibition affecting them does not extend to deriving benefit from them."*

[**I**.A] [As to putting] wine [having the status of heave-offering, which must be consumed and not permitted to go to waste] into fish brine, Rabbi permits doing so.

[B] R. Eleazar b. R. Simeon prohibits doing so [cf. M. Ter. 11:1].

[C] Therefore if one has transgressed and put wine [having the status of heave-offering into fish brine],

[D] Rabbi declares [the mixture] prohibited to nonpriests, [because the wine imparts flavor to the fish brine].

[E] R. Eleazar b. R. Simeon permits [the mixture] to nonpriests[, because the wine is destroyed by the fish brine and so is null, not in existence].

[F] R. Mana bar Tanḥum asked, "In accord with the opinion of the one who permits [a mixture of wine having the status of heave-offering and fish brine] to nonpriests, then why is fish brine belonging to a gentile prohibited? [Surely in principle, as at E, the wine is deemed null.]"

[G] R. Jeremiah in the name of R. Hiyya bar Ba: "It is on account of [the prohibition of] food cooked by gentiles."

[H] And has it not been taught: **[Brine made by] an expert—lo, this is permitted. That which is not made by an expert is prohibited [T. A.Z. 4:11U].**

[I] **If it is made by an expert, it is permitted**—is this not [only] when it has not been cooked? Similarly, then, brine not made by an expert is prohibited, even though it has [not] been cooked.

[J] Now what [is the reason that fish brine is prohibited]? [The reason is that wine is put in] to remove the smell, so on account of idolatry [a libation made with that wine, fish brine is forbidden].

[K] [On account of that small benefit enjoyed by idolatry, the rule] has stated that the enjoyment imparted to idolatry causes the prohibition of the fish brine. And yet the enjoyment involved in the consumption of heave-offering [by a nonpriest is so slight that] it is permitted. [So strict is the law against idolatry that a negligible volume of wine is taken into account.]

[L] Said R. Yoḥanan bar Madayya, "In accord with the opinion of the one who rules [H] that if the fish brine is made by an expert, it is permitted—that is the case only if the Israelite purchaser knows the gentile."

[M] And R. Yoḥanan and R. Eleazar—one of them ruled, "[The rule that one may not boil wine having the status of heave-offering] is because one diminishes it from its original volume [M. Ter. 11:1F–I]," and the other ruled, "[The reason is that] one diminishes it[s value] so far as those who will drink it are concerned[, since boiled wine is less desirable]."

[N] Now they did not know which authority stated this reason, and which one that.

[O] But from that which R. Yoḥanan said, "The opinion attributed to R. Judah has been confused," while R. Eleazar said, "It has not been confused," for there we speak of a priest, and here we speak of the owner, we must conclude that it is R. Yoḥanan who has ruled, "The reason for the prohibition is that one diminishes it so far as those who will drink it are concerned [and the operative consideration is the ultimate consumer of the wine and his interest, which will suffer if the wine should be boiled, since he then will receive a less desirable kind of wine for his drinking]." [Cf. Y. Ter. chapter 2.]

The reason that the Talmud treats the materials of Terumot in the present context is at **I**.F, the effort to draw out of the law of heave-offering a problem in the analysis of the present pericope of the Mishnah. H–J, K, then carry forward relevant discussion. Fish brine is prohibited because a small volume of wine is added (J), and then the contrast to the law of heave-offering, which treats so small a volume as null (**I**.E), is explained. M–O are to be considered in the context of tractate Terumot and need not detain us here.

2:7

[A] *Said R. Judah, "R. Ishmael asked R. Joshua as they were going along the road.*

[B] *"He said to him, 'On what account did they prohibit cheese made by gentiles?'*

[C] *"He said to him, 'Because they curdle it with rennet from carrion.'*

[D] *"He said to him, 'And is not the rennet from a whole offering subject to a more stringent rule than rennet from carrion, and yet they have said, 'A priest who is not squeamish sucks it out raw'?"*

[E] *(But they did not concur with him and ruled, "It is not available for [the priests'] benefit, while it also is not subject to the laws of sacrilege.")*

[F] *"He went and said to him, 'Because they curdle it with rennet of calves sacrificed to idols.'*

[G] *"He said to him, 'If so, then why have they not also extended the prohibition affecting it to the matter of deriving benefit from it?'*

[H] *"He moved him on to another subject.*

[I] *"He said to him, 'Ishmael, my brother, how do you read the verse: "For your [masculine] love is better than wine," or, "Your [feminine] love is better than wine" (Song of Sol. 1:2)?'*

[J] *"He said to him, "For your [feminine] love is better than wine.'*

[K] *"He said to him, 'The matter is not so. For its neighbor teaches concerning it, "Your [masculine] ointments have a goodly fragrance" (Song of Sol. 1:3).' "*

[**I**.A] [With reference to Meir's view that fish brine and Bithynian cheese belonging to gentiles are prohibited even as to deriving benefit,] R. Jacob bar Aḥa, R. Simeon bar Ba in the name of R. Joshua b. Levi [stated]: "It is because of the calves that are slaughtered there for the sake of idolatry[, and the rennet deriving from those calves is used for making cheese, and, because of that tiny amount, Meir prohibits even deriving benefit from the cheese (as at M. A.Z. 2:7F)]."

[B] Hearing this ruling, R. Yoḥanan stated, "Well has Rabbi [Meir] taught us. For so is the rule, that he who slaughters a beast for idolatry—even the excrement of such a beast is prohibited [for Israelite use or benefit]."

[C] R. Yoḥanan raised the question: "[If] one found a ring in [a beast slaughtered for idolatry, may an Israelite enjoy the use and benefit of that ring]?"

[D] Said R. Yosé, "A ring is distinct [from the beast, and so is permitted], while excrement is part of the very body of the beast [and so is prohibited]."

[**II**.A] R. Ḥiyya bar Ba in the name of R. Yoḥanan: "At first they ruled, 'They do not curdle [milk] with rennet from carrion [even of an Israelite] or with rennet deriving from gentile [preparation, since it is part of its body].' They reverted to rule, 'They curdle milk with rennet from carrion, but they do not curdle cheese with rennet deriving from gentile [preparation, for the rennet has the status of excrement].' "

[B] R. Ba bar Zabeda, R. Samuel bar R. Isaac raised the question: "Is this to exclude the opinion of R. Eliezer, for R. Eliezer says, 'The intention of a gentile is [invariably] for idolatry'? [At M. 2:3 we reject Eliezer's position and here appear to affirm it.]"

[C] R. Assi came and taught in the name of R. Yoḥanan, "In the beginning they would rule, 'They curdle milk with the rennet of carrion, but not with rennet prepared by a gentile.'

[D] **"They reverted to rule, 'They curdle milk whether with the rennet of carrion or with the rennet produced by a gentile [T. Hul. 8:12B].'** [This answers B: The rule is contrary to Eliezer's position.]"

[E] The language of the Mishnah supports the position of R. Ḥiyya bar Ba [who sees the carrion and the gentile's item as distinct]: *[The milk] in the stomach [of a beast slaughtered by] a gentile [which is carrion] and that [in the stomach] of carrion—lo, this is prohibited [M. Hul. 8:5].*

[F] This [cited teaching] is in accord with the first Mishnah: *A ṭerefah-beast that sucked from a valid one—milk in its stomach is permitted.*

[G] This is in accord with the latter version of the Mishnah: *A valid beast which sucked from a ṭerefah-beast—milk in its stomach is prohibited* [M. Hul. 8:5C–E].

[H] Even if the House of Shammai concur with the House of Hillel in regard to the version of the latter Mishnah, still, an egg is grown by the body [of the chicken itself], while milk in the stomach derives from another source [than the body of the beast].

[I] And this ruling is in accord with that which R. Yosé b. R. Bun said in the name of R. Yoḥanan: "MᶜŚH B: Wolves tore up more than three hundred sheep belonging to the son of R. Judah b. Shammua. Now the case came before sages, who permitted the stomachs of the sheep to be used for rennet [even though they were carrion].

[J] "They said, 'An egg is grown within the body of the chicken itself, while milk in the stomach derives from another source than the body of the beast, [so the cases are different].' "

[**III**.A] [Leiden MS and *editio princeps:* 2:8] [As at M. San. 11:4] associates in the name of R. Yoḥanan: [Leiden MS and *editio princeps:* Rabbi] "The words of scribes are more beloved than the words of Torah and more cherished than words of Torah: 'Your palate is like the best wine' (Song of Sol. 7:9)."

[B] Simeon bar Ba in the name of R. Yoḥanan, "The words of scribes are more beloved than the words of Torah and more cherished than words of Torah: 'For your love is better than wine' (Song of Sol. 1:2)."

[C] R. Ba bar Kohen in the name of Bar Pazzi: "You should know that the words of scribes are more beloved than the words of Torah. For lo, as to R. Tarfon[, to whom M. Ber. 1:3 refers as follows: *Said R. Tarfon, 'I was coming along the way, and I inclined to recite the Shemaᶜ, in accord with the opinion of the House of Shammai, and I endangered myself because of bandits.' They said to him, 'You deserved to be subject to such liability, because you transgressed the words of the House of Hillel'],* had he [merely] not recited the *Shemaᶜ*, he would have violated only a positive commandment [of the Torah, to recite the *Shemaᶜ* morning and night]. But because he transgressed the words of the House of Hillel, he turned out to be liable for the death penalty. This was by reason of the following verse: 'A serpent will bite him who breaks through a wall' (Qoh. 10:8)."

[D] R. Ishmael repeated the following: "The words of Torah are subject to prohibition, and they are subject to remission; they are subject to lenient rulings, and they are subject to strict rulings. But words of scribes all are subject only to strict interpretation, for we have learned there: *He who rules, 'There is no requirement to wear phylacteries,' in order to transgress the teachings of the Torah, is exempt. But if he said, 'There are five partitions in the phylactery, instead of four,' in order to add to what the scribes have taught, he is liable [M. San. 11:3].*"

[E] R. Ḥaninah in the name of R. Idi in the name of R. Tanḥum b. R. Ḥiyya: "More stringent are the words of the elders than the words of the prophets. For it is written, 'Do not preach'—thus they preach—one should not preach of such things (Micah 2:6). And it is written, '[If a man should go about and utter wind and lies, saying,] "I will preach to you of wine and strong drink," he would be the preacher for this people!' " (Micah 2:11).

[F] "A prophet and an elder—to what are they comparable? To a king who sent two senators of his to a certain province. Concerning one of them he wrote, 'If he does not show you my seal and signet, do not believe him.' But concerning the other one he wrote, 'Even though he does not show you my seal and signet, believe him.' So in the case of the prophet, he has had to write, 'If a prophet arises among you . . . and gives you a sign or a wonder . . .' (Deut. 13:1). But here [with regard to an elder:] '. . . according to the instructions which they give you . . .' (Deut. 17:11) [without a sign or a wonder]."

[**IV**.A] R. Jacob bar Aḥa, R. Simeon bar Ba in the name of R. Joshua b. Levi [stated]: "It is because of the calves that are slaughtered there for the sake of idolatry[, and the rennet deriving from those calves is used for making cheese, as above]."

[B] Hearing this ruling, R. Yoḥanan stated, "Well has Rabbi [Meir] taught us. For so is the rule, that he who slaughters a beast for idolatry—even the excrement of such a beast is prohibited [for Israelite use or benefit]."

[C] R. Yoḥanan raised the question: "[If] one found a ring in [a beast slaughtered for idolatry, may an Israelite enjoy the use and benefit of that ring]?"

[D] Said R. Yosé, "A ring is distinct [from the beast, and so is permitted,] while excrement is part of the very body of the beast [and so is prohibited]."

[**V**.A] What is the meaning of ŚWRPH ["sucks it out"; M. A.Z. 2:7D]?

[B] It means, "Quaff."

[C] R. Simeon b. Laqish said, "[The reason that the Mishnah rules that when one sucks it out, he does not derive benefit and does not commit an act of sacrilege is that] it is comparable to drinking from a dirty cup, for thus the law states, 'He who drinks [what belongs to the cult] from a dirty cup does not derive benefit and does not therefore commit an act of sacrilege[, since there is no complete enjoyment out of the act.' Still, the act is forbidden]."

[D] And why did he not reveal this reason to him [M. 2:7H]?

[E] Said R. Yoḥanan: "It was because in the near future they declared it forbidden, and, furthermore, R. Ishmael was a minor[, too young to know the reasons that lie behind the laws of the Torah]."

[**VI**.A] [*He moved him on to another subject (M. A.Z. 2:7H)].* R. Ḥoniah said R. Ḥama bar Uqba asked, "If it was his intent to put him off with words, he should have moved him on to the five puzzles that are in the Torah [in which it is possible to interpret a matter in two equally valid ways]. And these are they:

[B] " 'Lifted up' (Gen. 4:7:). 'If you do well[, good,] but you must bear the sin if you do not well.' Or, 'If you do well, there will be a lifting up of face, and if you do not do well, sin crouches at the door.'

[C] " 'Cursed' (Gen. 49:6, 7:). 'And in their self-will they houghed oxen. Cursed be their anger, for it was fierce.' Or, 'And in their self-will they houghed the cursed oxen. Their anger was fierce.'

[D] [41d] " 'Tomorrow' (Ex. 17:9:). 'Go out and fight with Amalek tomorrow. I will stand on the top of the hill.' Or, 'Tomorrow I will stand on the hill. . . .'

[E] " 'Like almond blossoms' (Ex. 25:33:). 'Three cups, make like almond blossoms in one branch, a knop and a flower.' Or, 'Three cups, like almond blossoms . . . a knop and a flower.'

[F] " 'Rise up' (Deut. 31:16:). 'Behold you are about to sleep with your fathers, and this people will rise up.' Or, 'Behold, you are about to sleep with your fathers, and will rise up. This people will go astray. . . .' "

[G] R. Tanḥuma added the following: "The sons of Jacob came from the field, when they heard of it." Or, "When they heard of it, the men were indignant and very angry" (Gen. 34:6–7).

[H] Said Rabbi, "No. There are matters on account of which one smacks his lips. This is in line with that which is said, 'Oh that he would kiss me with the kisses of his mouth' (Song of Sol. 1:2)."

[I] Said R. Isaac, " 'And me did the Lord command at that time' (Deut. 4:14: *and* me, thus:) Things were said to me that also were said to you, but things were said to me that were said only to me [and not to you]."

[J] R. Simeon b. Ḥalafta, R. Ḥaggai in the name of R. Samuel bar Naḥman: " 'The lambs will provide your clothing, and the goats the price of a field; there will be enough goats' milk for your food' (Prov. 27:26–27). KBŠYM is written [as if with a *shin,* meaning, hide [withhold], instead of *lambs,* thus:] How so? When the disciples are young, withhold the words of Torah from them. [You cannot reveal the secrets of the Torah to the young.] But after they grow up and become like goats, reveal to them the [real] secrets of the Torah."

[K] This teaching supports that which R. Simeon b. Yoḥai repeated: " 'These are the laws that you will set [TŚYM] before them' (Ex. 21:1). Just as this treasure [SYMH] is not revealed to everyone, so you have no right to devote yourself [to the exposition of] words of Torah except before suitable people."

Unit **I** prepares the way for unit **II** and also focuses upon M. 2:7F. What is critical is C, Yoḥanan's question about the difference between excrement found in the intestines and a ring found in the intestines. Yosé's answer provides the important distinction, the foundation of what is to follow. Unit **II** then introduces two distinct versions of the law as Yoḥanan has presented it. Ḥiyya bar Ba's view of Yoḥanan's version of the law is that at the outset there is a prohibition against two kinds of rennet, both that coming from carrion and that coming from a beast slaughtered by a gentile. Then the two were treated differently, the one permitted, the other prohibited. This presents a problem, for we turn out (B) to rule in accord with Eliezer's supposition that any act of slaughter performed by a gentile is for the sake of idolatry, so any part of such a beast—in line with M. 2:7F—will be forbidden. That accounts for the prohibition affirmed in the latter version of the Mishnah at **II**.A. Assi then has a different version of the matter (C–D) in which the final version of the Mishnah (D) permits both kinds of rennet, and thus prevents our assuming that Eliezer, an individual as against the opinion of the collectivity of the sages, stands behind the law. Now we notice that Ḥiyya bar Ba insists (**II**.A) that carrion and a beast slaughtered by a gentile are treated as distinct from one another. E–G point out that the language of the relevant pericope of the Mishnah yields essentially the same conception. The passage cited at **II**.F permits milk in the stomach of a *ṭerefah*-beast that has sucked from a valid beast. At **II**.G, the *ṭerefah*-beast is prohibited, just as Ḥiyya bar Ba said in Yoḥanan's name.

What follows at H now requires brief explanation. The reference of **II**.H is to M. Bes. 1:1, where the House of Shammai and the House of Hillel dispute about the status of an egg in the body of the chicken. The principle alone is relevant here. The House of Shammai regard the egg as part of the body of the dam. The Hillelites regard the egg as distinct from the body of the dam. Now the Talmud's reference (**II**.H) is to this dispute. The point the Talmud wishes to make is that the dispute is *not* pertinent to the case before us. The dispute of the Houses concerns that which has grown in the body of the chicken, the egg itself. The House of Shammai deny that the egg has the status of the body of the chicken itself. But the rennet in the belly of a beast derives from some other source than the body of the beast, so the Houses will not deem it part of the body of the beast. Both Houses, then, concur with the latter version of the Mishnah. I–J then make explicit the same position as is stated *vis-à-vis* the Houses by H. It goes without saying that the same materials recur at Y. Beṣ. 1:1 and there are to be dealt with at greater length.

III moves on to the matter of "words of scribes," in the assumption that scribes stand behind the rule of M. 2:7B. The entire passage is more suitable at M. San. 11:4, where it appears verbatim. **IV** repeats **I** verbatim; lower criticism surely will remove the entire passage, which is out of place. At **V** and

VI the Mishnah pericope before us is subjected to further careful exegesis. **V** includes the important explanation of the Mishnah's rule by Simeon b. Laqish. **VI** uses the Mishnah as a mere pretext to state a repertoire of other possible puzzles in biblical interpretation. **VI**.I–K allude to secret interpretations of Scripture.

2:8

[A] *These are things of gentiles that are prohibited, but the prohibition of which does not extend to deriving benefit from them:*

[B] *[1] milk drawn by a gentile without an Israelite watching him; [2] their [gentiles'] bread; and [3] their oil—*

[C] *(Rabbi and his court permitted their oil)—*

[D] *[4] stewed and pickled [vegetables] into which it is customary to put wine and vinegar; [5] minced fish; [6] brine without "kilbit-fish" floating in it; [7] "ḥileq-fish"; [8] drops of asafetida; and [9] sal conditum—*

[E] *lo, these are prohibited, but the prohibition affecting them does not extend to deriving benefit from them.*

[**I**.A] As to milk produced by a gentile['s cow]—why is it prohibited?

[B] R. Ba bar R. Judah, R. Simon in the name of R. Joshua b. Levi: "As to milk produced by a gentile['s cow]—why is it prohibited? Because of its having been left exposed[, for gentiles are not punctilious about covering up liquids and preventing their contamination]."

[C] And [why not] let [the Israelite] curdle [the milk, and if there is snake venom, it will be skimmed off]?

[D] Said R. Samuel bar R. Isaac, "[Still, this will have to be prohibited] because of the poison located in the cracks [of the cheese]."

[E] And so it is taught in a Tannaitic tradition: "There are three kinds of venom, one that floats, one that sinks, and one that [remains on the top of liquids] like a net-like film" [and the kind that sinks is that to which reference is made at D].

[F] Workers were farming in a field. A pitcher of water was left uncovered. They drank from it, but did not die. Then they went and drank again from the water, and they died.

[G] Now I say that it was because of venom that had sunk to the bottom [and that they did not drink the first time around].

[H] In the time of R. Jeremiah the water tank of the great school was left uncovered. They drank once and did not die, then went and did it again and died.

[I] Now I say that it was because of venom that had sunk to the bottom.

[J] So has it been taught in a Tannaitic teaching: A watermelon that was pierced, and from which ten people ate,

and so too, a jug of wine that was left uncovered, and from which ten people drank—it is forbidden to eat or drink after them.

[K] Now I say that it is because of venom that has sunk to the bottom [that it is prohibited to do so].

[L] Said R. Jeremiah, "Milk produced by a gentile['s cow]—why is it forbidden? Because of the mixture [of milk from] an unclean beast [together with that produced by a clean beast, since the gentile need not scruple about such considerations]."

[M] And so it has been taught in a Tannaitic tradition: **An Israelite may sit at the other side of his corral, and a gentile may milk the cows and bring the milk to him, and he need not scruple [T. 4:11P]** [so the issue of protecting the milk from contamination is not critical].

[**II**.A] *Their bread [M. A.Z. 2:8B(2)]: R. Jacob bar Aḥa in the name of R. Jonathan: "The law [permitting gentile bread for Israelite benefit, but not consumption] was an irregular measure [passed in an emergency, but contrary to the real law]."*

[B] For thus do I maintain: "In a place in which bread prepared by Israelites is readily available, it is logical that bread produced by gentiles should be forbidden. But they acted irregularly and permitted it."

[C] Or [perhaps the matter should be phrased in this way]: "In a place in which bread prepared by Israelites is not readily available, it is logical that bread produced by gentiles should be permitted. But they acted irregularly and prohibited it."

[D] [Now the issue is which of these two versions in explanation of A is sound.] Said R. Mana, "And does irregular legislation apply to a matter of prohibition? [Clearly, the issue of an irregular decision should not apply in a matter of prohibition, since that language is irrelevant. One may simply say that the authorities made a stringent decision.] And is not bread tantamount to that which a gentile has cooked? [Surely, therefore, it is the version of B, not the version of C, that is sound.]"

[E] Thus do we therefore state the matter: "In a place in which food is prepared by Israelites, it is logical that food produced by gentiles [should be forbidden. But they acted irregularly and] permitted it"!? [Clearly this is not the way to state the matter, since, expressed as a matter of prepared food in general, the matter leads to the absurd statement just now made.]

[F] "But thus is the proper version: In a place in which Israelite bread is not readily available, it was logical [nonetheless] that bread prepared by gentiles should be forbidden. But they acted irregularly and permitted it, because it is a matter of the preservation of life."

[G] Rabbis of Caesarea in the name of R. Jacob bar Aḥa: "[Even] in accord with the position of him who permits [using bread prepared by gentiles], this is on the condition that [it is purchased] from a baker [and not from a householder]."

[H] But they do not practice the law in such wise [but permit even home-baked bread].

[**III**.A] *[Stewed and pickled vegetables into which it is customary to put wine and vinegar (M. A.Z. 2:8D[4])]:* They said before R. Ḥiyya the Great, "R. Simeon b. Yoḥai taught, 'You shall purchase food from them for money, that you may eat; and you shall also buy water of them for money, that you may drink' (Deut. 2:6). [Now the statement by Moses explicitly permits Israelites to purchase and drink water from gentiles, and by analogy, we reason as follows:] Just as water is something that does not change from its natural state, so anything that is not changed from its natural state [may be purchased from gentiles and consumed by Israelites]."

[B] They objected, "Lo, their [gentiles'] liverwort, [pressed] apricots, pickled [vegetables], parched corn, and [boiled] water [cf. T. 4:11H] are permitted" [and these are all prepared and not in their natural state].

[C] All of them pose no difficulties, for they can be soaked and made to return to their original state.

[D] [But that clearly is not the case of] parched corn, [so] why [is that not forbidden, if whatever is cooked by gentiles in fact is prohibited by the law of the Torah cited at A]?

[E] R. Yosé b. R. Bun in the name of Rab: "[The reason that food cooked by gentiles is prohibited is a decree made by rabbis, and not by the Torah.] Any food that is eaten as is, raw, is not subject to the prohibition against eating food cooked by gentiles.

[F] "[But any food that is usually eaten] with bread is subject to the prohibition against eating food cooked by gentiles."

[G] How then does R. Ḥiyya the Great interpret the verse, "You shall purchase food from them for money, that you may eat; and you shall also buy water of them for money, that you may drink" (Deut. 2:6)?

[H] With food you shall purchase [Esau, that is, Rome, finding favor by providing food to him]. Once you have fed him, break him. If he is hard on you, purchase [his good will] with food. And if [that does] not [work], give him ample funds.

[I] They say that thus did R. Jonathan do: When a gentile of high standing came to town, he would send him [gifts]. If then a case of an orphan or a widow would come up, [in advocating their case] he would then find favor [with the ruler].

[**IV**.A] [*Their oil* (M. A.Z. 2:8B[3]):] Who forbade their oil? B. Judah said, "Daniel forbade it: 'And Daniel resolved [that he would not defile himself with the king's rich food or with the wine which he drank]' (Dan. 1:8)."

[B] Who permitted it? *Rabbi and his court [permitted their oil] (M. A.Z. 2:8C).*

[C] In three settings R. Judah the patriarch is referred to as "our rabbi," in the context of [rules covering] writs of divorce, oil, and producing an abortion in the shape of a sandal[, in all of which Rabbi and his court took a lenient position].

[D] In consequence they referred to his court as the court that permitted oil [made by gentiles].

[E] Any court that gave a lenient ruling in three matters is called a permissive court.

[F] Said R. Judan, "Rabbi's court differed from him in the matter of the writ of divorce." [In this case a man said, "Lo, this is your writ of divorce if I do not come back within twelve months" and died in that period. The man did not specify that the writ was valid from that moment, so it was as if a writ of divorce after death, so M. 7:8. T. 5:9C states, "Our rabbis instructed her to remarry," and this, we know, refers to Rabbi.]

[G] What is the law as to the woman's being permitted to remarry [forthwith on the strength of the writ of divorce under the stated circumstances]?

[H] R. Haggai said, "She is permitted to remarry."

[I] R. Yosé said, "She is forbidden to remarry."

[J] [As to Daniel's prohibition of the oil made by gentiles, why did that prohibition find acceptance?] R. Aḥa, R. Tanḥum bar Ḥiyya in the name of R. Ḥaninah, and some say it in the name of R. Joshua b. Levi: "Because they were going up to the Royal Mountain and being put to death on this account."

[K] Isaac bar Samuel bar Marta went down to Nisibis. He found Simlai, the southerner, sitting and expounding: *"Rabbi and his court permitted oil [prepared by gentiles]."*

[L] He said [the rule before] Samuel, [who thereupon] ate [oil prepared by gentiles]. [He did the same before] Rab, [who] did not accept the rule for himself or eat [such oil]. He said to him, "Samuel ate. If you do not do the same, I shall decree concerning you that you are a 'rebellious elder.' "

[M] [Rab] replied to him, "When I was still there [in the Land], I know that Simlai, the southerner, rejected [the prohibition against oil, so I do not trust this report of his]."

[N] [Samuel] said to him, "Did [Simlai] say this in his own name? Did he not say it in the name of R. Judah the patriarch?" Samuel nagged him about the matter until he too ate oil prepared by gentiles.

[O] R. Yoḥanan raised the question: "And have we not learned in the Mishnah [M. Ed. 1:5C]: *For a court has not got the power to nullify the opinion of another court unless it is greater than it in wisdom and in numbers.*

[P] "Now how is it possible that Rabbi and his court should [nullify the ruling and so] permit what Daniel and his colleagues had prohibited?"

[Q] R. Yoḥanan is consistent with his opinion expressed elsewhere [in denying that it was Rabbi and his court who permitted the oil, and in affirming that it was permitted on other grounds entirely].

[R] For R. Yoḥanan said, "I have received it as a tradition from R. Eleazar b. R. Ṣadoq that any decree a court should issue, and which the majority of the community should not accept upon itself, is no decree. [What in fact happened was that] they looked into the matter and found out in the case of the decree against oil [prepared by gentiles] that the majority of the community had not accepted [the decree, and so they nullified the rule on those grounds, and not on the grounds of Rabbi's decision]."

[**V**.A] An egg roasted by [gentiles]—

[B] Bar Qappara permitted.

[C] Hezekiah prohibited.

[D] Now the foregoing dispute concerns an egg that a gentile deliberately roasted. What about one that was not deliberately roasted by a gentile [but that happened, through his action, to be roasted]?

[E] Let us infer the rule from the following: MʿŚH Š: A fire [set by a gentile] broke out in a reed thicket and in a date grove, and there were locusts there, which got roasted. The case then came before R. Mana, who prohibited [Israelites from eating the locusts, because they had been roasted by a gentile, even though it was not the gentile's deliberate action that had led to the locusts' being roasted].

[F] Said R. Abbahu, "[But that is hardly probative. The reason that the locusts were prohibited was not that a gentile had originally set the fire, but] because of the mixture of unclean locusts [with the clean ones, with the consequence that Israelites could not consume the acceptable ones because of the presence of unclean ones]."

[G] Said R. Yosé b. R. Bun, "But this was one of the strict rulings imposed by Rab" [in the circumstance to be explained now].

[H] Rab went down to that place [Babylonia], He saw that they followed lenient rulings, so he imposed strict rulings on them. [Here are two examples.]

[I] A man was walking in the market place and tasting a piece of meat. A *diata*-bird flew down and snatched it up from his hand. [As the bird flew off, the meat] fell down [beneath the bird]. [The man] went [and] wanted to take it [and eat it].

Rab said to him, "It is forbidden to you. For I say it was carrying a piece of carrion meat, and it fell down, and then the bird swiped this piece of yours in its stead. [So the piece of meat you found is the carrion which the bird had been carrying, and that is why you may not eat the meat.]"

[J] A man went and wanted to wash off in the river meat hanging on a crosspiece. The meat came out of his grip and floated away. He went and planned to get it back.

Rab said to him, "It is forbidden to you. For I say the piece you had was swept off by the river, which brought in its stead a piece of carrion."

[**VI**.A] What is the law governing [Israelite consumption of] their [gentiles'] lupines?

[B] [42a] Rabbi prohibits.

[C] Geniba permits.

[D] Said Rabbi, "I am an elder, and he is an elder. I intend to prohibit them, and he intends to permit them."

[E] R. Mana bar Tanḥum went to Tyre and permitted [Israelites to make use of] lupines prepared by [gentiles].

[F] R. Ḥiyya bar Ba went to Tyre and found that R. Mana bar Tanḥum had permitted lupines prepared by [gentiles]. He went to Yoḥanan. [Yoḥanan] said to him, "What sort of case came to your hand?"

[G] He said to him, "I found that R. Mana bar Tanḥum had permitted [Israelites to eat] lupines prepared by [gentiles]."

[H] [Yoḥanan] said to [Ḥiyya], "And did you punish him [by declaring him to be excommunicated]?"

[I] He said to him, "He is a great man, for [so wise is he that] he knows how to sweeten [the water of the] Mediterranean sea."

[J] He said to him, "It is not so, my son. He merely knows how to take the measure of the water. For when the water praises God who created it, [the water] turns sweet. [So his knowledge is not so impressive.]"

[K] Said R. Isaac bar Eleazar, "[Nonetheless,] he came intending to discredit him and ended up praising him."

[L] Said R. Yosé b. R. Bun, "It is a great piece of knowledge. R. Zakkai of Alexandria knows that wisdom."

[M] He said, "If I wanted, I could have gone and learned it from him."

[**VII**.A] Dumpling prepared by them—what is the law?

[B] Let us infer the rule from the following:

[C] R. Ami went up with R. Yudan the patriarch to the hot springs of Gedar and permitted [Israelites to eat] dumplings [prepared by] them.

[D] R. Ba bar Memel raised the question: "Then what is the difference between dumplings [which Israelites may eat] and lupines [which Rabbi prohibited, **VI**.A–C]?"

[E] Said R. Yosé, "Dumplings are not subject to cooking over a fire [since they are made by pouring on hot water, and hot water prepared by a gentile is permitted for Israelite use], while lupines are subject to cooking over a fire."

[F] Fish hash is not subject to the prohibition of cooking by gentiles, but [nonetheless, even though it is not cooked], by means [of that sort of hash] they carry out the obligation of setting out cooked food [for continuing to cook on a festival day].

[G] R. Ba in the name of R. Aḥi: "A hash of small fish preserved in salt is not subject to the prohibition of cooking by gentiles, but by means [of that sort of hash] they carry out the obligation of setting out cooked food [for continuing to cook on a festival day]."

[H] R. Yosé b. R. Bun in the name of R. Huna: "Any sort of food that is eaten raw, as is, is not subject to the prohibition of cooking by gentiles, but by means [of that sort of food] they carry out the obligation of setting out cooked food [as above]."

The first four units seek reasons for rulings given in the Mishnah, treated in order, and the concluding three then ask about edibles not mentioned in the Mishnah. The sequence of topics is orderly and reasonable. The point of special interest to the Mishnah, the fact that Israelites indeed may derive benefit from the listed foods even though they may not eat those foods (by contrast to M. 2:7 and 2:9), is not analyzed by the Talmud. This is particularly striking in the discourse of unit **II**, which asks not about the reason for what is permitted (in contrast to M. 2:7), but for what is prohibited. In this regard unit **I**, with its stress upon the prohibition and the basic reasons, is exemplary. There are two possible considerations, either the matter of leaving liquids uncovered, or the issue of gentiles' mixing of milk from both valid and prohibited beasts. The point of interest of unit **II**, in fact, is the analysis of a peculiarly worded tradition on the matter. How **II**.F would like to read the pericope of the Mishnah before us is difficult to imagine. It surely does not speak about what is before us. For the prohibition of cooked vegetables that contain wine and vinegar a reason is adduced that ignores the presence of the wine or vinegar. First we have an exegetical exercise, then a restatement of the rule. Once more it is difficult to see how the Talmud has constructed its ideas in response to the sentence of the Mishnah supposedly under discussion. Unit **IV** takes as its point of interest the fact that gentiles' oil had been prohibited but now has been permitted. The materials of the unit are strung together, but a second glance shows that they are coherent. Unit **V** sets forth sayings and stories relevant to a common theme, but not tied together into coherent discourse. The same may be said of units **VI** and **VII**. The overall impression of this set of materials is that someone has used the themes of the Mishnah pericope as a pretext for gathering pertinent, already available units of thought and stringing them together. What we have gives the impression, overall, of serving as an anthology or even an encyclopedia, rather than as a sustained and truly analytical inquiry into the exegesis of what is important to the Mishnah pericope.

2:9

[A] *These [to begin with] are permitted for [Israelite] consumption:*

[B] *[1] milk that a gentile drew, with an Israelite watching him;*

[C] *[2] honey; and [3] honeycombs,*

[D] *(even though they drip with moisture, they are not subject to the rule of imparting susceptibility to uncleanness as liquid)—*

[E] *[4] pickled vegetables into which it is not customary to put wine or vinegar; [5] unminced fish; [6] brine containing fish; [7] a [whole] leaf of asafetida, and [8] pickled olive cakes.*

[F] *R. Yosé says, "Those that are sodden are prohibited."*

[G] *Locusts that come from [the shopkeeper's] basket are forbidden.*

[H] *Those that come from the stock [of his shop] are permitted.*

[I] *And so is the rule for heave-offering [purchased from an untrustworthy priest].*

[**I**.A] Said R. Eleazar, "[It follows from the teaching] that you have given [that it is permitted to consume] food in which it is not customary to put wine or vinegar, [that] lo, [if] it is entirely clear that [a gentile indeed] has put [wine or vinegar into food, that food] is forbidden, even for Israelite benefit [e.g., through sale to a gentile]."

[B] R. Jacob bar Aḥa, R. Ḥiyya in the name of R. Yoḥanan: "[In the case of] an Israelite and a gentile who share [in the] cooking [of food], the Israelite sets [the pot onto the fire], and the gentile stirs the pot."

[C] Who [tastes the food in the pot and] puts it back [so that it will cook further]?

[D] It is reasonable to suppose that the Israelite [tastes the food in the pot and] puts it back [so that it will cook further].

[E] Said R. Benjamin bar Leoai, "And that rule [requiring the Israelite to put the food back into the pot for further cooking] applies [even in the case of food that is only] a third cooked."

[F] R. Yosé raised the question: "[Now] if when the food is only a third cooked, why should an Israelite be the one to return it to the pot? Even a gentile [should be permitted] to return [the scarcely cooked food to the pot]."

[**II**.A] What is *ḥileq*-fish [M. A.Z. 2:8D(7)]?

[B] Rab said, "It is *sultanit*-fish [a kind of anchovy]."

[C] Said R. Yoḥanan, "*Ḥileq*-fish is the same as minced fish."

[D] R. Zeira, Kahana bar Taḥelipa, Ḥanan bar Ba in the name of Rab: "*Laḥeluḥeta* is forbidden because of the mixture [therein] of unclean fish."

[E] R. Ba in the name of R. Judah: "That which you have stated applies to that sort of fish caught in a pool in which the water is not running, but as to that sort of fish caught in a running stream, the clean fish [in any case] does not swim along with unclean fish."

[F] And lo, the Sea of Tiberias is an example of running waters [and yet unclean and clean fish are caught together]!

[**III**.A] [As to minced fish, which, prepared by a gentile, Israelites may not eat (M. 2:8D[5]),] said R. Yosé b. R. Bun, "But [that prohibition applies] specifically when the fish is chopped up[, and the body of the fish is not discerned at all]."

[B] Said Samuel, "As to mud-fish [to determine whether or not it has scales and so is permitted for Israelite consumption], one puts it into its shell. If it produces brine, it is permitted, and if not, it is prohibited[, since the moisture indicates the presence of scales]."

[C] What is pickled fish in which the [shape of the fish] can be recognized? Any in which the head and backbone are present.

[D] R. Eleazar in the name of R. Ḥaninah: MʿŚH B: "A fishing vessel belonging to the household of Rabbi had more than three hundred kegs [of fish]. Rabbi inspected all of them. He found only one in which the heads and backbones [of the fish] were visible [in which case this sort of fish, prepared by a gentile, was permitted for Israelite use, and on the strength of that single keg], he permitted the whole lot of them [to be sold to, and eaten by, Israelites]."

[E] R. Jacob bar Aḥa said R. Asi raised the question concerning [this story]: "It is reasonable that only that particular keg should have been permitted, and all the rest of the kegs should have been forbidden. But I say, through some accident the kegs were upset."

[F] R. Haggai asked R. Ba bar Zabeda [about such a case]. He said to him, "A matter of considerable [value] is not going to be prohibited [so as to cause substantial damages solely by reason of doubt]."

[G] R. Jacob bar Zabedi and R. Isaac raised the question: "Now [if by reason of the pretext that, in a case of doubt, one will permit the food so that a considerable loss will not be incurred, then what about the case, at Y. Git. 1:1, in which] documents [were found] in which obviously gentile names such as Lucas were inscribed [as the witnesses? Now what is the difference between this case before us, in which, on account of some pretext, you permit the food whose status is in doubt, and the case involving bonds of indebtedness, in which case the law is that testimony is required to validate the signatures of the witnesses bearing gentile names and so possibly not valid witnesses at all?] [If] you invoke a mere pretext [in the present case], then [surely you should invoke] a mere pretext [e.g., the Israelite court is not likely to permit gentiles to sign the bonds, and hence, even though the names are gentile, the bonds belong to Israelites] in this other case." [The question is not answered.]

[H] Ulla Shikepa taught before R. Dosa: "Unclean fish are viviparous, and clean fish eject eggs."

[I] [Ulla] further taught before him, "Fish entrails and roe are to be eaten only on the advice of an expert."

[J] He said to him, "Retract one [of these two teachings, which contradict one another, since, in the light of I, an unclean fish also may lay eggs]."

[K] He wanted to retract [one of the two statements].

[L] Said to him R. Zeira, "Do not retract. [When the unclean fish] come out, they are completed [and emerge from eggs within the womb]."

[M] R. Ba in the name of R. Judah: "If [the seller] says to you, 'I personally salted them,' he is to be believed [that the fish is clean and acceptable for Israelite consumption]."

[N] Nathan bar Ba said before Samuel, "I know how to tell the difference between the roe of unclean fish and the roe of clean fish. The roe of unclean fish are round, and the roe of clean fish are elongated."

[O] He showed him [the roe of] a *salpita*-fish[, which is clean]. He said to him, "Now what is the law pertaining to this sort of fish?"

[P] He said to him, "It is unclean."

[Q] He said to him, "It does not bother me so much that you have declared a clean one to be unclean, but in the end you are going to declare an unclean one to be clean."

[R] It has been taught in a Tannaitic tradition: **Fish entrails and roe are to be purchased only on the advice of an expert. Purple dye is to be purchased only on the advice of an expert. Bithynian cheese is to be purchased only on the advice of an expert. Wine in Syria is to be purchased only on the advice of an expert. Meat bearing no mark is to be purchased only on the advice of an expert. But any of these may be eaten in the home of one who is not an expert, and one need not scruple on that account [cf. T. A.Z. 4:13].**

[S] R. Aḥa, R. Tanḥum in the name of R. Joshua b. Levi: "[If someone] sent asafetida [as a gift], he is believed [to testify that the leaves have not been cut up by a knife belonging to a gentile]."

[T] R. Jacob bar Aḥa, R. Jacob bar Idi in the name of R. Joshua b. Levi: "[If one] sent purple dye, he is believed [to testify that this is valid dye for its purpose]."

[U] The child of Levi Ṣanbarayya would sell produce [in the assumption that it had been tithed, because his father was reliable about tithing].

[V] R. Jacob bar Aḥa, in the name of R. Yassa, "The slave belonging to a reliable Israelite himself is tantamount to a reliable person."

[W] Germana, the slave of R. Yudan the patriarch, had purple dye [for sale].

[X] R. Yassa in the name of R. Yoḥanan: "The slave belonging to a reliable Israelite himself is tantamount to a reliable person[, so it is permitted to purchase this purple dye from Germana]."

[**IV**.A] *Sal conditum [M. 2:8D(9)]:*

[B] There are Tannaitic tradition teachers who teach, "Black is forbidden and white is permitted."

[C] There are Tannaitic tradition teachers who teach, "White is permitted and black is forbidden."

[D] The one who says that the black kind is forbidden [maintains that the salt is prepared by] putting into it a black dead creeping thing [which is not to be eaten by Israelites].

[E] The one who says that the white kind is forbidden [maintains that the salt is prepared by] putting into it a white dead creeping thing.

[F] R. Hanania b. Gamaliel said in the name of R. Judah b. Gamaliel, "Both this kind and that kind are prohibited."

[G] Said R. Hanania, "[The reason is that] we had a neighbor [who prepared this kind of salt] by putting pig fat into it."

[**V**.A] *[Pickled olive cakes, M. A.Z. 2:9E(8)].* All the same are the objects referred to by the following words: Those for overhanging boughs and protruding growths; for loose lattice work and vibrating slats; for mouldings and rims; for cups and mugs; for a place for placing cups and a place for leaving pieces [of food, (M. Kel. 22:1)]; for pickled olive cakes and circles of pressed olives.

[**VI**.A] *Those that are sodden are forbidden (M. A.Z. 2:9F).*

[B] R. Ḥiyya in the name of R. Yoḥanan said, "[This refers to] a certain kind of olives into which they put vinegar so as to extract the pit."

The Talmud's treatment of the Mishnah suggests that M. 2:8 and M. 2:9 are addressed as a single unit, since units **II**, **III**, and **IV** take up items of M. 2:8. On the other hand **I**.A takes up M. 2:9E[4]. The principal interest of unit **I** is in the matter of cooking done by an Israelite and a gentile together, which does not interest the Mishnah at all. Units **II** and **III** speak of fish prepared by gentiles and assemble relevant materials on that theme. The sole point of special attention is at **III**.F–G, at which a principle adduced in explanation of a pertinent case is challenged by reference to an unrelated case. **III**.H–X then take up clean and unclean fish, without reference to gentiles' preparation of them. The entire set of materials is irrelevant to the Mishnah. Units **IV**, **V**, and **VI** rather perfunctorily treat items on the Mishnah's lists, but, as we see, there is no sustained and systematic treatment of the materials of the Mishnah. (For that purpose, one should have to consult the Tosefta's examination of the same pericopes of the Mishnah.)

3 Yerushalmi Abodah Zarah Chapter Three

3:1

[42b/A] *"All images are prohibited,*

[B] *"because they are worshiped once a year," the words of R. Meir.*

[C] *And the sages say, "Prohibited is only one that has in its hand a staff, bird, or sphere [orb]."*

[D] *Rabban Simeon b. Gamaliel says, "Any that has anything at all in its hand."*

[**I**.A] Said R. Ḥiyya bar Ba, "[The reason all images are prohibited] is that in the great city of Rome they are worshiped twice in a septennate."

[B] If that is the operative reasoning, then in a locale in which they are worshiped they should be forbidden, while in a locale in which they are not worshiped they should be permitted [for Israelite commerce].

[C] Said R. Yosé, "Once they are prohibited in a single locale, the prohibition applies in every locale."

[D] How shall we explain [the dispute between Meir and the sages]?

[E] [Here is the problem:] If it is a matter of certainty that [statues are] of kings [and hence made for worship], then all will have to concur that they are forbidden.

[F] If it is a matter of certainty [that the statues are] of local authorities [and hence not for worship], then all will have to concur that they are [made merely for decoration and hence] permitted.

[G] But thus we must interpret the dispute: in the case of a statue lacking all specification [as to its clear-cut purpose].

[H] R. Meir says, "When they lack all specification, they are of kings."

[I] And rabbis maintain, "When they lack all specification, they are of local rulers."

[J] Asyan the carpenter in the name of R. Yoḥanan: "As to icons, why are they prohibited?

[K] "Because the [idolators] offer up incense before them when they set them up."

[L] Said R. Yoḥanan, "It is permitted to look upon them when they come down.

[M] "What is the scriptural basis for that ruling? 'You will look upon the destruction of the wicked' (Ps. 37:34)."

[N] One has written: He who strolls below portraits or icons—they do not gaze upon them on the Sabbath, and not only so, but also on a weekday they do not gaze upon icons.

[O] What is the scriptural basis for that rule? "Do not turn to idols" (Lev. 19:4)—do not [42c] turn to them who make them[, thus, to those portrayed as icons].

[P] R. Judah says, "[The meaning of the verse is], 'Do not turn to gaze upon them' literally [not merely upon the icons of those who make them, but on the idols themselves]."

[Q] When R. Naḥum bar Simai died, they covered up the icons with mats. They said, "Just as he did not set eyes upon them when he was alive, so let his eyes not set upon them after death."

[R] Now [do the dead] know a thing?

[S] Said R. Simeon b. Levi, "We have nothing in common with the truly righteous except the power of speech [which both we and they lose upon death. But their other powers remain, so a man so holy as Naḥum bar Simai will see them, if they can be seen]."

[T] Said R. Zeira, "The deceased hears words of praise for himself as if in a dream."

[U] Said R. Asyan, "The deceased hears words of praise for himself as if in a dream."

[V] And why was he [Q] called "Naḥum, the most holy"? Because he never gazed upon the face of a coin in his entire life [to avoid seeing the idol inscribed thereon].

[W] And why was he called "our holy rabbi"? Because he never laid eyes upon the mark of his circumcision in his entire life.

[**II**.A] When R. Aḥa died, a star appeared at noon.

[B] When R. Ḥanan died, the statues bowed low.

[C] When R. Yoḥanan died, the icons bowed down.

[D] They said that [this was to indicate] there were no icons like him [so beautiful as Yoḥanan himself].

[E] When R. Ḥanina of Bet Hauran died, the Sea of Tiberias split open.

[F] They said that [this was to commemorate the miracle that took place] when he went up to intercalate the year, and the sea split open before him.

[G] When R. Hoshaiah died, the palm of Tiberias fell down.

[H] When R. Isaac b. Eliasheb died, seventy [infirm] thresholds of houses in Galilee were shaken down.

[I] They said that [this was to commemorate the fact that] they [were shaky and] had depended on his merit [for the miracle that permitted them to continue to stand].

[J] When R. Samuel bar R. Isaac died, cedars of the land of Israel were uprooted.

[K] They said that [this was to take note of the fact that] he would take a branch [of a cedar] and [dance, so] praising a bride [at her wedding, and thereby giving happiness to the bride].

[L] The rabbis would ridicule them [for lowering himself by doing so]. Said to them R. Zeira, "Leave him be. Does the old man not know what he is doing?"

[M] When he died, a flame came forth from heaven and intervened between his bier and the congregation. For three hours there were voices and thunderings in the world: "Come and see what a sprig of cedar has done for this old man!"

[N] [Further] an echo came forth and said, "Woe that Samuel b. R. R. Isaac has died, the doer of merciful deeds."

[O] When R. Yasa bar Ḥalputa died, the gutters ran with blood in Laodicea.

[P] They said [that the reason was] that he had given his life for the rite of circumcision.

[Q] When R. Abbahu died, the pillars of Caesarea wept.

[R] The [gentiles] said [that the reason was] that [the pillars] were celebrating. The Israelites said to them, "And do those who are distant [such as yourselves] know why those who are near [we ourselves] are raising a cry?"

[S] When R. Abbahu lay dying, they brought before him thirteen lamps kindled with balsam wood. He said to them, "For whom are all these?"

[T] They said to him, "They are for you."

[U] He said to them, "And are all these for Abbahu? 'I have labored in vain, I have spent my strength for nothing and vanity; yet surely my right is with the Lord, and my recompense with my God' (Is. 49:4). The Holy One, blessed be he, in this world shows the righteous the reward that is coming to them, so that when their soul is satisfied, they may go into their sleep. It may be compared to a king who made a banquet, and on a cloth he made a design of all of the foods to be served at the banquet. When the guests entered, they saw them, and their souls were sated, so they went into a deep sleep."

[V] Zabedai bar Levai and R. Yosé bar Piteres and R. Joshua b. Levi respectively cited [one of the following] three verses when they were dying:

[W] One of them said, "Therefore let every one who is godly offer prayer to thee" (Ps. 32:6).

[X] And one of them said, "But let all who take refuge in thee rejoice, let them ever sing for joy" (Ps. 5:11).

[Y] And one of them said, "O how abundant is thy goodness, which thou has laid up for those who fear thee and wrought for those who take refuge in thee" (Ps. 31:19).

[Z] R. Jacob bar Idi in the name of R. Joshua b. Levi: MʿSH Š: Elders went into the upper room in the house of Gedaya in Jericho. An echo went forth and said to them, 'There are among you two who are worthy of receiving the Holy Spirit, and Hillel the Elder is one of them.' They gazed upon Samuel the Small.

[AA] "ŠWB: Elders went into the upper room in [a house in] Yabneh, and an echo went forth and said to them, 'There are among you two who are worthy of receiving the Holy Spirit, and Samuel the Small is one of them.' They gazed upon R. Eliezer. And they were overjoyed that their own [prior] opinion agreed with the opinion of the Holy Spirit."

[BB] One of the members of the patriarchate died, and the [burial] cave folded over [and received the bier], so endangering the lives [of those who had come to bury him]. R. Yosé went up and took leave [of the deceased], saying, "Happy is a man who has left this world in peace."

[CC] When R. Yasa died, the castle of Tiberias collapsed, and members of the patriarchate were rejoicing. R. Zeira said to them, "There is no similarity [between this case and the miracle described at BB]. The peoples' lives were endangered, here no one's life was endangered. In that case, no pagan worship was removed, while here, an idol was uprooted [so, consequently, the event described in BB was not a miracle, while the event described here was a miracle and a sign of divine favor]."

[DD] R. Jacob bar Idi in the name of R. Joshua b. Levi: "When Rabban Yoḥanan ben Zakkai lay dying, he said, 'Clear out the house [of objects that will receive] uncleanness [when I die, leaving my corpse under the roof of this house], and prepare a throne for Hezekiah, king of Judah.'

[EE] "R. Eliezer, his disciple, when he lay dying, said, 'Clear out the house [of objects that will receive] uncleanness [when I die], and prepare a throne for Rabban Yoḥanan ben Zakkai.' "

[FF] And there are those who say, "Just as his master had seen [Hezekiah in a vision], so too did he see [the same vision]."

[GG] One of the members of the household of R. Pazzi did the members of the patriarchate seek to [engage for] marriage [into the family of the patriarchate], but he did not wish [to enter the marriage]. He said, "They should not so degrade me [by such a marriage proposal]."

[HH] When he lay dying, he said, "Clear out the house [of objects that will receive] uncleanness [when I die], and prepare a throne for Jehoshaphat, king of Judah."

[II] They said, "Let this one come, who ran after glory, in the aftermath of that one, who fled from glory."

[**III**.A] *And the sages say, "Prohibited is only one that has in its hand a staff, bird, or sphere" [M. A.Z. 3:1C].*

[B] A staff—for [what is intended is that] it rules the world with [a staff].

[C] A bird—"My hand was found like a nest the wealth of the peoples" (Is. 10:14).

[D] A sphere—for the world is shaped like a sphere.

[E] Said R. Jonah, "When Alexander of Macedon wanted, he could wing upward, and he would go up. He traveled upward until he saw the world as a sphere, and the sea as a dish. That is why they represent the world as a sphere in the hand [of an idol]."

[F] So let them depict a dish in [the idol's] hand too?

[G] [The idol] does not rule over the ocean.

[H] But the Holy One, blessed be he, rules over sea and land, saving [those who are in need] at sea and saving [those in need] on dry land.

[I] R. Zeira son of R. Abbahu expounded the following verse in the presence of R. Eleazar: " 'Happy is he whose help is the God of Jacob, whose hope is in the Lord his God' (Ps. 146:5).

[J] "Now what is written immediately thereafter? 'Who made heaven and earth, the sea and all that is in them' (Ps. 146:6).

[K] "Now what has one thing got to do with the other?

[L] "But a mortal king has a patron [to whom he is subservient]. In this hyparchy he does not [truly] rule. Is it possible that he [really] rules in some other? And if you would claim that there is the cosmocrator [who rules the world], he rules only on dry land, but not on the sea. But the Holy One, blessed be he, is not so. He is ruler by sea and ruler by land.

[M] "And not only so, but if there is a sword hanging over the neck of a man, the Holy One blessed be he saves him.

[N] "That is the meaning of what Moses said: 'He delivered me from the sword of Pharaoh' (Ex. 18:4). What is written here is, 'from the sword'—meaning: even if a sword is hanging over above one's neck, the Holy One, blessed be he, saves him from it."

[O] They added [to the list of items stated by the sages] **a sword, crown, ring[, image, or snake] [T. A.Z. 5:1B].**

[P] A sword—with which [the idol] kills.

[Q] A crown—with which [an idol] is crowned.

[R] A ring—with which [an idol] seals [its decrees].

[S] **A ring on which there is an idol is prohibited [Tosefta: permitted] for use as a seal. R. Judah says, "If the seal was incised, it is prohibited for use as a seal, because an image is made thereby. If it projects, it is permitted to make a seal with it" [T. A.Z. 5:2F–G].**

[T] **R. Haninah b. Gamaliel says, "The members of father's establishment would use a seal on which there were figures."**

[U] **R. Eleazar b. R. Simeon says, "Any sort of figure would have been found in Jerusalem, except for the figure of a man alone" [T. A.Z. 5:2N–O].**

[**IV**.A] *Rabban Simeon b. Gamaliel says, "Any that has anything at all in its hand" [M. A.Z. 3:1D]—*

[B] but this is on condition that it be something that is a matter of honor [respectable to hold].

[C] A thorn, a wooden prick, or shears are matters of common use [and so will not fall into the category of objects indicating the idol is honored].

[D] Paper and quill are matters of honor.

[E] As to an inkstand, [the item is in doubt and] requires [investigation].

Unit **I** opens in a promising way, carrying out the expected exegesis of the Mishnah's statements. There is an extension of the rule, at **I**.N–V , prohibiting even gazing upon icons or statues. In the illustrative fables, at Q, a death scene is mentioned. That is the only reason for the intrusion of the whole of unit **II**, which catalogues various kinds of death scenes, speeches, and stories. The whole clearly was built out of materials joined together before interpolation into the present setting, to which it scarcely relates. Units **III** and **IV** return to the citation and gloss of the Mishnah. **III**.A–D do a fine job. Once more, however, an allusion in what is relevant provokes the framers of the Talmud to tack on a great deal that is not, at E–N. Then O takes up a passage found in the Tosefta, as indicated, and performs an exegesis of its items, parallel to the earlier exegesis of the Mishnah's. In a Talmud organized more rigorously around the Mishnah's materials, we should have had A–D, then O–R. S–U then presents further materials found in the Tosefta, without any sort of comment at all. At the end **IV** presents a truly satisfying exegesis of the Mishnah's materials, a suitable amplification of the law itself.

3:2

[A] *He who finds the sherds of images—lo, these are permitted.*

[B] *[If] one found [a fragment] shaped like a hand or a foot, lo, these are prohibited,*

[C] *because objects similar to them are worshiped.*

[**I**.A] R. Yosé in the name of R. Yoḥanan: "[The reason that sherds are permitted is] that most of them come from Delphic tables[, which are decorated with images, and there is no reason to suppose they have been worshiped as idols]."

[B] If that is the case, then even the image of a hand or a foot [should be permitted].

[C] These are different, *because objects similar to them are worshiped.*

[D] [Adducing evidence that hands or feet are worshiped, the Talmud cites Scripture:] It is written, "The men of Babylon made Succoth-benoth" [meaning] a chicken and its eggs.

[E] "The men of Cuth worshiped Nergal" (2 Kings 17:30)—Jacob's foot and Joseph's foot [which they worshiped].

[F] ([Laban said to Jacob,] "If you will allow me to say so, I have learned by divination [42d] that the Lord has blessed me because of you" [Gen. 30:27].)

[G] "And the Lord blessed the Egyptian's house for Joseph's sake" (Gen. 39:5). [So their relics too were worshiped.]

[H] "The men of Hamath worshiped Ashima" (2 Kings 17:30)—a lamb, as it is said, "And the priest shall make atonement for him with the ram of the guilt-offering [*asham*]" (Lev. 5:16).

[I] "And the Avvites worshiped Nibhaz and Tartak" (2 Kings 17:31). The former was a dog, and the latter an ass.

[J] "And the Sepharvites burned their children in the fire to Adrammelech and Anammelech, to gods of Sepharvaim" (2 Kings 17:31)—[this refers to] a peacock and a pheasant.

[**II**.A] An idol that was [found] smashed—

[B] R. Yoḥanan said, "[The sherds are] forbidden."

[C] R. Simeon b. Laqish said, "[The sherds are] permitted."

[D] Now how shall we interpret this dispute? If at some point in the future the sherds are going to be restored to their former, whole condition, in the opinion of all parties [they must be] forbidden.

[E] And if at some point in the future the sherds are not going to be restored to their former, whole condition, in the opinion of all parties [they must be] permitted.

[F] But thus we interpret the dispute, [to deal with a case in which the disposition of the sherds is left] unspecified.

[G] R. Yoḥanan said, "[Sherds, the disposition of which is left] unspecified are equivalent to sherds that are destined to be restored to their former, whole condition."

[H] R. Simeon b. Laqish said, "[Sherds, the disposition of which is left] unspecified, are equivalent to sherds that are not destined to be restored to their former, whole condition."

[I] (Said R. Yudan, father of R. Mattenaiah, "If they were left in their original place, they are equivalent to sherds that are destined to be restored to their original condition.")

[J] R. Simeon b. Laqish objected to R. Yoḥanan, "And lo, it is written, 'This is why the priests of Dagon and all who enter the house of Dagon do not tread on the threshold of Dagon in Ashdod to this day' (1 Sam. 5:5) [which would indicate that it is not customary to restore the sherds to their former, whole condition]."

[K] He said to him, "This teaches that they behaved [with greater respect] for the threshold than they did for Dagon himself."

[L] R. Jeremiah in the name of R. Ḥiyya bar Ba said, "The nations of the world made a single threshold, but Israel made a great many thresholds. The scriptural proof for this statement is as follows: 'On that day I will punish every one who leaps over the threshold' (Zeph. 1:9)."

[**III**.A] He who comes across an idol—

[B] Rab said, "He shatters it limb by limb, and it is thereby nullified."

[C] Samuel said, "It is never subject to nullification [and its pieces are always prohibited for Israelites]."

[D] *[If one found a fragment of a hand or a foot (M. A.Z. 3:2B)]—*

[E] R. Abin in the name of R. Simeon: "That rule applies to a case in which there is no pedestal with them, but if there is a pedestal with them, I claim that the hand or foot come from the sherds [of the statue, and one who says that a broken idol is permitted will permit an Israelite to derive benefit from these sherds, while the one who rules that a broken idol is never permitted will not do so]."

The mode of argument of unit **I** is parallel to that of 3:1's opening unit. The extensive proof texts are relevant at only one point, E. Unit **II** is equally well formulated into a cogent analytical argument (**II**.A–G, I–J). If **III**.D belongs with A–C, then the interpolated materials indicate why.

3:3

[A] *He who finds utensils upon which is the figure of the sun, moon, or a dragon, should bring them to the Salt Sea [for disposal].*

[B] *Rabban Simeon B. Gamaliel says, "[Those that are found] on objects of value are prohibited, but [those that are found] on objects of no worth are permitted."*

[C] *R. Yosé says, "One breaks them into pieces and throws the powder to the wind or drops them into the sea."*

[D] *They said to him, "Also: they may be made into manure, as it is said, 'And there will cleave nothing of a devoted thing to your hand' (Deut. 13:18)."*

[**I**.A] They repeated [the rule of M. 3:3A] only in the case of *utensils upon which is the figure of the sun, moon. . . .* Lo, [if the representations] of any other heavenly bodies [should be found on utensils, the stated rule does] not [apply].

[B] They repeated [that same rule] only in the case of *utensils upon which is the figure of . . . a dragon.* Lo, [if the representations] of any other serpents [should be found on utensils, the stated rule does] not [apply].

[C] What is a dragon? It is any from the neck of which fringes come forth. And so it has been taught: R. Simeon b. Azzai says, "What is a dragon? It is any from the neck of which fringes come forth."

[D] [A utensil bearing the image of one the neck of which is] smooth is permitted.

[E] He who finds [a utensil bearing] a dragon made in the shape of a reptile—[the utensil] is forbidden.

[F] [He who finds a utensil bearing] a reptile made in the shape of a dragon removes the [part of the utensil in the shape of] a reptile, and tosses out the [part of the utensil marked with the figure of a] dragon.

[G] Samuel said, "[If] the cup forms the pedestal for a dragon, it is prohibited. And [if] the dragon forms the pedestal for a cup, it is permitted."

[H] R. Ba in the name of Rab: "The sherds of a dragon—lo, these are permitted. [If there was] a whole dragon that was shattered—lo, [the sherds] are prohibited."

[I] But the sherds [referred to above] to begin with came from a whole [dragon, did they not]?

[J] R. Hezekiah in the name of Rab: "Thus [the situation under discussion is one in which] one saw [idolators] prostrating themselves before a whole dragon, which then was shattered. [In this case the sherds are] prohibited [for Israelite use or benefit]."

[**II**.A] Now how shall we interpret the matter [of M. 3:3B]? If it is a matter of certainty that [the sherds] were worshiped, then even those that are found on objects of no worth must be forbidden. And if it is a matter of certainty that they have not been subjected to worship, then even those that are found on objects of value should be permitted.

[B] Then we must interpret the rule to apply to an object in which the matter is unspecified [as to whether or not the object has been subject to veneration].

[C] Said R. Qerispai: "Cups are objects of no worth. For R. Ḥiyya bar Ba had metal cups on which was incised the silhouette of Rome. He went and asked R. Yoḥanan [whether or not he might keep these cups], who said to him, 'Since water flows over [the silhouette of Rome], it is an object of no worth, and this ladle, since you dip it into water, is a matter of no worth.' "

[D] In the days of R. Yoḥanan [Israelites] began to paint on the walls, and [the sages] did not stop them.

[**III**.A] **R. Yosé [who rules that one breaks them into pieces and throws the powder into the wind or drops them into the sea] objected to the rabbis [who said the objects may be pulverized and made into manure], "And is it not written: 'Then I took the sinful thing, the calf which you had made, and burned it with fire and crushed it, grinding it very small until it was as fine as dust, and I threw the dust of it into the brook that descended out of the mountain' (Deut. 9:21). [This would indicate that the object must be broken into pieces and thrown into the sea or into the river.]"**

[B] **They said to him, "This verse [does not indicate how idols in general must be discarded, but serves to] teach that Moses planned to test them just as they test wives accused of adultery: 'And he took the calf which they had made and burnt it with fire and ground it to powder and scattered it upon the water and made the people of Israel drink it' (Ex. 32:20).**

[C] **"And has it not been written, 'He also removed Maacah his mother from being queen mother because she had an abominable image made for Asherah; and Asa cut down her image and burned it at the brook Kidron' (1 Kings 15:13). [But he did not pulverize it, so it can have been used for manure.]"**

[D] He said to them, "Is there any proof from that verse? **'Asa cut down her image, crushed it, and burned it at the brook Kidron' (2 Chr. 15:16). [This explicitly states that Asa did pulverize the idol.]"**

[E] **He said to them, " 'And he broke in pieces the bronze serpent that Moses had made, for until those days the people of Israel had burned incense to it'** (2 **Kings 18:4). [This was an idol, and it had to be pulverized, and clearly could not be used for manure.]"**

[F] **[They said to him,] "Now was the serpent an idol? And did not Moses himself make it? But it teaches that the Israelites strayed after it [as if it were an idol], so that Hezekiah came along and removed it."**

[G] **One verse of Scripture states, "And the Philistines left their idols there, and David and his men carried them away"** (2 Sam. 5:21).

[H] **And yet another verse of Scripture states, "And they left their gods there, and David gave command, and they were burned"** (1 Chr. 14:12) [T. A.Z. 3:19].

[I] [This conflict in the account of the disposition of the idols is dealt with by] R. Yosé bar Ḥalputa and the rabbis. R. Yosé bar Ḥalputa says, "As to what was of metal: 'And David and his men carried them away.' And as to what was of wood: 'And David gave command, and they were burned.' "

[J] And the rabbis say, "What Itti the Githite nullified [since he was a gentile and so had the power to nullify the power of an idol]: 'And David and his men carried them away.' And what Itti the Githite did not nullify: 'And David gave command, and they were burned.' "

[K] Now how does R. Yosé ben Ḥalputa interpret the passage, "And David and his men carried them away" [seeing that Israelites cannot derive benefit from idols]? They took them as small chips [once they had been nullified and no longer had the status of idols].

Unit **I** provides both a simple exegesis of the language of the Mishnah and further relevant rules. The systematic analysis of the Mishnah is undertaken at **II**, which carries out a familiar exercise. **III** supplies a debate between Yosé and the sages of the Mishnah, as indicated. The debate is effected through contradictory verses, each providing proof of the proposition of one party to the dispute.

3:4

[A] *Peroqelos b. Peloselos asked Rabban Gamaliel in Akko, when he was washing in Aphrodite's bathhouse, saying to him, "It is written in your Torah, 'And there shall cleave nothing of the devoted thing to your hand' (Deut. 13:18). Why are you taking a bath in Aphrodite's bathhouse?"*

[B] *He said to him, "They do not give answers [to serious questions] in a bathhouse."*

[C] *When he went out, he said to him, "I never came into her domain. She came into mine. They don't say, 'Let's make a bathhouse as an ornament for Aphrodite.' But they say, 'Let's make Aphrodite as an ornament for the bathhouse.'*

[D] *"Another matter: Even if someone gave you a lot of money, you would never walk into your temple of idolatry naked or suffering a flux, nor would you piss in its presence.*

[E] *"Yet this thing is standing there at the head of the gutter and everybody pisses right in front of her."*

[F] *It is said only, ". . . their gods" (Deut. 12:3)—that which one treats as a god is prohibited, but that which one treats not as a god is permitted.*

[**I**.A] How shall we interpret [the discourse with the nonbeliever]? If he asked him a question about the laws of the bathhouse, then [even in the bathhouse] he should have answered him [since, as we shall see, B, it surely is permissible to answer a question about the laws of the bathhouse when one is in the bathhouse]. And if it was not about the laws of the bathhouse, he should not have answered him at all.

[B] For R. Jacob bar Idi said in the name of R. Joshua b. Levi, "It is permissible to ask questions about the laws of the bathhouse in the bathhouse itself, laws of the privy in the privy itself."

[C] [A relevant precedent is] as follows: R. Simeon b. Eleazar went up to bathe with R. Meir [on the Sabbath in the hot springs of Tiberias]. He said to him, "What is the law as to our rinsing off?"

[D] He said to him, "It is forbidden."

[E] "What is the law as to our wiping ourselves off?"

[F] He said to him, "It is forbidden." [This proves that one may reply to questions pertaining to the laws of the bathhouse when in the bathhouse.]

[G] But [to the contrary] did not Samuel ask Rab, "What is the law as to answering, 'Amen,' in a filthy place [e.g., such as a privy]?"

[H] He said to him, "It is forbidden. And, furthermore, it is forbidden for me to say to you, 'Forbidden'!" [This proves, to the contrary, that one may not engage in such a discussion in that location.]

[I] It is found taught [in a Tannaitic tradition]: They do raise questions about the laws of the bathhouse in the bathhouse, and about the laws of the privy in the privy. [So the law necessitates answering, A.]

[J] Said Yudan, father of R. Mattenaiah, "[It is quite so that] concerning the laws of the bathhouse did [the nonbeliever] ask [Gamaliel]. But it is not customary to give answers in a bathhouse."

[K] Said R. Samuel bar Abedimi, "Indeed concerning the laws of the bathhouse did he ask him, but the steam of the bathhouse is bad for the teeth. [Consequently, he did not want to engage in discussion until he got outside, so as to avoid having to open his mouth.]"

[**II**.A] Associates, R. Ḥama bar Yosé in the name of R. Hoshaiah, R. Zeira in the name of R. Joshua b. Levi: "[Gamaliel] gave the nonbeliever an answer merely meant to put him off [but not a serious reply].

"For if [he really wanted to give a serious reply], the nonbeliever should have answered him by reference to the incident of Baal Peor, the worship of which was only through self-exposure ["flashing"], [and there is no more disgraceful deed, and yet this was deemed a mode of worship]. [So Gamaliel's reply about not urinating before the idol is of no account, and the entire argument adds up to nothing.]

[B] What is the upshot of the matter [since there really is a problem facing Gamaliel]?

[C] *That which one treats as a god is prohibited, but that which one treats not as a god is permitted.*

To the central concern of the Mishnah the question raised by **I** is hardly so pertinent as that of **II**. The problem of why Gamaliel did not give an answer in the bathhouse, in the light of the diverse rules on the matter, is solved by J and K. The point of **II** comes at the citation of the Mishnah, on which account M. 3:4F should not be treated as part of Gamaliel's answer. This is a particularly fine example of the role, in the Talmud's interpretation of the Mishnah, of criticism based on acute and sensitive analysis of the substance and language of the Mishnah.

3:5 [Leiden MS and *editio princeps:* 3:6]

[A] *Gentiles who worship hills and valleys—*

[B] *these [hills or valleys] are permitted, but what is on them is forbidden [for Israelite use],*

[C] *as it is said, "You shall not covet the silver or gold that is upon them nor take it for yourself" (Deut. 7:28).*

[D] *R. Yosé the Galilean says, "Their gods are 'on the mountains,' and the mountains are not their gods. Their gods are 'in the valleys,' and the valleys are not their gods."*

[E] *On what account is an "asherah" prohibited? Because it has been subject to manual labor, and whatever has been subject to manual labor is prohibited.*

[F] *Said R. ʿAqiba, "I shall explain and interpret the matter before you:*

[G] *"In any place in which you find a high mountain, a lofty hill, or a green tree, you may take for granted that there is an idol there."*

[**I**.A] R. Zeira, R. Yasa, R. Yosé bar Ḥanina in the name of R. Hoshaiah: "One Scripture states, 'You shall not covet the silver or gold that is upon them, nor take it for yourself' (Deut. 7:25). And yet another verse of Scripture says, 'And you have seen their detestable things, their idols of wood and stone, of silver and gold which were among them.' Now if [it says] 'upon them,' then why does it say 'among them,' and if it says 'among them,' why does it say 'upon them'?

[B] "Just as 'upon them' refers to something that is set aside as an ornament for them, so that which is 'with them' [which is forbidden] is anything that is set aside as an ornament for them."

[C] R. Yoḥanan in the name of R. Yannai: "Anything that is located within the hangings [in the sanctum] of the temple have they declared forbidden, for example, [even something that is not set aside as an ornament for the idol itself such as] money chests."

[D] Said R. Yasa, "We have a mnemonic [to remember that there is a dispute between A–B and C,] and it is this: R. Hoshaiah disputes the position of R. Yannai."

[E] But that is not so. Indeed the one position supports the other, as follows:

[F] Just as that which is "upon them," something that is set aside as an ornament for them, [is forbidden,] so that which is "with them," something that is set aside as an ornament for them, is forbidden. This then excludes money chests [if located outside of the veils of the sanctum].

[G] R. Ba in the name of R. Judah: "And even water and salt [pertaining to an idol will be forbidden]—salt for rubbing down the idol, and water to rinse it."

[H] And as to this "even" it should be: *for example* [of what is set aside as an ornament], water and salt.

[**II**.A] [The following discussion assumes knowledge of M. Kil. 7:4, which is as follows: *He who trellises his vine over the grain of his neighbor, lo, (by violating the law against mixing grain in a vineyard) this one has sanctified (the grain underneath the vines) and is liable. R. Yosé and R. Simeon say, "A man does not sanctify something that is not his own."* It is established elsewhere that the former position belongs to Judah and Meir.] As to [a beast] that has been worshiped [by a man]—

[B] there are Tannaim who repeat, "Whether it belongs to the man [who worshiped it] or whether it belongs to his fellow, [that beast] is prohibited."

[C] And there are Tannaim who repeat, "[If it belongs] to the man [who worshiped it], it is prohibited, but if it belongs to his fellow, it is permitted."

[D] The one who rules that, whether or not the beast belongs to the man [who committed idolatry] or to his fellow, it is prohibited, is R. Judah. And the one who rules that if it belongs to the man [who worshiped it], it is prohibited, but if it belongs to his fellow, it is permitted, is R. Yosé and R. Simeon. [The reference, as noted, is to M. Kil. 7:4, and the basis for this conclusion is self-evident.]

[E] R. Yosé in the name of [43a] R. Ila, "In point of fact, it is the position of all parties [including Yosé and Simeon]. This is in accord with that which the law states, 'As to a living creature, even though [if it is worshiped by a third party] it is not forbidden to an ordinary person, it is forbidden to the Most High.' " [Thus even Yosé and Simeon concur that the beast that has been worshiped is forbidden, A, whether it belongs to the one who has committed the act of idolatry with the beast or whether it belongs to another party. But then the owner, if it is not the idolator, has the use of the creature for other purposes—so Yosé and Simeon.]

[F] And similarly, as to something [you worship] that does not belong to you, even though it is not forbidden to an ordinary person, it is forbidden to the Most High.

[G] R. Bun bar Ḥiyya said, "Even fine flour [that one has used for idolatrous purposes]—that which belongs to the man [who committed the act of idolatry] is forbidden, but that which belongs to his fellow is permitted [for ordinary use]." [This rule applies even to inanimate objects.]

[H] Is this in accord with the opinion of the one who ruled, Whether it belongs to himself or to his fellow, it is forbidden? [The point is that] the argument does not pertain to something that is inanimate[, for all parties concede that someone cannot sanctify what is not his].

[I] Or perhaps R. Bun bar Ḥiyya comes to tell you that the Mishnah addresses the case of an animate creature, [on which all parties agree,] [and] concerning what do [the authorities] differ [if not] concerning an inanimate object?

[J] No, lo, [if] an animate object is prohibited [under the stated circumstances], will an inanimate object not all the more so be forbidden! [So I's version is not possible.]

[K] [But the real meaning of G is this:] The point is that you should *not* say, Just as you have ruled there, an animate object, even though it is not forbidden to an ordinary person, is forbidden to the Most High, similarly [you should not maintain that] an inanimate object not your own [that you have worshiped], even though it is not forbidden to an ordinary person, is forbidden to the Most High[, for that is not the case of an inanimate object in the view of Bun bar Ḥiyya].

[**III**.A] [If a gentile] prostrated himself in worship before an egg—

[B] Hezekiah said, "He has not prohibited it [for Israelite use or benefit]."
R. Yoḥanan said, "He has prohibited it."

[C] Said R. Zeirah, "Concerning an [actual] egg do they dispute."

[D] Associates say, "Concerning boulders in a valley [and not an actual egg] do they dispute."

[E] Said R. Huna, "And Scripture itself supports the position held by associates: 'Among the smooth stones of the valley is your portion; they, they are your lot' (Is. 57:6)".

[F] The lenient position of Hezekiah is on the basis of this statement: *On what account is an asherah prohibited? Because it has been subject to manual labor, and whatever has been subject to manual labor is prohibited [M. 3:5E].* [Now the stones of a valley have not been worked by man, so the stones or the egg will not be prohibited, in line with B.]

[G] All agree in the case of wheat [that a gentile has worshiped,] that it is prohibited[, for it is subject to manual labor].

[H] For R. Haninah bar Yasa in the name of R. Judah: "The roots of wheat extend into the earth by fifty cubits; the roots of a young fig extend into a rock."

[I] What is the scriptural proof for that statement? "I the Lord am its keeper; every moment I water it" (Is. 27:3).

[J] It was taught by a Tannaitic tradition: R. Simeon b. Eleazar says, "This verse teaches that the earth drinks [the rains] only as far as its upper layer goes."

[K] If so, what should the roots of a carob or a sycamore do?

[L] Said R. Ḥaninah, "Once every thirty days the great deep rises up and waters them."

[**IV**.A] An egg belonging to an idol that hatched and produced a chick—

[B] R. Ḥaggai in the name of R. Josiah: "Kahana and Hezekiah dispute about this matter.

[C] "Kahana said, 'It is permitted.'

[D] "And Hezekiah said, 'It is forbidden.' "

[E] Now a question to be addressed to the position of Hezekiah is this: How is it possible that an egg belonging to an idol should hatch and produce a chick?

[F] For how shall we interpret the case? If it is a case in which one has beaten out of shape the face of the idol [and so nullified it], there is no question of a chick [for the egg will have been destroyed with the idol].

[G] If it is a case in which one brought the egg inside of the hangings [into the sanctum as an offering to the idol], do [we] go and see whether one has bowed down to it! [That is irrelevant in light of M. A.Z. 3:5E. Hezekiah on that count has not forbidden it.]

[H] But because one has brought it within the hangings, [Hezekiah] has forbidden it.

[I] Said R. Yudan father of R. Mattenaiah: "Interpret the dispute to concern a case in which one has rolled the egg in toward the altar [in which case the condition of M. A.Z. 3:5E—an act of manual labor—has been met].

[**V**.A] A nut subject to the ʿ*orlah* taboo [that is, deriving from a tree subject to the taboo against using the fruit of a tree in the first three years of its growth] that one planted,

[B] and so too: an egg subject to a vow of sanctification that hatched and produced a chick—

[C] R. Yasa: "Kahana and R. Yoḥanan disputed about this matter.

[D] "Kahana said, 'It is forbidden.'

[E] "And R. Yoḥanan said, 'It is permitted.' "

[F] Said R. Zeira before R. Yasa, "And has not R. Yoḥanan said, 'It is permitted,' [but] even he [requires that] one redeem it at [its value at] the time that he planted it."

[G] There came R. Ḥananiah, R. Yonah, R. Eleazar in the name of Kahana: "One redeems it at [its value at] the time at which he planted it."

[H] R. Ḥananiah in the name of R. Pinḥas said, "The matter must be corrected as follows:

[I] "Kahana said, 'It is forbidden, and one redeems it as is.'

[J] "R. Yoḥanan said, 'It is permitted, and one redeems it at [its value at] the time that he planted it.' "

[Leiden MS and *editio princeps:* 3:7]

[**VI**.A] *Said R. ʿAqiba, "I shall explain and interpret ('WBYN) the matter before you: In any place in which you find a high mountain, lofty hill, or green tree, you may take for granted that there is an idol there" [M. A.Z. 3:5F–G].*

[B] [In reference to the language ʿAqiba uses, 'WBYN, translated, "explain and interpret,"] we repeat the tradition, 'WBYN.

[C] But there are Tannaim who repeat the tradition as "'WBYL before you," that is, "I shall discuss before you."

[D] He who said [that it is correct to read] 'WBYN means, "Let us understand the subject."

[E] And one who said, "'WBYL" means, "Let us discuss the subject."

[F] R. Boreqai taught before R. Mana, "This verse [Deut. 7:28] teaches that the Canaanites did not leave a single mountain or valley on which they did not perform an act of idolatrous service."

[G] Now have we not reasoned and ruled, Something that is animate, even though it is not forbidden to an ordinary person, is forbidden to the Most High?

[H] [If so, how did they know] where the Chosen House [of the temple] was to be built?

[I] It was in accord with the instruction of the prophet: "So David went up at Gad's word, which he had spoken in the name of the Lord" (1 Chr. 21:19).

The opening exercise, unit **I**, appears to wish to contrast miniscule elements of verses of Scripture, but at **I**.B, C an important dispute is presented. So far as I can see, the claim that the two opinions do conflict is valid, unless, as we must, we interpolate the added language at the end of F. G–H form an appendix to the whole. Unit **II** deals with the worship of inanimate and animate objects, well within the thematic frame of the Mishnah. The exposition from A–F is smooth. While Bun bar Ḥiyya's saying poses no problems of interpretation, H–J are somewhat complicated, and I may not have done full justice to the rhetorical shifts. The outcome is clear at J. Unit **III** carries forward the established problem of the disposition of an object worshiped as an idol by a gentile. At issue are an egg and wheat, and what we have is the elucidation of the extent to which the Mishnah's principle applies. The same intent is clear at unit **IV**, which introduces a dispute demanding coordination with the Mishnah's critical principle. Without that principle it is not possible, in the Talmud's view, to interpret the dispute at hand, thus **IV**.F, G, I. Unit **V** focuses upon a different problem, namely, the value imputed to an object subject to redemption at the time at which the object is used. If one wishes to utilize the nut or the egg, he pays for that object and so transfers the sanctity inhering in it to the money he hands over, leaving the object itself available for common use. He pays either the value of the object at the moment of redemption (Kahana), or the value of the object at the moment of utilization (Yoḥanan). None of this pertains to the pericope of Mishnah before us, and unit **V** is introduced solely because of **V**.B. Unit **VI** returns us to the interpretation of the present passage of the Mishnah, interpreting alternate readings of the language attributed to ʿAqiba.

3:6 [Leiden MS and *editio princeps:* 3:8]

[A] *He [the wall of] whose house was adjacent to [and served also as the wall of the temple of] an idol, and [whose house] fell down—*

[B] *it is forbidden to rebuild it.*

[C] *What should he then do?*

[D] *He pulls back to within four cubits inside his own property and then rebuilds his house.*

[E] *[If there was a wall belonging] both to him and to [the temple of an] idol, it is judged to be divided half and half.*

[F] *The stones, wood, and mortar deriving from [the wall belonging to a temple] impart uncleanness having the status of a dead creeping thing, for it is said, "You will utterly detest it" (Deut. 7:26).*

[G] *R. ʿAqiba says, "Having the status of a menstruant['s uncleanness], as it is said, 'You shall cast them away as a menstrous thing; you shall say unto it, Get you hence' (Is. 30:22).*

[H] *"Just as a menstruating woman imparts uncleanness to the one who carries her, so an idol imparts uncleanness to the one who carries it."*

[**I**.A] "Abomination" is written in connection with the menstruating woman, "abomination is written in connection with dead creeping things, and "abomination" is written in connection with an idol.

[B] In connection with the menstruating woman: ". . . for whoever shall do any of these abominations—[the persons] that do them shall be cut off . . ." (Lev. 18:29). [Lev. 18:19 explicitly includes under the stated curse one who has sexual relations with a menstruating woman.]

[C] In connection with dead creeping things: "You shall not eat any abominable thing" (Deut. 14:3).

[D] In connection with idolatry: "And you shall not bring an abominable thing into your house and become accursed like it; you shall utterly detest and abhor it; for it is an accursed thing" (Deut. 7:26).

[E] But I do not know to which matter an analogy is to be drawn.

[F] R. ʿAqiba said, "It is to be compared to the abomination stated with reference to the menstruating woman:

[G] *"Just as a menstruating woman imparts uncleanness to the one who carries her, so an idol imparts uncleanness to the one who carries it."*

[H] Or perhaps: Just as a menstruating woman imparts uncleanness [by the pressure of her weight when she is seated] on top of a large stone [to objects located beneath said stone], so an idol imparts uncleanness when located on top of a large stone [and not in direct contact with objects underneath the stone].

[I] R. Zeriqa in the name of R. Ḥaninah, and there is he who holds he said it in the name of R. Ḥisda, "R. ʿAqiba concurs with the sages that an idol does not impart uncleanness to [what is beneath] a large stone."

[J] And the rabbis state [that an idol is analogous] to the "abomination" stated with regard to dead creeping things.

[K] Just as a dead creeping thing imparts uncleanness to the one who merely shifts its position [without bearing its weight], so the idol imparts uncleanness to the one who merely shifts its position.

[L] Or perhaps should we argue: Just as a dead creeping thing imparts uncleanness when it is merely of the size of a lentil, so an idol should impart uncleanness when a sherd of it is so small as a lentil?

[M] [That possibility is rejected in the following proof.] R. Zeira, R. Isaac bar Naḥman, R. Eleazar, R. Abbahu in the name of R. Yoḥanan: " 'Then they attached themselves to the Baal of Peor, and ate sacrifices offered to the dead' (Ps. 106:28). Just as a corpse imparts uncleanness through a piece of corpse matter the size of an olive's bulk, so an idol will impart uncleanness when its sherd is the size of an olive's bulk."

[N] Or perhaps [the verse of M should be interpreted to mean]: Just as a corpse imparts uncleanness once one has brought in [under the roof of a house so small a part of the corpse as] the tips of its fingers, might one say, "Also an idol should impart uncleanness when one has brought [under the roof of a house so small a part of the idol as] the tips of its fingers"?

[O] The word "tear down" [NTYṢH] is used both with reference to an idol and with reference to a house afflicted with plague. ["You shall tear down their altars" (Deut. 12:3), "And he shall break down the house, its stones and timber and all the plaster of the house" (Lev. 14:45).]

[P] [So one may] learn [the following rule] from the matter of the house afflicted with plague:

[Q] Just as in the case of a house afflicted with plague, once one has poked in his head and the greater part of his body, [he has become unclean], so in the case of an idol, once one has poked in its head and the greater part of its body[, it imparts uncleanness to objects under the roof of the house].

[**II**.A] Said R. Ḥaninah, "That is to say that the uncleanness imputed to an idol is not clear[ly derived from the Torah]. For if that were not so, would one compare it to a lesser [source of uncleanness], and not compare it to a more severe [source of uncleanness]?!"

[B] Said R. Mana, "It is clear [that the source of uncleanness to which the idol is comparable is the Torah, even though the analogy is drawn to both a minor and a major source of uncleanness].

[C] "Now why does one compare it to a corpse and to a dead creeping thing? To derive evidence therefrom for the minor [forms] that apply to [both these sources of uncleanness]. [That is, the purpose is to impose on the idol the small volume sufficient to impart uncleanness that applies in the case of a corpse, an olive's bulk, and to compare the idol to the dead creeping thing in that the idol will not impart uncleanness to the one who carries it.]"

[D] This [comparison to the corpse] is in line with the following: [The minimum volume to impart uncleanness, an olive's bulk, applies] to an idol that is broken, but in the case of an unbroken idol, whatever size it is[, it imparts uncleanness].

[E] This is in line with that which R. Yosé b. R. Bun said, R. Ḥama bar Gurion in the name of Rab: "[There was an idol] in the shape of the head of a penis, and there was one in the shape of a bean."

[F] Now what is the scriptural basis [for this statement about the kind of idol just now described in the shape of a penis]? "And they made as their god the master of the mark of circumcision [Baal berith]" (Judges 8:33). [This indicates that there can be an idol in the stated shape.]

[**III**.A] What is the scriptural basis of R. ʿAqiba['s position, comparing the idol to a menstruating woman as to uncleanness]? "You shall [utterly detest and] abhor it" (Deut. 7:26)—like menstrual uncleanness.

[B] What is the scriptural basis of the rabbis? "You shall utterly detest [and abhor it]" (Deut. 7:26)—like a dead creeping thing.

[C] How do the rabbis interpret the language adduced in evidence by R. ʿAqiba? ["Abhor it" means] treat it like excrement or carrion.

[Supply: And how does R. ʿAqiba interpret the language adduced in evidence by the rabbis? "Detest it" means deface it.]

[D] And how do the rabbis provide scriptural proof that one must deface an idol?

[E] R. Samuel, R. Abbahu in the name of R. Eleazar: "[They cite this verse: 'Then you will defile your silver-covered graven images and your gold-plated molten images. You will scatter them as unclean things;] you will say to them, 'Begone!' (Is. 30:22)."

[F] **The one whom they call "Face of God" [Israelites must call] "Face of Dog." "Spring of the well" do they call "Spring of the thorn" [KWS, QWṢ]. "Fortune" [GDDY'] do they call "Heap" (GLYY') [T. A.Z. 6:4B–D].**

[G] R. Tanḥuma asked in the name of R. Huna, "It is written, '[Joshua sent men from Jericho to] Ai, which is near Beth-aven, east of [MQDM] Bethel' (Joshua 7:2). Formerly [MQDM] they called it Beth El (house of God), but now they call it Beth-aven (house of falsehood)."

[H] It was taught in the name of R. Eleazar, "[If a person] did not want to call it by [an honorable name such as ʿ*omdah*, then let people call it ʿ*amidah* ('piss-pot')]."

[I] And they call urine-soaked dung an ʿ*amidah* [as above].

[J] Now how do the rabbis interpret the verse in Isaiah, "You will say to them . . ."?

[K] R. Yosé b. R. Abun, R. Huna in the name of R. Joseph: "How do we know that one does not say to a person, 'Get out,' before he pokes in his head and the greater part of his body [where he is not wanted]? [From the verse in Isaiah just now cited.]" [That is, they interpret the verse in a quite different context.]

[**IV**.A] There is a version of the Mishnah tradition that states, "An idol is like a menstruating woman [as to uncleanness], and the appurtenances of an idol [also] are like a menstruating woman."

[B] And there is a contradictory version of the Mishnah tradition that states, "An idol is like a menstruating woman [as to uncleanness] but its appurtenances are like a dead creeping thing [as to uncleanness]."

[C] For the one [43b] who maintains, "An idol is like a menstruating woman and the appurtenances of an idol are like a menstruating woman," [the verse adduced in evidence by ʿAqiba] poses no problems [in comparing the idol to a menstruating woman (Is. 30:22)].

[D] But the one who says, "An idol is like a menstruating woman, but the appurtenances of an idol are like a dead creeping thing"—the very essence of the cited verse refers as a menstruous thing only to the appurtenances of the idol [e.g., the gold plating]! [So the verse adduced in evidence contradicts this view of the status of the appurtenances.]

[E] Interpret the verse to refer to that which is hammered into the body [of the idol itself].

[F] For R. Jacob of Kefar Hanan said, "Interpret the statement to apply to a case in which one prostrates himself to the ephod [of an idol], as it is said, 'And Gideon made an ephod [of the golden pieces given to him by the people] . . . ; and all Israel played the harlot after it there' (Judges 8:27)."

[G] The Mishnah [in regard to ʿAqiba's position] follows the opinion of the one who rules, "An idol is like a menstruating woman [as to uncleanness], but its appurtenances are like a menstruating woman, for thus have we repeated the Mishnah pericope: *The stones, wood, and mortar deriving from [the wall belonging to a temple] impart uncleanness in the status of a dead creeping thing [M. A.Z. 3:6F].* [And this differs from M. A.Z. 3:6G–H, so ʿAqiba will not concur.]

[H] Interpret the statement to apply to a case of one's prostrating himself in worship to the house itself [and not merely to what is in it]. [For even though the house is attached to the ground, as at unit **VI**, and so not subject to prohibition, it was originally not so, and was only attached later on.]

[I] This is in line with that which R. Ba, R. Huna in the name of Rab [stated]: "He who prostrates himself in worship to a house has prohibited [Israelite use or benefit from that house]."

[J] R. Zeira, R. Abbahu in the name of R. Yoḥanan "He who sanctifies a house—the laws of sacrilege do apply to it."

[K] And the one who said, "The laws of sacrilege do apply to it" [maintains that] the one who has worshiped it has rendered it forbidden for Israelite use or benefit.

[L] R. Ḥaggai objected before R. Yosé, "And lo, the Mishnah takes a position at variance with that of Rab:

[M] *"A trough that is hewn in the bedrock—they do not draw [water for the purification ashes] with it, they do not mix [water with purification ashes] in it, they do not sprinkle [the mixture] from it, it does not require a tightly sealed stopper, and it does not render an immersion pool unfit [since it is not an autonomous utensil].*

If it was a movable utensil, and one then joined it with plaster to the ground, they do draw with it, they do mix with it, they do sprinkle from it, it does require a tightly sealed stopper, and it renders unfit in the case of an immersion pool [since it is an autonomous utensil in all regards] [M. Par. 5:7A–D].

[N] "Now the reason that the utensil is regarded as a utensil [in the second half of the rule and so] invalidates an immersion pool [if drawn water is poured from it into an immersion pool lacking the requisite volume of fit water] is that one has hewn it out and afterward attached it to the bedrock. Lo, if one attached it to the bedrock and afterward hewed out a container, what would be the rule governing the object?"

[O] Interpret the matter in line with the view of R. Yoḥanan: "Hewing stones is the completion of the act of manufacturing them [and at that point they are appurtenances of idolatry, even before being made part of the house]."

[**V**.A] Now does this statement [of M. A.Z. 3:6F] not stand at variance with that which R. Simeon b. Laqish said, "An idol that was broken is permitted"?

[B] And we have had the theory: If in the future one plans to put the sherds back together, all parties concur that it is forbidden. [But here we do not know what will be done with the sherds.]

[C] Interpret the matter to apply to a case in which one has prostrated himself in worship to each stone, and afterward put them all together. [Thus each stone was forbidden as an idol before the idol itself was made. When the idol broke, the sherds remained prohibited.]

[D] Does this same rule not stand at variance with the position of R. Yoḥanan, for R. Yoḥanan said, "An idol that was shattered is forbidden"?

[E] And we had the theory: "If one is not going in the future to put the sherds back together to their former, whole condition, then all parties should concur that [the sherds of the shattered idol are] permitted. [But here we do not know what will be done with the sherds.]

[F] Interpret the rule to apply to a case in which one has prostrated himself in worship to a root and afterward planted it in the ground.

[**VI**.A] Levi said, "One who prostrates himself to a house has forbidden it. But if he did so to a cave, he has not prohibited it."

[B] What is the difference between a house and a cave?

[C] Said R. Ḥaninah b. R. Hillel, "A house had a time in which it was distinct from the ground, but a cave never had a time at which it was distinct from the ground. [This is in line with **IV**. H ff.]

[**VII**.A] R. Yoḥanan interpreted the Mishnah [M. A.Z. 3:6A: *He whose house was adjacent to a temple*] to speak of a case of a convert [to Judaism] and a gentile who shared in the inheritance of their gentile father. [The gentile took a house containing an idol, the Israelite took the house next door, which had none.]

[B] Now why did he not interpret the Mishnah to speak of a case in which the temple containing the idol was brought and placed next to the house of the Israelite?

[C] [The reason Yoḥanan did not imagine so simple a case is that] it was taught: A temple containing an idol was next to a house and afterward it was removed [since the wall fell down]—it is permitted [for the Israelite to use the wall's materials].

[D] But a convert [to Judaism] and a gentile who shared in the inheritance of the estate of their gentile father [and the wall fell down]—[the use by the Israelite of the wall's materials] is forbidden.

[E] It was taught: A temple containing an idol was next to a house and afterward it was removed—[use of the other house] is permitted.

[F] But if the Israelite came along and set his house up against the wall of the temple to an idol, the entire house is deemed to be for the sake of the idol [and is prohibited for Israelite use or benefit].

[G] Said R. Yosé, "The Mishnah itself speaks of exactly that sort of case, when it states, *If there was a wall belonging both to him and to the temple of an idol, it is judged to be divided half and half" [M. A.Z. 3:6E].*

The dispute as to the uncleanness of an idol and its sherds or appurtenances occupies the principal part of the Talmud's treatment of this Mishnah pericope, units **I–IV**. M. 3:6A–E are treated only at the end (**VI–VII**), and then in a perfunctory way. The concrete difference between M. 3:6F and G–H, by contrast, hardly would lead us to expect such a sustained exegetical treatment. The sole difference is expressed at H, a position rejected by F. So far as F is concerned, one who carries but does not actually touch a piece of an idol (e.g., carrying a sherd in a brown paper bag) will not be unclean. The first exercise is spelled out at **I**.A–E, repeated at unit **III**. It is possible to draw an analogy, through the utilization of common language, among the idol, the menstruating woman, and the dead creeping thing. This statement allows for a review of the Mishnah's dispute between ᶜAqiba and the anonymous authority of M. 3:6F. The dialectic begins at H, at which contrary possibilities are raised for the principal assertions of ᶜAqiba and the sages. This is clearly expressed at K, challenged by L. L then is rejected by M. M is tested by N. N then is refuted by O–Q, a moving argument that in no way loses coherence. Ḥanina's question, at the outset of unit **II**, carries forward the discussion of unit **I**. He points out that we have compared the idol to the uncleanness imputed to a corpse, in that sherds impart uncleanness like limbs of a corpse, and to a dead creeping thing, in that a bit so small as a lentil contaminates. The remainder of unit **II** fills out this point. Reverting to the point at which we started, **III** returns to the scriptural bases for the conflicting positions, allowing each party to interpret in his own way the evidence adduced by the other. Unit **IV** presents a compilation in the foregoing discussion, since it concedes ʿAqiba's position about the status, as to uncleanness, of the idol, but then raises the distinct question about the status of the appurtenances of an idol. Then it goes back over the original dispute, now with regard to these appurtenances. The center of interest is ʿAqiba's position on the status of the appurtenances. G settles that question by showing that he differs as much about the appurtenances as about the idol itself. Now to reject that obvious proof, H replies that the case of the stones, wood, and mortar, in fact it is not relevant to the present question. Why not? Because these, in context, are not appurtenances of an idol, but constitute idols themselves. They were worshiped, and so the disagreement of ʿAqiba and the sages deals solely with the idol—here stones, wood, and mortar—and not necessarily the appurtenances of an idol. Now what makes that position difficult is that the house is attached to the ground, and we already know that things deemed part of the earth—hills and valleys—are not prohibited as objects of idolatry, but only what is on them. So the matter requires introducing Rab's position that a house can be worshiped as an idol and so prohibited. What is not stated but necessary for understanding what is to follow, is that the theory behind this rule is that the house is not essentially part of the earth at all, a fact stated explicitly at **VI**. It was originally not attached to the ground, that is, the wood, stone, and mortar were distinct from the ground and then reattached thereunto, that is, when the house was built. Ḥaggai (L–N) points out a Mishnah pericope that rejects Rab's theory of the status of what originally was not part of the ground but then became part of the ground. The cited passage (M) is shown to relate through the elucidation supplied at N. Then O dismisses the objection, which, to begin with, is hardly essential to the argument. The discussion of **V**.A–C poses no problems, but the text of D–F is inferior. The better version will be given in due course; meanwhile Pené Moshe should be consulted. Unit **VI**, by contrast, presents no problems. Unit **VII** has Yoḥanan interpret in a rather farfetched way the case to which the Mishnah rule applies (A–D). This is dealt with by Yosé at G; he sees no reason for the approach proposed by

Yoḥanan. It is a simple case. An Israelite came and set his house up next to a building in which there was an idol. If the wall falls down, it is prohibited to rebuild it, just as the Mishnah says. The part belonging to the temple of the idol is forbidden. There is then no need to invent a case of a joint inheritance of a gentile idolator and a convert to Judaism to explain the Mishnah's reference.

3:7 [Leiden MS and *editio princeps:* 3:9]

[A] *There are three sorts of houses [so far as use as a shrine for idolatry is concerned]:*

[B] *[1] a house that was built to begin with for the purposes of idolatry—lo, this is prohibited.*

[C] *[2] [If] one stuccoed and decorated it for idolatry and renovated it, one removes the renovations [added for idolatry and then may use the house].*

[D] *[3] [If] one brought an idol into it and took it out—lo, this is permitted.*

[**I**.A] Rab and R. Yoḥanan—both of them say "The Mishnah pericope speaks of the situation prevailing when the Israelites entered the land [in which case there were houses built to begin with for idolatry, and these were forbidden, as at M. A.Z. 3:7B. Both authorities wish to explain why the Mishnah does not merely state, 'He who prostrates himself in worship to a house has forbidden it,' rather than the Mishnah's specification of building the house for idolatrous purposes]."

[B] Now in accord with the position of Rab, who said, "He who prostrates himself in worship to a house has prohibited [the house for Israelite use or benefit]," it is a suitable explanation to explain the Mishnah to refer to the period at which the Israelites entered the land.

[C] But in accord with the position of R. Yoḥanan, who said, "He who declares a house to be sanctified—the laws of sacrilege do not apply to it" [because the house to begin with is not truly sanctified, since it is attached to the ground, how is the Mishnah's rule to be interpreted]?

[D] [Yoḥanan] may interpret the passage to refer to one who prostrates himself in worship to a house. [Now this is different from a house built to begin with for idolatrous purposes.]

[E] [This then is the point of the Mishnah in Yoḥanan's view:] He who prostrates himself in worship to a house—there is the possibility of nullifying the effects of his action. [But what was already subject to idolatry] when the Israelites entered the land is not subject to the possibility of nullifying the effects of idolatrous worship.

[F] What should one do [in the case of a house originally built for idolatry]? One must take apart the doorposts, and it is then permitted.

[**II**.A] [With regard to M. A.Z. 3:7C] R. Ila in the name of R. Eleazar: "And this rule applies to the case of one who has brought an idol into the house."

[B] [If that is the case, then] so far as the view of R. Eleazar is concerned, there are two categories of house [M. A.Z. 3:7C and D are the same].

[C] And yet we have learned in the Mishnah, *There are three sorts of houses.*

[D] In the one case [M. 3:7D] the idol was brought in for the interim, in the other [M. 3:7C] it was brought in permanently.

Unit **I** takes its beginning from the question of why the Mishnah asks about a house built to begin with for idolatrous purposes. For, the two authorities note, merely worshiping the house as an idol suffices to prohibit its use to Israelites. Building it for that purpose to begin with hardly requires specification and contributes nothing. By referring the Mishnah's discourse to the situation prevailing when the Israelites conquered the land, the two authorities allow the Mishnah to make a point in addition to the one that is expressed by the statement "He who worships a house has forbidden it." Now, as we notice, Yoḥanan's position on sanctifying a house is that the house is not sanctified, because it is attached to the ground. So, once again, that familiar problem has to be confronted. The answer this time, in the present context, is to claim that Yoḥanan treats a house built for the purposes of idolatry differently from a house that has been worshiped. E expresses this differentiation and explains Yoḥanan's view of the Mishnah's meaning. If a house is built for idolatrous purposes, it cannot ever be used for Israelite ones; now that is not a rule that can be expressed merely by stating "He who prostrates himself to a house has forbidden its use by Israelites." The discourse thus makes a good and valid point of differentiation and satisfactorily explains within diverse principles—Rab's and Yoḥanan's—why the Mishnah pericope before us expresses an important and fresh point. The second unit poses no problems. Eleazar's point is that merely intending to beautify the house for an idol is insufficient; one must actually bring an idol into the house, and in that case the improvements to the house, made for idolatrous purposes, must be removed before an Israelite may use or derive benefit from the house. So mere intention is insufficient in this area of the law.

3:8 [Leiden MS and *editio princeps:* 3:10]

[A] *There are three sorts of stones:*

[B] *[1] a stone which one hewed to begin with for a pedestal [for an idol]—lo, this is forbidden.*

[C] *[2] [If] one plastered it and adorned it for an idol, and did something new to it,*

[D] *one may remove that which he made which is new [and use the stone].*

[E] *[3] [If] he set up an idol on [an existing] stone and then took it off, lo, this is permitted.*

[**I**.A] R. Ba in the name of Rab: "On the basis of [this law of the Mishnah we infer that] slags that are smelted for use in idolatry are prohibited forthwith."

[B] R. Jeremiah in the name of R. Eleazar: "On the basis of [this law of the Mishnah we infer that] he who smelts metal for a cup for idolatry—it is forbidden forthwith."

[C] R. Hila in the name of R. Eleazar, "And that is the case if one has then set up an idol on top of it."

[**II**.A] The opinions imputed to Rab are confused. There he has said, "On the basis [of this law of the Mishnah we infer that] he who smelts metal for a cup for idolatry—it is forbidden forthwith."

[B] And here has he said this [statement]?

[C] Interpret the passage in the manner of the following Mishnah law which we have learned there: *An idol belonging to a gentile is prohibited forthwith. But one belonging to an Israelite is prohibited only once it has been worshiped [M. A.Z. 4:4A–B].*

[D] Now is it so that the argument concerns an idol? Perhaps it refers to its appurtenances.

[E] R. Simeon in the name of R. Eleazar: "Also with regard to the apurtenances of an idol is there a dispute."

[F] R. Hila in the name of R. Eleazar, "And that is the case if one has then set up an idol on top of it."

[G] In regard to the opinion of R. Eleazar, there will be two types of stones!

[H] And lo, we have learned, *Three stones?*

[I] In the one case we speak of what is temporary, in the other, of what is permanent.

The dispute of unit **I** has to do with the prohibition, even before it is used for idolatrous purposes, of ore smelted for the purpose of making a pedestal for an idol. Rab at **I**.A maintains that that prohibition applies forthwith, before idolatry has taken place. Jeremiah-Eleazar interpret Rab's position to mean that the appurtenances of an idol, such as a cup, fall under the same rule. As soon as the ore is mined and smelted for a cup, it is prohibited. Then, reading C as continuous with A–B, we find that Hila-Eleazar takes the opposite position. The appurtenances are prohibited only when used for idolatry. Then they will be forbidden. But the appurtenances are not prohibited if they are not worshiped. Mere intent is null. Unit **II** turns its attention to M. 4:4, on which Rab comments that a pedestal made for an idol, from which the idol has been removed, is *not* nullified on that account. Now we must assume in that context that the gentile plans to put some other idol on it. So the intention of the gentile in regard to the pedestal *is* operative, despite the present facts of the matter. If then we look at **I**.B, C, we note that Rab takes the view that the mere intention is null. The solution to this problem is at C. At M. 4:4 we speak of a gentile's idol, and here, of an Israelite's one, so Eleazar's qualification of Rab's position (the cup must be actually prepared, the idol must actually set on top of it) pertains to something belonging to an Israelite. D proposes a different solution, that in the one place the idol is prohibited forthwith, while in the other the appurtenances of the idol are prohibited only once they serve in an act of worship. The answer, E, is that the argument applies to both sorts of objects, idol and appurtenance. Unit **II** goes over a familiar exercise, now interpreting M. 3:8E. This yields two types of stones, not three, and the distinction is offered familiar from the foregoing pericope.

3:9 [Leiden MS and *editio princeps:* 3:9]

[A] *There are three kinds of "asherahs":*

[B] *[1] A tree that one planted to begin with for idolatry—lo, this is prohibited.*

[C] *[2] [If] he chopped it and trimmed it for idolatry, and it sprouted afresh, he may remove that which sprouted afresh [and use the remainder of the tree. The growth alone was for idolatry].*

[D] *[3] [If] he set up an idol under it and then annulled it, lo, this is permitted.*

[**I**.A] R. Ami in the name of R. Simeon b. Laqish said, "If one incised markings in it [gashed the sides of the tree], it is not subject to nullification.

[B] [This point is obvious.] But is is needed to make the point, "Even if he removed the gashes [the tree is still prohibited]."

[**II**.A] It was taught in a Tannaitic teaching: If one grafted [something onto the tree], for the sake of an *asherah*, he removes that which he grafted onto the tree.

[B] Said R. Yannai, "And that rule applies to the case in which one has grafted on something for idolatry."

[**III**.A] R. Hila in the name of R. Simeon b. Laqish: "And the law applies in a case in which one set up an idol under the tree."

[B] The theory of R. Simeon b. Laqish appears to be confused.

[C] There R. Ami said [in his name], "If one incised markings on it, it is not subject to nullification." And we reasoned and ruled that, even if one has then removed the gashes [it is not nullified as an idol].

[D] Yet here he has said this[, that if there is no idol under the tree, the tree is not prohibited]!

[E] The rule is more strict in the case of incisions on the tree.

[**IV**.A] It was taught, "If one has grafted onto the tree [a branch for an *asherah*], one removes what he has grafted onto the tree."

[B] Said R. Hila in the name of R. Eleazar, "And that is the case if one has set up an idol underneath the tree."

[C] In respect to the thesis of R. Eleazar, there are two sorts of *asherah*-trees, and yet we have learned, *There are three kinds of asherahs* [M. A.Z. 3:9C–D, vs. A].

[D] In the one case we speak of an *asherah* that is temporary, in the other, permanent.

Unit **III**, in which two opinions of Simeon b. Laqish are contrasted, is of particular interest. In the one case (unit **I**) we maintain that if one has trimmed a tree for idolatry, M. 3:9C, one removes what has been done only in the case in which one has actually set an idol under the tree. Then his actions show that the purpose of the new growth of the tree was for idolatry. But at **I**.A/**III**.C, we impute to the same authority the position that no act of nullification is valid, e.g., even removing the idol from underneath the tree. The answer is, as expected, at **III**.E: the rule is more strict in the case of **I**.A/**III**.C, than in the present instance. Unit **IV** once more goes over familiar ground.

3:10

[A] *What is an asherah? Any tree under which is located an idol.*

[B] *R. Simeon says, "Any [tree] that people [actually] worship."*

[C] *MʿŚH: In Sidon there was a tree that people worshiped, and they found a pile of stones underneath it.*

[D] *Said to them R. Simeon, "Investigate the character of this pile of stones."*

[E] *They did investigate it and found an image in it.*

[F] *He said to them, "Since they are worshiping the image [and not the tree], let us permit them to make use of the tree [itself]."*

[**I**.A] Said R. Ḥisda, "In respect to a tree that is lacking in specification are the authorities [of M. A.Z. 3:10A, B] in dispute."

[B] [Explaining Ḥisda's point, we proceed:] Now how shall we interpret the matter?

[C] If it is a matter of certainty that they are worshiping the image and the tree, then all parties concur that [the tree] is forbidden.

[D] And if it is a matter of certainty that they are worshiping the image and not worshiping the tree, then all parties must concur that [the tree] is permitted.

[E] But thus we must interpret the matter, in a case lacking in all specification [as Ḥisda said].

[F] R. Simeon says, "In the case of those trees that are not specified, they are worshiping the image and the tree."

[G] And the rabbis say, "In the case of those trees left without specification, they are worshiping the image, and they are not worshiping the tree."

[H] But there is a question [to be raised against this interpretation of the matter].

[I] [If so,] is it possible that R. Simeon differs from the sages and yet makes a concrete decision in accord with their view [for, at M. 3:10F, he distinguishes worship of the image from use of the tree, and this is a case of a tree left without specification, as at F, G? So the present view is that Simeon rules at M. A.Z. 3:10F, in practice, in accord with sages, G. That then is the question announced at H].

The mode of inquiry into the Mishnah is a familiar one, pointing out the extreme possibilities (C, D) and then harmonizing them at an excluded middle, at which we are not sure of the facts of the case and so can consent to the presence of a dispute based on essentially a shared principle.

3:11 [Leiden MS and *editio princeps:* 3:13]

[A] *One should not sit in [an asherah's] shade, but if he sat in its shade, he is clean.*

[B] *And he should not pass underneath it, but if he passed underneath it, he is unclean.*

[C] *[If] it was overshadowing public domain [taking away property from public use], and one passed beneath it, he is clean.*

[D] *And they sow seeds underneath it in the rainy season, but not in the dry season.*

[E] *But as to lettuce, neither in the dry season nor in the rainy season [may one plant it there].*

[F] *R. Yosé says, "Also: not vegetables in the rainy season,*

[G] *"because the foliage drops on them and serves as manure for them."*

[**I**.A] There [in Babylonia] they say in the name of R. Ḥisda, "The shade [of an *asherah*] is forbidden, but the shadow cast by its shade is permitted."

[B] What is the shadow cast by its shade, and what is its shade?

[C] There they said, "Any space that, if the tree should fall down, [its branches] would reach—this is [the area of its] shade.

[D] And any space that, if the tree should fall down, [its branches] would not reach—this is [the area of the] shadow of its shade.

[E] On what account is the shadow [of an *asherah*-tree] prohibited?

[F] Because it is subject [to the prohibition of deriving] benefit [from an object of idolatry].

[G] [If that is the criterion, then] lo, the grave is prohibited for benefit, yet its shadow is permitted.

[H] Lo, there is the temple pile, [the shadow of which] is prohibited for benefit. And yet Rabban Yoḥanan b. Zakkai would sit and teach in the shadow of the temple pile [so it is merely to begin with that the prohibition applies (Pené Moshe)].

[I] So the reason cannot be that [the shade of an *asherah*] is prohibited because of a prohibition of deriving benefit therefrom [for these cases do not run parallel].

[J] R. Abin in the name of the rabbis from over there [in Babylonia]: "That is to say that the uncleanness of corpses is not clear[ly based on the rules of the Torah], for if that were not the case, then [how could we rule that] a grave that was overshadowing the public domain and beneath which one passed—he is clean [M. A.Z. 3:11C]! [So the decree concerning uncleanness derives from rabbinical and not scriptural authority.]"

[**II**.A] Gamaliel Zuga was walking along, leaning on the shoulder of R. Simeon b. Laqish. They came across an image.

[B] He said to him, "What is the law as to passing before it?"

[C] He said to him, "Pass before it, but close [your] eyes."

[D] R. Isaac was walking along, leaning on the shoulder of R. Yoḥanan. They came across an idol before the council building.

[E] He said to him, "What is the law as to passing before it?"

[F] He said to him, "Pass before it, but close [your] eyes."

[G] R. Jacob bar Idi was walking along, leaning upon R. Joshua b. Levi. They came across a procession in which an idol was carried. He said to him, "Naḥum, the most holy man, passed before this idol, and will you not pass by it? Pass before it but close your eyes."

[**III**.A] Does this statement [M. A.Z. 3:11G: the foilage manures the crop] not stand at variance with the position of R. Yoḥanan, for R. Yoḥanan said, "An idol that was shattered remains prohibited."

Now did we not reason and rule, "If one was not going to restore it to its original, whole condition, all parties concur that it is permitted. [So why should we care about the foilage at all?]

[B] Interpret the rule to speak of an idol belonging to an Israelite.

[C] Does [43c] this then not stand at variance with the position assigned to Rab [at M. A.Z. 3:14], "[If he trimmed the *asherah*] for its own good, it is forbidden, but its chips are permitted," [so once more why are we concerned about the chips]?

[D] Once again interpret the rule to apply to an idol belonging to an Israelite.

[E] On what account does everyone want to keep away from [an idol belonging to an Israelite]?

[F] Because [an idol belonging to an Israelite] is bad even when disfigured.

The question raised at unit **I** is not directly answered, but the answer is contained at I–J. The prohibition of the shade of an *asherah*-tree is proved to be not based on the scriptural prohibition against deriving benefit from idolatry, but rather on the rabbis' decree alone. Unit **II** then goes on to what is at best a marginally relevant theme, walking by idols. The triplet of patterned stories makes no important point. Unit **III** asks the necessary question of why, at the Mishnah, we should care about the foilage of such a tree, seeing that it is no longer part of the *asherah*. Yose's position appears to be extreme. The Talmud hypothesizes that the *asherah* belongs to an Israelite, in which case it is never subject to nullification, and whatever pertains to it remains permanently prohibited for Israelite use or benefit.

3:12 [Leiden MS and *editio princeps:* 3:14]

[A] *[If] one has taken pieces of wood from [an asherah], they are prohibited for benefit.*

[B] *[If] he lit a fire in the oven with them, if it is a new oven, it is to be overturned. If it is an old oven, it must be allowed to cool down.*

[C] *[If] he baked a loaf of bread in [the oven heated by the wood of an asherah], it is prohibited for benefit.*

[D] *[If] it was mixed up with others, all of them are prohibited as to benefit.*

[E] *R. Eliezer says, "Let him take the [funds received for the sale as a] benefit [from the tree] to the Salt Sea."*

[F] *They said to him, "There is no form of redemption for an idol."*

[**I**.A] Said R. Ḥisda, "It is in the case of a piece of wood, the purpose of which is unspecified, that they differ [at M. A.Z. 3:12D–F]."

[B] How shall we interpret the dispute?

[C] If it is intended to burn it up, all parties concur that it is permitted.

[D] If it is to create smoke [and incense], all parties agree that it is prohibited.

[E] But thus must we interpret the rule to deal with one that is not specified [of its purpose].

Ḥisda interprets the dispute of M. 3:12D–F as dealing with the wood of A. The absence of an antecedent, to be sure, does not obscure M. 3:12D's clear intent, which is to speak of loaves of bread, not pieces of wood.

3:13 [Leiden MS and *editio princeps:* 3:13]

[A] *[If] one took wood for a shuttle, it is forbidden for benefit.*

[B] *[If] he wove a garment with the shuttle, the garment is forbidden for benefit.*

[C] *[If] it was mixed up with other garments, and other garments with still others, all of them are forbidden for benefit.*

[D] *R. Eliezer says, "Let him take the funds derived from the benefit to the Salt Sea."*

[E] *They said to him, "There is no redemption price for a matter of idolatry."*

[**I**.A] Said R. Ḥaggai, "When I got off the boat, I found R. Jacob bar Aḥa sitting and raising the question, '*If one took wood for a shuttle it is forbidden for benefit. If he wove a garment with the shuttle, the garment is forbidden for benefit' [M. 3:13A–B].*

[B] "And [Jacob added] have we not learned: 'Let him sell the whole of it to a gentile, except for the value of the libation wine that is in it [which value he may not enjoy. But the rest is permitted].' "

[C] Said R. Jacob bar Aḥa, "Ḥaggai raised the question, and Ḥaggai interpreted the law:

[D] "What is the difference between the two cases? There it is not common for people to purchase [wine] from a gentile, but here it is common for people to purchase clothing from a gentile, [so we impose a strict rule, to take account of the possibility that a gentile will purchase the garment and resell it to an unsuspecting Israelite, who will be guilty of deriving benefit from the part of the cloth woven with an object belonging to an idol]."

The Talmud's treatment of the Mishnah is clear.

3:14 [Leiden MS and *editio princeps:* 3:16]

[A] *How does one desecrate [an asherah]? [If] one trimmed it or pruned it, took from it a branch or twig, even a leaf—*

[B] *lo, this constitutes desecration.*

[C] *[If] one has trimmed it for the good of [the tree], it remains forbidden.*

[D] *[If he trimmed it] not for the good of the tree, it is permitted.*

[**I**.A] Rab said [with reference to M. A.Z. 3:14D], "If [the trimming] was for the need of the man, both the tree and the chips are permitted.

[B] "If it is done for the sake of the tree, the tree is forbidden, but the chips are permitted."

[C] Samuel said, "If it is done for the need of the tree, both the tree and the chips are forbidden.

[D] "If it was done for the convenience of the man, the tree is forbidden, but the chips are permitted."

[E] R. Yoḥanan said, "If it was done for the need of the tree, it is prohibited, but the chips are permitted."

The Talmud adds the matter of the chips produced in trimming the tree. B and E concur against C.

4 Yerushalmi Abodah Zarah Chapter Four

4:1

[A] *R. Ishmael says, "Three stones, one beside the other, beside Merkolis are forbidden.*

[B] *"But two are permitted."*

[C] *And sages say, "Those that appear to belong to it are forbidden,*

[D] *"and those that do not appear to belong to it are permitted."*

[**I**.A] Said R. Ami, "The reason of R. Ishmael is that [when there are three stones beside a statue of a Merkolis, they signify] a large Merkolis alongside a small Merkolis [and not because we take account of the possibility that the three stones have fallen from the idol itself, as is the reasoning of the sages, M. A.Z. 4:1C–D]."

[B] And the rabbis say [that the reason is that the nearby stones appear to serve as] the feet of Merkolis [which have fallen from the idol but are an integral part of it].

[C] And [up to] how long a distance [from the idol will rocks be deemed] the feet of Merkolis?

[D] R. Ba in the name of the rabbis from over there [Babylonia]: "[Those found within] fifty cubits [distance from the idol]."

[E] The law governing the proper construction of Merkolis is thus: two stones, one beside the other, with yet a third situated on top [of both of them].

[F] [If an Israelite] put on the second stone [thus not completing the idol, and also slaughtered a beast before the incomplete idol, and the beast was the dam of an offspring that had been slaughtered on that day, or the offspring of a dam that had been slaughtered on that day, so that there are two transgressions in view, one, building an idol, the other, slaughtering a dam and its offspring on the same day], and they had warned [the Israelite] concerning violation of the law against slaughtering the dam and its offspring on the same day, [the Israelite] is given a flogging [on the count of violating the prohibition against slaughtering the dam and its offspring on the same day], but on the count of idolatry he is not stoned to death. [On this the authorities cited below concur. Their dispute is now to be spelled out.]

[G] [If an Israelite] set the third stone [on the pile, so completing the idol], then we come to a dispute of R. Yoḥanan and R. Simeon b. Laqish. For thus do they argue:

[H] He who slaughters a dam and its offspring for the sake of idolatry—

[I] R. Yoḥanan said, "If [others] gave warning to the man [43d] on the count of not slaughtering a dam and its offspring on the same day, he is given a flogging. If they gave warning on the count of idolatry, he is stoned to death [and not flogged]."

[J] R. Simeon b. Laqish said, "Even if [others] should give him warning on the count of not slaughtering the dam and offspring on the same day, he is not given a flogging, since, if they warned him on the count of idolatry, he would be stoned to death."

[**II**.A] What then is [the definition of stones set up as] a Merkolis?

[B] It is any object [set up to serve as] a protective measure at the sea or by the wayside.

[C] The law [for serving a Merkolis is carried out] through tossing [a stone onto the pile].

[D] [If a gentile] prostrated himself in worship before such a statue, what is the law [since this is not the normal mode of worship]?

[E] Said R. Yosé, "The very essence of its being deemed a Merkolis is only through a gesture of respect such as prostration[, so even though that is not the normal mode of worship, it indeed is effective]."

[F] "[You shall make for yourselves no idols and erect no graven image or pillar, and] you shall not set up a figured stone in your land to bow down to them" (Lev. 26:1).

[G] Is it possible to rule that one should not set two stones side by side and place his basket on top of them [so forming something like a Merkolis statue]?

[H] Scripture states, ". . . to bow down to them."

[I] To it you may not bow down, but you may place your basket on it [since this is no sign of respect].

[J] "To it" you may not prostrate yourself, but you may prostrate yourself on the stones of the house of the sanctuary.

[K] Rab instructed the household of R. Aḥa, R. Ami instructed the members of his household, "When you go out to a public fast, do not prostrate yourselves in your normal way [of doing so at home, because in the public place there is a mosaic floor]."

[L] R. Yonah lay down on his left side. R. Aḥai lay down on his left side.

[M] Said R. Samuel, "I personally saw R. Abbahu lying down in his normal manner."

[N] Said R. Yosé, "I raised this question before R. Abbahu, [phrasing it as follows:] Is it not written, 'You shall not set up a figured stone in your land to bow down to them'?"

[O] [He replied,] "Interpret the matter to prohibit establishing a permanent location [for prostration, outside of the temple]."

[P] "And is it not written, 'When David came to the summit, where he would prostrate himself to God' (2 Sam. 15:32) [this being the summit of the Mount of Olives, and this would indicate that this was a place where prostration usually took place, and it was not the temple mount]?"

[Q] "But this was a prostration that was not on the earth [and such is not subject to the prohibition of which the Scripture speaks]."

[R] "And is there a prostration that is not on the earth?"

[S] "[Yes, as it is written:] '[When all the children of Israel saw the fire come down . . . upon the temple,] they bowed down [but did not prostrate] with their faces to the earth on the pavement . . .' (2 Chr. 7:3)."

[T] [The following is added in connection with the interpretation of M. Shebu. 2:3, which states, *If one was made unclean in the temple courtyard, and [unwittingly] he prostrated himself, or remained therefore an interval sufficient for prostrating himself, if he then went out by the longer way, he is liable.*] The duration of tarrying then is to be specified. It is the time taken to recite the verse, "And all the children of Israel looked on, when the fire came down, and the glory of the Lord was upon the house; and they bowed themselves with their faces to the ground upon the pavement, and prostrated themselves, and gave thanks to the Lord" (2 Chr. 7:3). To this stated interval [the time taken to recite the verse], R. Abbahu added, "For he is good, for his mercy endures forever."

[U] [To this interval] R. Mana added to "For he is good, for his mercy endures forever" [the further words] "upon Israel."

[V] R. Yoḥanan said to R. Ḥiyya bar Ba, the Babylonian, "Two rulings came up from your midst[, which we have accepted]:

[W] "The total prostration spreading out of hands and feet, on the fast day;

[X] "and the custom of using the willow branch on the seventh day of the festival of Tabernacles."

[Y] The rabbis of Caesarea say, "Also [the rules as to which day one may and which day one may not] let blood."

[Z] [And this ruling about total prostration on a fast day that came up from Babylonia] is in accord with that which R. Ami, the Babylonian, stated in the name of the rabbis of that locale, "They permitted prostration only at a public fast, and this is on condition that one did so lying on the side."

[AA] R. Yannai, Zeira in the name of his father: "Whoever is not so worthy as Joshua, to whom, if he should fall on his face, God will say, 'Arise' (Joshua 7:10), should not fall on his face.

[BB] "But this is excepting an individual [worshiping] apart from the congregation."

[**III**.A] *And the sages say, "Those that appear to belong to it are forbidden, and those that do not appear to belong to it are permitted" [M A.Z. 4:1C–D].*

[B] *Those that appear to belong to it [are forbidden* as part of] its body, and *those that do not appear to belong [to it are not forbidden as they are]* not part of its body.

[C] *Those that appear to belong to it are forbidden*—does this rule not stand at variance with the position of R. Simeon b. Laqish?

[D] For R. Simeon b. Laqish said, "An idol that was broken—[the sherds] are permitted."

[E] Now did we not reason and say, "If one was going to put them together whole, then in the view of all parties, [the sherds are] forbidden? [Now here, since the stones are near the idol, they evidently are going to be reassembled and reconstituted as the idol was to begin with.]

[F] And does it not also stand at variance with the position of R. Yoḥanan?

[G] For R. Yoḥanan said, "An idol that was broken—[the sherds] are forbidden."

[H] Now did we not reason and say, If one was not going to put them together again, then in the view of all parties [the sherds are] permitted?

[I] [In this same connection] R. Yudan father of R. Mattenaiah said, "If the sherds were lying in their place, it is as if one plans to restore them to their original whole condition. And these stones are in their place." [Now these stones are permitted, even though they are in essentially their own place, M. A.Z. 4:1D].

[**IV**.A] R. Ba in the name of Rab: "Sometimes one may infer that the sherds of an idol are not subject to nullification [and always are forbidden], and sometimes you may infer that the appurtenances of an idol are not subject to nullification [and eternally forbidden]."

[B] He who states the rule in regard to the appurtenances [that they are always prohibited] the more so will deem the idol itself [to be perpetually prohibited].

[C] But the one who states that the sherds of an idol are perpetually prohibited—lo, the appurtenances are not [always going to be subject to prohibition of Israelite use or benefit].

[D] R. Samuel, R. Abbahu in the name of Rab: "Stones of a Merkolis that were scattered are never subject to nullification at any time, on the count of having been part of an idol."

[E] R. Yoḥanan heard this statement and said, "Well did Rabbi teach us, for thus it is the rule: 'He who prostrates himself to an idol made up of an offering of food—[the produce] never can be nullified [from its status as part of an idol]' "

[F] How then does one nullify it?

[G] R. Ḥiyya bar Ada said, "By spitting [at it]."

[H] And has it not been taught, R. Ḥiyya taught, "Stones of a Merkolis that were scattered are never subject to nullification at any time"? [So how do F–G apply?]

[I] Said R. Pinḥas, "In the one case, [in which the stones were] tossed toward the idol, [there can be no nullification, because the stones themselves constitute offerings to the god]. In the other case, in which the stones were not tossed toward the idol[, there can be nullification, because the stones themselves do not constitute offerings to the god but are merely sherds thereof]."

[J] This is in accord with the following: R. Simeon, son of Rabbi, had a Merkolis [built by gentiles] in a forest belonging to him. A station guardsman came to him and said to him, "Since I have heard that the ruler of the city wants to pass by here tomorrow [I have to remove the stones from the road]."

[K] He said to him, "By your life! You should remove these stones from them."

[L] After he had removed them, he went and wanted to take them [for himself].

[M] [Simeon] said to him, "They belong to me."

[N] R. Ḥiyya bar Vada heard and commented, "Now that man's mother has a real son!"

[O] Now did not R. Ḥiyya the Great teach this tradition [that an idol that has been nullified is available for Israelite use]?

[P] But when R. Ḥiyya the Great heard this story, he fortified the law and established it as the norm. [And the deed was praiseworthy because Simeon had made the distinction between stones that had been tossed at the idol, which were permanently prohibited as an offering, and stones of the Merkolis itself, which were permitted once they had been nullified by gentile action.]

The opening unit accomplishes both the exegesis of the Mishnah and also the extension of the facts provided in the present pericope to a fresh range of issues, nicely spelled out at **I**.F–J. What we should have expected is an amplification of the secondary dispute. Still, the positions possible in regard to the conundrum confronted at G are exhausted. Unit **II** runs on because of the allusion to prostrating oneself before a Merkolis, not the usual mode of worship (**II**.E). Once this point is introduced, it becomes possible to discourse on matters having to do with prostration, in a smooth movement from the stated topic to closely related ones, then to ones still less clearly connected (**II**.G–H, then I–J). From this point the issue of prostration takes over; the one of the Merkolis passes from view. The discourse on Abbahu's view that prostrating oneself in the normal way is permissible (M) demands that we deem O, Q, and S to belong to Abbahu, at least for the purposes of argument. Then T, relevant both to Abbahu and to the theme of prostrating oneself, but not relevant to what has gone before, is tacked on. V–Z form yet another collection of miscellanies on prostrating oneself. Unit **III** stands more closely in relationship to the exegesis of the Mishnah. Its interest, by now not unexpected, is in testing the established positions of Yoḥanan and Simeon b. Laqish against the fresh materials supplied by the present pericope. The result is that the rule can be shown to conflict with both viewpoints. Unit **IV**, finally, takes up the subject of nullifying the status of idolatry as it applies to a given object. A–C are familiar, but not relevant at the outset. The important point comes at D, and the rest is clear. The issue of A–C then becomes pertinent, since we have to sort out those parts of an idol that can be rendered fit for Israelite use (through a gentile's treating them as null) from those that can never be used by an Israelite. An offering remains perpetually prohibited, even a stone tossed at a Merkolis—a suitable ending for a reasonably coherent discussion of the Mishnah.

4:2

[A] *[If] one found on its head coins, clothing, or utensils, lo, these are permitted.*

[B] *[If one found] bunches of grapes, garlands of corn, jugs of wine or oil, or fine flour,*

[C] *or anything the like of which is offered on the altar—*

[D] *it is forbidden.*

[**I**.A] Said R. Jonathan, "Bunches of grapes are not the end of the matter, but even bunches of roses [will be forbidden as something left as an offering on the altar]."

[B] Said R. Yosé, "A Merkolis with coins on its head is not the end of the matter [of what is permitted], but even if, in the case of an idol not surrounded by a veil, one found inside of the idol clothing or utensils, lo, these are permitted."

The Talmud glosses the Mishnah by expanding the negative and positive application of its principle.

4:3

[A] *A pagan cult place that had a garden or a bathhouse—*

[B] *they derive benefit from them [when it is] not to the advantage [of the temple],*

[C] *but they do not derive benefit from them [when it is] to the advantage [of the temple].*

[D] *If it belonged to [the pagan cult place] and to others, they derive benefit from it both to advantage and otherwise.*

[**I**.A] Thus is the meaning of the Mishnah passage: When it is to the advantage of the priests, when it is not to the advantage of the priests [of the temple of idolatry].

[**II**.A] **As to bagpipes belonging to an idol, it is forbidden to sell them [Tosefta: to make a lamentation with them]. If they were rented from the state, even though they were made for use of an idol, it is permitted to make lamentation using them. Shops belonging to an idol's [temple]—it is prohibited**

to rent space in them. But if they provided a rental for the state, even though they were built for the use of an idol['s temple], it is permitted to rent them. Charity collectors for a temple of idolatry—it is prohibited to give anything to them. But if they provided funds to the state, even though they are working for the welfare of an idol—it is permitted to give a contribution to them [as at M. A.Z. 4:3D].

[B] Now the Mishnah also has stated the same rule: *If it belonged to the [pagan cult place] and to others, they derive benefit from it when it is both to its advantage and otherwise [M. A.Z. 4:3D].*

The Talmud glosses the Mishnah at unit **I** and vastly expands it at unit **II**'s massive citation of the Tosefta.

4:4

[A] *An idol belonging to a gentile is prohibited forthwith [when it is made].*

[B] *And one belonging to an Israelite is prohibited only after it will have been worshiped.*

[C] *A gentile has the power to nullify an idol belonging either to himself or his fellow.*

[D] *But an Israelite has not got the power to nullify an idol belonging to a gentile.*

[E] *He who nullifies an idol has nullified its appurtenances.*

[F] *[If] he nullified [only] its appurtenances, its appurtenances are permitted, but the idol itself [remains] prohibited.*

[**I**.A] R. Simeon b. Laqish said, "The Mishnah [M. A.Z. 4:4A] refers to a case of a gentile craftsman who manufactures [idols] for sale in the market place, for once he has completed the idol, it is a matter of certainty that he has prostrated himself in worship to it."

[B] [Since the Mishnah has stipulated, at M. 4:4B, that an idol made by an Israelite is prohibited only after it has been worshiped, the Mishnah author appears to take for granted that the idol in general is not worshiped forthwith upon the completion of its manufacture. That is what prompts] R. Yosé [to] ask, "If it [really] is a matter of certainty that he has prostrated himself to it, then is it in such a case that we have learned in the Mishnah: *An idol belonging to a gentile is prohibited forthwith, and one belonging to an Israelite is prohibited only after it will have been worshiped?"*

[C] R. Hila in the name of R. Simeon b. Laqish: "He who hews [stone for] a statue for idolatry, even though you have ruled 'The earth is not prohibited [by reason of idolatry, so what is yet attached to the earth is not subject to prohibition on account of serving for an idol],' nonetheless they pronounce a warning to him [against his actions] for each act of hewing stone. When [the idol] is [then] detached [from the ground, once it is fully sculpted], he is to be given a flogging."

[D] Said R. Yosé, "From the stated rule, you may infer the following: He who makes a statue for an idol [e.g., for decorating a beast, which is an idol], even though you have ruled, 'Something that is animate is not prohibited [so the beast is not prohibited],' they nonetheless pronounce a warning to him [against his actions] for each blow with the hammer. When the idol is completed, he is given a flogging."

[**II**.A] *An idol belonging to a gentile is prohibited forthwith* [M. A.Z. 4:4A]. Therefore it is subject to nullification.

[B] *And one belonging to an Israelite is prohibited only after it will have been worshiped [M. A.Z. 4:4B].* Therefore it is not subject to nullification.

[C] Said R. Zeira, "There is no 'therefore' applicable here. But [one should state the rule], 'It is not subject to nullification,' or, 'It is subject to nullification.' "

[**III**.A] *An idol belonging to a gentile is prohibited forthwith,* in line with the following verse of Scripture: "You shall surely destroy [all the places where the nations whom you shall dispossess served their gods]" (Deut. 12:2)—forthwith.

[B] *And one belonging to an Israelite is prohibited only after it will have been worshiped,* in line with the following verse of Scripture: "Cursed be the man who makes a graven or molten image, an abomination to the Lord, a thing made by the hands of a craftsman, and sets it up in secret" (Deut. 27:15)—when he will set it up.

[C] There are those who reverse the matter:

[D] An idol belonging to an Israelite is prohibited forthwith, as it is written, "Cursed be the man who makes a graven or molten image."

[E] And one belonging to a gentile is prohibited only after it will have been worshiped, as it is written, "You shall surely destroy all the places where the nations whom you shall dispossess served their gods."

[F] R. Isaac bar Naḥman in the name of Samuel derived that same view [that an idol belonging to a gentile is prohibited only after it will have been worshiped] from the following: If one has inherited [the idol] when it [already] is deemed a god, "in fire will you burn it," and if not: "whom the nations whom you shall dispossess . . . their gods." ["You shall tear down their altars and dash in pieces their pillars and burn their Asherim with fire . . ."] (Deut. 12:2–3). [That is, if you have inherited the idol at a point at which it has already been served as a god, you must burn the idol. But if not, then those not already worshiped which you inherit are yours and may be sold, with the profits for Israelite benefit.]

[**IV**.A] [With reference to the following passage of the Mishnah: *A gentile has the power to nullify an idol belonging either to himself or his fellow, but an Israelite has not got the power to nullify an idol belonging to a gentile,*] R. Yoḥanan in the name of R. Yannai derived that view from the following verse of Scripture: "You shall not covet the silver or the gold that is on them or take it for yourselves" (Deut. 7:25). "You may not covet and take [that gold], but other may covet [the gold], and then you may take it."

[B] R. Yoḥanan said to Bar Derosai, "Go, break all the idols that are in the public baths [of Tiberias]," and he went and broke all of them except for one.

[C] And why so?

[D] Said R. Yosé b. R. Bun, "Because a certain Israelite was suspected of going and offering incense on that one[, and an idol worshiped by an Israelite is not subject to nullification at all]."

[E] R. Ḥiyya bar Ashi in the name of Rab: "Rabbi was sitting and repeating to R. [44a] Simeon, his son, the following tradition: '*A gentile has the power to nullify an idol belonging either to himself or to his fellow[, but an Israelite has not got the power to nullify an idol belonging to a gentile]* [M. A.Z. 4:4C–D].'

[F] "He said to him, 'While you are still in your youth, I repeated the tradition [to you] as follows: '*A gentile has the power to nullify an idol belonging either to himself* or to an Israelite.'

[G] "He said to him, 'No, my son. An idol that an Israelite has worshiped is never subject to nullification!' "

[H] And there is a Tannaitic teaching along these same lines:

[I] R. Simeon b. Menassia says, "An idol that an Israelite has worshiped is never subject to nullification."

[J] Rab taught the tradition in the name of this Tanna who adduced in evidence the following Scripture: "Cursed be the man who makes a graven or molten image, [an abomination to the Lord, a thing made by the hands of a craftsman, and sets it up in secret]" (Deut. 27:15)—[cursed be he] forever.

[K] Bar Qappara found a ring bearing an image. An Aramaean shepherd boy was running after him, wanting to pick it up. [Bar Qappara] pressed the boy despite it [nullify it through disrespect]. He told him to spit on it [and so nullify its status as an idol], but the boy would not agree to do so. He urged him then to piss on it, but he would not agree to do so.

[L] This [story] is in line with the rule: *A gentile has the power to nullify an idol belonging either to himself or to his fellow* [even if] this is under coercion.

[M] And this applies only in the case of [a gentile] who knows the character of the idol belonging to him [as in the story of K].

[N] The law states: An idol that an Israelite has worshiped is never subject to nullification.

[O] But why not let it be treated as an idol the worshipers of which have abandoned [in peacetime] [M. A.Z. 4:6], and let it be nullified on that count?

[P] Said R. Zeira, "Over any [idol] that, on its own, may be subject to nullification, does an Israelite have the power to nullify, and over any idol that, on its own, may not be subject to nullification, does an Israelite not have the power of nullification."

[**V**.A] Rab said, "A pedestal [from which the idol is removed still] is not subject to nullification."

[B] Lo, if [gentiles] nullified it, it indeed is null [as an idol. So it is regarded as an idol].

[C] The opinions attributed to Rab are confused.

[D] There [3:8, above, p. 143] we said, "On this basis, 'He who smelts ore and pours a metal cup for the purposes of idolatry—it is forbidden forthwith.' [So the appurtenance, the cup, is forbidden forthwith. Then the pedestal is an appurtenance.] And here he has said this [that the pedestal is deemed an idol itself]?"

[E] In the one case, it is an instance in which the idolator has offered incense [to the pedestal], and in the other case it is an instance in which he has not offered incense [to the cup].

[F] And even if you rule, "Both statements refer to cases in which the idolator offered up incense," nonetheless Rab is consistent, for Rab has said, "On this basis: If one has smelted ore and poured a metal cup for idolatry, the cup is prohibited forthwith."

[G] Rab said, "A pedestal is never subject to nullification." Lo, its appurtenances [by contrast] *will* be subject to nullification.

[H] The opinions attributed to Rab are confused.

[I] In the one case, R. Sheshet said in the name of Rab, "[In regard to the rule of M. A.Z. 4:6C–D: *Pedestals set up for kings, lo, these are permitted, since they set images up on them only at the time kings pass by,*] this rule applies to a case in which the kings went their way by a different route."

[J] And yet where has he said this?

[K] In the one case, it is an instance in which the idolator has offered incense, and in the other case it is an instance in which he has not offered incense.

[L] And even if you rule, "Both statements refer to cases in which the idolator offered up incense," nonetheless, Rab is consistent, for Rab has said, "On this basis: If one has smelted ore and poured a metal cup for idolatry, the cup is prohibited forthwith."

[**VI**.A] Said R. Yoḥanan, "When Scripture speaks of a statue, it refers to any sort of thing, even an individual rock. An altar is any that has numerous stones [brought together]."

[B] Hezekiah said, "A statue—once one has damaged it, he has nullified it. An altar requires [for nullification that one] damage each stone [used to constitute the object]."

[C] A Mishnah teaching of Hezekiah himself contradicts this ruling of his: "If you have torn down an altar, leave it; if you have broken a statue, leave it. [Thus no further action against the individual stones is required.]"

[D] R. Zeira, R. Isaac bar Naḥman in the name of R. Hoshaiah, R. Ḥiyya R. Ba, R. Eleazar in the name of R. Hoshaiah: " '[Therefore by this the guilt of Jacob will be expiated, and this will be the full fruit of the removal of his sin]: when he makes all the stones of the altars like chalkstones crushed to pieces[, no Asherim or incense altars will remain standing]' (Is. 27:9). Pursue them until you wipe out their sperm from the world."

[E] But here: "If you have [merely] torn down an altar, leave it; if you have broken a statue, leave it"?

[**VII**.A] It is written, "You shall make for yourselves no idols and erect no graven image or pillar, and you shall not set up a figured stone in your land, to bow down to them" (Lev. 26:1).

[B] Is not the act of *making* them equivalent to *setting* them up? [So why shift word choices?]

[C] Said R. Hila, "Making them is at the beginning of the prohibited act. Setting them up applies to any case in which the idol falls. One should not restore it to its original upright position."

[D] It is written, "You shall tear down their altars, and dash in pieces their pillars, and burn their Asherim with fire" (Deut. 12:3).

[E] Now how do we know that the law stated here [breaking an altar] applies to the case described in the other setting [dashing pillars in pieces], and that what is stated in the other setting applies in the present case?

[F] Said R. Bun bar Ḥiyya, "Each rule surely applies to the case of the other: either break, or chop down, or tear down, in every case [of idolatry]."

The Talmud opens with a close reading of the rule of the Mishnah. The focus of interest is the contrast of M. A.Z. 4:4A and

B, and again C and D. Units **I** and **II** present no problems of interpretation. The question of **II**.A, B is whether there is a clear link between one rule and the other, but the dispute is not spelled out at all. Unit **III** provides proof texts for the present rule of the Mishnah and for its exact opposite. Unit **IV** then moves on to the next segment of the Mishnah's law. The program of unit **IV** is strikingly apt: first, an exegesis of Scripture to prove the same point; second, a story illustrating how the law was kept; third, some secondary material, at E–G, about the formulation of the law, leading to material relevant to the secondary, not the primary, topic of discourse, now the impossibility of nullifying an idol worshiped by an Israelite. The story told about Bar Kappara (K) yields several legal observations (L, M ff). At this point the discourse broadens to include objects other than the idol itself. At unit **V** we deal with a pedestal for an idol, in line with M. 4:4E–F, nullifying the status of idolatry imputed to the appurtenances of an idol. So here too the progression through the topics of the Mishnah pericope is smooth and systematic. Unit **V** focuses upon whether or not the appurtenance is deemed an idol unto itself; the whole rehearses the views of Rab on the question, and goes over materials familiar from M. A.Z. 3:8, above. Lower criticism will sort out what is repetitious and what belongs. Units **VI** and **VII** form a bridge from one pericope of the Mishnah to the next. Unit **VI** explains how one is supposed to nullify an idol, the topic of what is to follow. The focus of interest is contradictory teachings of Hezekiah, and the contradiction is not resolved.

4:5

[A] *How does one nullify it?*

[B] *[If] he has cut off the tip of its ear, the tip of its nose, the tip of its finger,*

[C] *[If] he battered it, even though he did not break off [any part of] it,*

[D] *he has nullified it.*

[E] *[If] he spit in its face, urinated in front of it, scraped it, threw shit at it, lo, this does not constitute an act of nullification.*

[F] *[If] he sold it or gave it as a pledge on a loan—*

[G] *Rabbi says, "He has nullified it."*

[H] *And the sages say, "He has not nullified it."*

[**I**.A] Said R. Zeira, "This rule you have stated [M. A.Z. 4:5F–H, that if one has sold it, there is a dispute] applies when one has sold it in times of peace. But if one has sold it by reason of wrath [against the idol, e.g., for not performing], then it is deemed by all parties to have been nullified."

[B] "And when they are hungry, they will be enraged and will curse their king [and their God and turn their faces upward; and they will look to the earth, but behold, distress and darkness, the gloom of anguish; and they will be thrust into thick darkness]" (Is. 8:21–22).

[C] Zeʿora bar Ḥinenah in the name of R. Ḥananiah, "When one has sold it on account of need is the case under dispute [M. 4:5F–H].

[D] "But if one has sold it to one who will worship it, then all parties concur that this does *not* constitute a valid act of nullification."

[E] R. Jeremiah in the name of Rab: "If one has sold it to those who will worship it, then the parties to the dispute disagree.

[F] "But if one has sold it by reason of need, all parties concur that this is a valid act of nullification."

[G] R. Jacob bar Aḥa in the name of R. Yoḥanan: "All parties concur."

[H] R. Hila in the name of R. Simeon b. Laqish: "It is subject to dispute."

[I] And R. Ḥaninah is in accord with R. Yoḥanan, and R. Jeremiah is in accord with R. Simeon b. Laqish.

[J] What is the upshot of the matter?

[K] If one has sold the idol by reason of need, the parties to the dispute differ.

[L] But if one has sold it to those who worship it, all parties concur that this does not constitute a valid act of nullification.

The Talmud takes up only the matter of the dispute of M. A.Z. 4:5F–H, attempting to locate the matter among the following possibilities of the point of difference: (1) it is not when the gentile got angry with the idol; (2) it is when the gentile sold it on account of need; (3) it is when the gentile has sold it to those who will worship it. There is a unfilled-out secondary development at G, H, and I (cf. Pené Moshe). K–L settle the matter.

4:6

[A] *An idol, the worshipers of which have abandoned at a time of peace, is permitted.*

[B] *[If they abandoned it] in time of war, it is forbidden.*

[C] *Idol pedestals set up for kings—lo, these are permitted,*

[D] *since they set [images up on them only] at the time kings go by.*

[**I**.A] It was taught[, There are idols that gentiles left behind, expecting to return], in the war of Joshua, [and such idols are] prohibited, while [there are idols that gentiles left behind, not expecting to return,] in the wars of Joshua, and [such idols are] permitted.

[B] Similarly, [there are idols that gentiles left behind] in the wars of David, [and these they did not expect to recover, so these are] permitted. [There are, further, idols that gentiles left behind] in the wars of David, [and these they did expect to recover, so such an idol would be] prohibited.

[C] [An idol left behind] in the war of Joshua[, which would be] forbidden [is referred to in the following verse of] Scripture: "[In the cities of those peoples that the Lord your God gives you for an inheritance, you shall save alive nothing that breathes,] but you shall utterly destroy them" (Deut. 20:16). [These idols were never finally abandoned. Their owners were killed.]

[D] [Those left behind] in the war of Joshua would be permitted, for the people left them behind for a moment [expecting to return, and since the people have had a chance to return and get them and have not done so, they are permitted].

[E] [There are those left behind] in the wars of David, which are permitted, [for example,] the sort that Itti the Gittite would nullify.

[F] And there are those left behind in the wars of David, which are forbidden [because they were abandoned] forever, [because the people could not get back to retrieve them].

The Talmud's treatment of the Mishnah's rule is an expansion of the law through historical examples.

4:7

[A] *They asked the sages in Rome, "If [God] is not in favor of idolatry why does he not wipe it away?"*

[B] *They said to them, "If people worshiped something of which the world had no need, he certainly would wipe it away.*

[C] *"But lo, people worship the sun, moon, stars, and planets.*

[D] *"Now do you think he is going to wipe out his world because of idiots?"*

[E] *They said to them, "If so, let him destroy something of which the world has no need, and leave something that the world needs!"*

[F] *They said to them, "Then we should strengthen the hands of those who worship these[, which would not be destroyed], for then they would say, 'Now you know full well that they are gods, for lo, they were not wiped out!' "*

[**I**.A] Philosophers *asked the sages in Rome, "[If God] is not in favor of idolatry, why does he not wipe it away?" They said to them, "[If] people worshiped something of which the world had no need, he certainly would wipe it away. But lo, people worship the sun, moon, and stars. Now do you think he is going to wipe out his world because of idiots?"]* [M. 4:7A–D]. **["But let the world be in accord with its accustomed way, and the idiots who behave ruinously will ultimately come and give a full account of themselves.] If one has stolen seeds for planting, are they not ultimately going to sprout? If one has had sexual relations with a married woman, will she not ulti-**

mately give birth? But let the world follow its accustomed way, and the idiots who behave ruinously will ultimately come and give a full account of themselves" [T. A.Z. 6:7].

[**II**.A] Said R. Zeira, "If it were written, 'Those who worship them are like them,' there would be a problem. Are those who worship the sun like the sun, those who worship the moon like the moon?! But this is what is written: 'Those who *make* them are like them; so are all who trust in them' (Ps. 115:8)."

[B] Said R. Mana, "If it were written, 'Those who worship them are like them,' it would pose no problem whatsoever. For it also is written, 'Then the moon will be confounded, and the sun ashamed' (Is. 24:23)."

[C] R. Naḥman in the name of R. Mana, "Idolatry is destined in the end to come and spit in the face of those that worship idols, and it will bring them to shame and cause them to be nullified from the world."

[D] Now what is the scriptural basis for that statement?

[E] "All the worshipers of images will be put to shame, who make their boast in worthless idols" (Ps. 97:7).

[F] R. Naḥman in the name of R. Mana, "Idolatry is destined in time to come and to bow down before the Holy One, blessed be He, and then be nullified from the world."

[G] What is the scriptural basis for that statement?

[H] "[All worshipers of images will be put to shame . . . ;] all gods bow down before him" (Ps. 97:7).

The dispute at **II**.A, B, fills out M. A.Z. 4:7C, the fate of sun-worshipers. C–H follow an obvious pattern.

4:8

[A] *They purchase from gentiles [the contents of] a winepress that has already been trodden out,*

[B] *even though [the gentile] takes [the grapes] in hand and puts them on the heap ["apple"],*

[C] *[for] it is not made into wine used for a libation until it drips down into the vat.*

[D] *[But if wine has] dripped down into the vat, what is in the cistern is prohibited,*

[E] *while [to be sure] the rest [remains] permitted.*

[**I**.A] R. Ḥanan taught [in connection with the rule that one may purchase contents of a winepress that has already been trodden out], "And that [lenient ruling] applies to a case in which an Israelite has not removed his eyes [from the press during the treading]. But if [an Israelite] has removed his eyes from it, it was not in such a case [that permission was granted to purchase the dregs of the winepress from the gentile]."

[B] [Is the law to be treated as strict] to such an extent?

[C] [Such a strict ruling as A's applies to] a case in which the gentile was taking wine and grapes together and putting them on the "apple." [Here there is wine to be protected from being used for a libation.]

[D] [If] he was putting [onto the "apple"] these by themselves and those by themselves [what is the law? Do we maintain that since the gentile was picking grapes out of the wine, the wine is treated as if it is by itself and is deemed libation wine?]

[E] Even as to what is left in the depressions of the vat—

[F] that which is under the grape clusters is permitted[, since it is not distinct from the grapes].

[G] That which is on the sides is forbidden[, since it is separate and distinct from the pulp] [cf. T. A.Z. 7:5D–E].

[H] R. Yosé b. R. Bun in the name of R. Yoḥanan: "[The wine in the depressions under the grape clusters] itself is forbidden[, for once the clusters are removed, this wine too remains separate from the pulp]."

[**II**.A] A winepress that a gentile stopped up [filling in the cracks]—

[B] [if he stopped up the vat from] the inside, [the wine] is forbidden, [and if he stopped up the vat] from the outside, it is permitted.

[C] [The basis for this distinction is that] it is not possible that there was not there a single moist drop [of wine in one of the cracks], which the gentile will touch and offer as a libation, thus rendering into libation wine whatever thereafter flows into the cistern.

[**III**.A] R. Huna in the name of Rab: "The jet [of wine flowing from the press] has the status of [the wine that already is in] the cistern. [That is, if a gentile touched the wine in the vat, it is as if he touched wine in the jet, and the wine is deemed libation wine.]"

[B] R. Zeira raised the question, "In every other place you do not treat that which flows as connected [to that from which the flow comes], but here do you treat that which flows as connected to the spout from which it flows? [This then contradicts M. Toh. 8:9.]"

[C] R. Huna considered [ruling that if] the vat was deemed to be prohibited as libation wine, the jet [of wine flowing into the vat likewise] was deemed to be prohibited as libation wine.

[The order of the above three entries should be C, opening the discourse, A, illustrating what Huna has just said, and then, at B, Zeira raising the question about this egregious position.]

[D] R. Ba did not rule thus, but rather [he maintained]: "[If] the wine in the vat has been turned into libation wine, wine flowing into the vat from the spout has not been turned into libation wine. But if wine in the spout was turned into libation wine, what is in the vat also has been turned into libation wine."

[E] What then is the meaning of that which R. Huna said in the name of Rab: "The spout has the same status as the vat[, so wine in the one has the same status as wine in the other]?"

[F] The thinking of R. Huna is this: "Just as wine in the vat may be turned into libation wine [in line with M. 4:8C], so wine in the spout may be turned into libation wine."

[**IV**.A] There they say in the name of Rab, "The very touch of a gentile turns wine into libation wine [without his stirring the wine at all]."

[B] R. Naḥman b. Jacob said, "But that is on condition that he stirs the wine a bit."

[C] An Aramaean fell into a vat of wine. The case came before R. Huna. He ruled, "They press down on him [so that he may not move about and stir the wine] until they can cause the wine in the vat to flow out."

[D] Said R. Ḥaninah, "[But did we not see that] he spread his hand out [in a gesture of making a libation]?"

[E] He said, "Bring wicker baskets and strain out the wine that is under [44b] his hands [keeping it separate from the rest]."

[**V**.A] Simeon bar Ḥiyya was teaching Ḥiyya bar Rab: "A gentile—from what age does he [have the power to] make wine into libation wine?"

[B] He said to him, "From the age at which he knows the meaning of idolatry [and so carries out his obligation to do so, that is, at a young age]."

[C] R. Josiah produced the relevant chapter [of law, the one before us,] saying to him, "That which you have said applies to a case in which *one purchases from gentiles the contents of a winepress that has already been trodden out,* but as to a gentile himself, once he is one day old [his very touch has the power to] turn wine into libation wine."

[**VI**.A] As to a gentile, what is the law covering his turning wine into libation wine through [the action of his] mouth [alone], [that is, merely drinking the wine, in which case he has no mind to make a libation]?

[B] R. Ada in the name of R. Eleazar, "A gentile does not turn wine into libation wine through the action of his mouth alone."

[C] R. Jeremiah in the name of R. Abbahu: "A gentile turns wine into libation wine through the action of his mouth alone."

[D] And so it has been taught in a Tannaitic tradition: **A market inspector who tasted what was in a cup and then poured it back into the jug or who stuck in his siphon, and a drop in any measure at all flowed back from it into the jug—it is forbidden [T. A.Z. 7:6D–E].**

[E] In the view of R. Ada in the name of R. Eleazar: "[That ruling applies to a case] in which the gentile put the wine back into the jug," [for his merely tasting it does not make it libation wine].

[F] In the view of R. Jeremiah in the name of R. Abbahu, "[That rule applies] even in the case in which an Israelite put the wine back into the jug," [for once the gentile has merely tasted the wine, it becomes libation wine].

The discourse of unit **I** imposes upon the lenient rule of the Mishnah a rather stringent condition, thus **I**.A. B then asks why this is so, and C answers that the qualification applies when there is a mixture of wine and pulp. Then the disposition of the wine requires supervision. D asks a question that flows from C. E–G can be read as an answer. That is, when the wine is distinct from the pulp, then, "as to what is in depressions of the vat," and F–G complete the thought. But it seems to me that E–G originally should have stood as a separate discourse, parallel to **II**.A, B. Then D should be deemed to be answered by H. That is, if the wine and the pulp are separate, then wine in the depressions under the grape clusters (that is, wine not mixed with pulp) will be forbidden for the reason given. This is precisely that sort of wine that the gentile will offer as a libation, in line with M. 4:8C. A glance at the Tosefta's version of **I**.E–F shows that the pericope serves a separate purpose from that imposed upon it by its present location in the Talmud. Unit **II** poses no problems, and its distinction is clear. It is a suitable complement to unit **I**. Unit **III** brings us to the rule of M. Toh. 8:9D–E: *A jet of liquid, water on an incline, and flowing liquid, do not form a connector between the utensil from which they flow and the one into which they flow, either for uncleanness or for cleanness. A rut of water [with no flow] does form a connector for both,* so that if a bit of water in the rut becomes unclean, all the water in the rut is unclean. The relevance to the present rule is at M. 4:8C, D, E, that is, the interest in the flow of liquid from the press to the vat. If what is in the press is invalid, then, in accord with M. Toh. 8:9, what is in the vat will be invalid. But if what is in the vat is invalid, the stream or jet of liquid pouring into the vat is not thereby contaminated. With these facts in mind, the dialectic of unit **III**, read in the order, C, A, and B, then D–F, presents no problems at all, and further explanation is unnecessary. Unit **IV** goes over a secondary question, now expanding the frame of discourse on the issues relevant to the Mishnah. Along these same lines, unit **V** employs the Mishnah's law to clarify a distinct question. Unit **VI** then appends supplementary information, not required or provoked by the Mishnah's rule, but relevant to its larger theme. So the entire construction relates closely to the Mishnah and admirably expands and explains its law.

4:9

[A] *[Israelites] tread a winepress with a gentile [in the gentile's vat],*

[B] *but they do not gather grapes with him.*

[C] *An Israelite who prepares [his wine] in a state of uncleanness—*

[D] *they do not trample or cut grapes with him.*

[E] *But they do take jars with him to the winepress, and they bring them with him from the winepress.*

[**I**.A] "[The rule that Israelites may tread a winepress with a gentile applies in a case in which,]" said R. Jonah, "[gentile] grape-treaders had already thoroughly trampled the grapes, warp and woof. But [if gentile] grape-treaders had not already trampled the grapes thoroughly, warp and woof, it is not in such a case [that it is permitted to tread a winepress with a gentile, since, as noted, in such a case, the Israelite joins in contaminating the produce of the Holy Land]."

[B] R. Yosé raised the question, "If the law applies only in a case in which gentile grape-treaders had already thoroughly treaded out the vat, warp and woof, then even in accord with the first Mishnah[, such an act should be prohibited to Israelites]:

[C] **"At first they ruled, 'They do not gather grapes with a gentile [vs. M. A.Z. 4:9A], and they do not press grapes with an Israelite who prepares his wine in a state of uncleanness [M. A.Z. 4:9C–D]; they do press grapes with a gentile' [M. A.Z. 4:9A; cf. T. A.Z. 7:1A–B].**

[D] "They reverted to rule, 'They do not press grapes with a gentile [*vs.* M. A.Z. 4:9A] and they do not press grapes with an Israelite who does the work in a state of uncleanness' [= M. A.Z. 4:9C].

[E] **"But they gather grapes with a gentile. And they assist him until he passes out of sight. Once he has passed out of sight, he may to be sure turn the wine into libation wine [but Isra-**

elites do not bear responsibility for that fact]" [T. A.Z. 7:1C, F].

[F] What is the reason for the ruling given by R. Jonah[, who maintained that the permission to tread grapes applies only at the end of the pressing of the grapes and not before? For from his viewpoint one could have taught that they may not press grapes with a gentile, meaning at the outset of the pressing. To be sure, one may not impart uncleanness to produce having an unconsecrated status. How is it possible to maintain that one may not cut grapes but may tread them? Why not simply say one may not *tread* them at all, for the reason that applies at the end is equally valid for the contrary decision at the outset]?

[G] [The reason is] that the grapes have already been made unclean by reason of their having been made susceptible to uncleanness at the point at which the grapes were picked [and so, once the grapes are susceptible, the gentile has made them unclean, and there is no further reason for an Israelite to refrain from working with the gentile on the grapes. The uncleanness derives from the harvesting of the grapes, and, as is clear, there is no reason for taking further protective measures at the stage of treading out the grapes, since they now are unclean anyhow].

[H] And what is the reason for the ruling given by R. Yosé, [who does not deem the Mishnah law to refer solely to the point at which the grapes have already been trodden out]?

[I] His reason is that [the grapes in fact] were clean [as a matter of] the law of the Torah, and you [the rabbis] are the one[s] who declared them to be susceptible to uncleanness to begin with. [For the fact that grapes when cut are made susceptible to uncleanness is a decree of scribes, not a rule of the Torah. Consequently, the prohibition must apply not only at the end of the process of treading out the grapes, but throughout the prior processes as well.]

[J] An argument for the position of R. Yosé [that it is prohibited to impart uncleanness to produce from which heave-offering has not yet been removed] derives from that which R. Yosé said in the name of R. Hila [in reference to M. Hal. 3:2]: "In point of law, a person should be able to declare his produce from which heave-offering has not yet been removed to be exempt from liability to heave-offering as a matter of Torah law.

[K] "[And the basis for this statement is as follows:] It is written, 'And from it you shall give the Lord's offering to Aaron the priest' (Num. 18:28).

[L] "The law has treated giving the heave-offering to Aaron the priest as a matter dependent upon the priesthood of the priest himself.

[M] "Now here, since you cannot hand over the produce to Aaron the priest in full justice to his priesthood [because there is a matter of doubt affecting the dough of M. Hal. 3:2], you are permitted to impart uncleanness to the produce that has not yet had its heave-offering taken out of it. [This then supports the position of Yosé, who has given as his reason for the rule that one may not tread grapes with an Israelite who does not observe the cleanness laws the fact that one may not impart uncleanness to the produce of the land.]"

For the Talmud, the Mishnah's sole point of interest is at M. 4:9A–B, C–D. The distinction between treading a winepress with a gentile, which is permitted, and gathering grapes with him, which is forbidden, is simple. When one cuts the grapes, they are in a state of cultic cleanness but are susceptible to becoming unclean. The gentile will contaminate them by his mere touch. If an Israelite works alongside, then he collaborates in rendering unclean produce of the Holy Land, and this Israelites may not do. But once the grapes are cut and are trod in a winepress, then they have already been made unclean. The Israelite cannot be accused of participating in making them unclean. That accounts for the contrast between M. 4:9A and B. Now a further fact must be introduced before we turn to the Talmud itself. As T. A.Z. 7:1 claims—and this is cited in the Talmud—there is a prior law that cutting grapes for the vat does not leave them susceptible to receiving uncleanness. In that case, the distinction made by M. 4:9A and B will require explanation in some terms other than those set forth just now.

With this in mind we turn to the Talmud. At **I**.A Jonah maintains that only in a vat that already has been completely contaminated may Israelites tread grapes with gentiles. Then (B–C) the issue of the earlier law, alluded to just now, is raised. What Yosé wants to know (B) is why Jonah's position would not be just as suitable in the context of the earlier version of the law as it is in the present one. B–D then cite this earlier version of the law. This law prohibited pressing grapes with a gentile, but (and this is the point) *also* prohibited gathering grapes with him. Now, the reason for the latter rule is that when grapes are gathered, they are rendered susceptible to uncleanness, and one may not cooperate with a gentile in contaminating produce of the Holy Land—just as is the supposition of A. So Yosé's observation is sound. His own position is not yet specified. F then goes back to Jonah's position (A) and explains it. Yosé's position is to be inferred at H. So far as he is concerned, the limitation stated at A does not apply. That is to say, in Yosé's conception, there is no reason to protect the produce from uncleanness at all, and this is explained at I. J–M then give exegetical materials pertinent to M. Hal. 3:2 and dealt with there, in support of this view that, so far as the Torah is concerned, there is no susceptibility to be imputed to the grapes when they are cut (I).

4:10

[A] *A baker who prepares bread in a state of uncleanness—*

[B] *they do not knead or cut out dough with him.*

[C] *But they may take bread with [assisting] him to the wholesale dealer.*

[**I**.A] And on this law [M. 4:10B] it has been taught: They do not stir grain in water, or mix with him.

[B] Said R. Hila, "[With reference to M. Sheb. 5:9:] *A woman may lend a sifter, sieve, handmill, or oven to her neighbor who is suspected of transgressing the seventh year law, but she may not winnow or grind grain with her. The wife of a fellow [who keeps cultic purity] may lend a sifter or sieve to the wife of an ʿam Ha'areṣ [who does not] and may winnow, grind, or sift grain with her].* In the case [in which one is *permitted* to winnow, grind, or sift grain with someone who will not preserve the cultic purity of the food], we deal with unconsecrated food, and in the case [in which one is *not* permitted to do so, as at M. 4:10A–B] we deal with food having the status of heave-offering. [So unconsecrated food need not be kept cultically clean, and food having the status of heave-offering must be kept clean.]"

[C] Now [the Mishnah refers explicitly to] a baker. Can you claim that a baker deals in grain having the status of heave-offering?

[D] The associates state, "Here [where one may *not* deal with someone who does not observe the rules of cultic purity for ordinary food], we deal with grain that has been wet down [and so is susceptible to uncleanness], and there [where one may deal with someone who does not observe those same rules], we deal with grain that has not been wet down [and so is not susceptible to become unclean anyhow]."

[E] Now has it not been taught [in the context of M. Sheb. 5:9, in which it *is* permitted to work with a person not careful about cultic cleanness of food], *But when she pours water over the flour, she may not draw near to her, since one may not help those who commit transgression.* [It follows that the associates' point of differentiation is false, since the right to deal with someone who does not and someone who does keep the law in both instances involves insusceptible food.]

[F] R. Ḥiyya and R. Ami [in discussing the statement at M. Sheb. 5:9, *One may help gentiles working in the fields in the seventh year, but not Israelites, and one may greet gentiles in the interests of peace*], one said, "[One may say to the gentile], 'Plough well, and I shall purchase it from you after the year of release.' " And one said, "[One may say to the gentile], 'Do well.' "

[G] In the view of the one who said, "[One may say to the gentile], 'Plough well, and I shall purchase it from you after the year of release' what is the law as to asking after their welfare? One says, 'Be well.' "

[H] And in the view of the one who said, "[One may say to the gentile only] 'Be well'—in what language do they ask after the welfare of an Israelite? One says, 'Peace be unto you.' "

[I] One time R. Ḥaninah bar Papa and R. Samuel bar Naḥman passed by someone who was ploughing in the seventh year.

[J] R. Samuel bar Naḥman said to him, "Be well."

[K] Said to him R. Ḥaninah bar Papa, "And did not Rabbi teach us, 'while those who pass by do not say, "The blessing of the Lord be upon you!" (Ps. 129:8)—[this verse means] that it is prohibited to say to those who plough in the seventh year, 'Be well.' "

[L] He said to him, "To cite Scripture you know full well, but to explain the meaning of Scripture you do not know at all. For have they not said: 'Those who pass by'—these are the nations of idolatry, who pass from the world, for they did not say to Israel, 'May the blessing of the Lord be upon you.'

[M] "And what do the Israelites reply to them? 'We bless you in the name of the Lord!' (Ps. 129:8).

[N] "For the Israelites say to them, 'It is not enough for you that all good things and consolation come into the world on our account, and yet you do not say to us, 'Come and take for yourselves some small part of the blessings.'

[O] " 'Not only so, but you impose upon us taxes and excises, head-taxes and corvées.' "

[**II**.A] R. Ami gave instructions: "To remove the bread from the oven with him [who prepares bread in a state of cultic uncleanness] is prohibited.

[B] "And similarly, to sprinkle [water] on the dough with him is prohibited."

The Talmud's focus is upon a parallel law, at M. Sheb. 5:9, which allows those who preserve the cultic cleanness of ordinary food to collaborate with those who do not. This law then stands in contrast to the one before us. The point of contact—for the Mishnah does not refer to the matters important at M. Sheb. 5:9—is at **I**.A. From there the need to harmonize the two rules is demonstrated. There are then two successive efforts, B–C, D–E, neither of which succeeds. F proceeds to the exegesis of yet another element of the cited pericope, followed by the expected cases, I–J and K ff. The whole sequence of thought therefore flows naturally, but along the lines of M. Sheb.'s interests, not those of the Mishnah pericope before us. By contrast, unit **II** deals directly with the present law.

4:11

[A] *A gentile who is found standing beside a cistern of wine—*

[B] *if he had a lien on the vat, it is prohibited.*

[C] *[If] he had no lien on it, it is permitted.*

[D] *[If] he fell into the vat and climbed out,*

[E] *or [if gentiles] measured it with a reed—*

[F] *[or if] he flicked out a hornet with a reed,*

[G] *or [if] he patted down the froth on the mouth of a jar—*

[H] *in regard to each of these there was a case,*

[I] *and [the sages] ruled, "Let it be sold."*

[J] *And R. Simeon permits [Israelites even to make use of it].*

[K] *[If] he took a jar and [in a fit of temper] threw it into the vat—*

[L] *this was a case,*

[M] *and they declared it valid [for Israelites to drink].*

[**I**.A] R. Sheshet in the name of Rab: "And this rule applies in a case in which [the gentile] had a lien on that particular vat [in which case it is prohibited, M. A.Z. 4:11A–B]. But if he had no lien on that particular vat [it is permitted], for it is the manner of lien-holders to stand over the winepress or threshing floor [of the borrower, to see how the debtor is doing in general, so that they can make certain of retrieving what has been lent; but the lender will not touch the wine not subject to a lien in particular]."

[B] They contemplated ruling, "He who said, 'And this rule applies in a case in which [the gentile] had a lien on that particular vat [means one that stands] within the man's grasp.'

[C] "And the one who ruled, 'This rule applies even in a case in which he did not have a lien on that particular vat,' will extend the rule even to a vat that lies outside of the man's grasp."

[D] Now did not R. Ba in the name of R. Sheshet say, "Just as they applied the measure of 'the grasp of the hands' [so far as one can reach] in cases involving food to be preserved in cultic cleanness, so they laid down that same measure of 'grasp' [as far as one can reach] in cases involving wine possibly used for a libation."

[E] But thus is the upshot of the matter: The one who said, "And this rule applies in a case in which one had a lien on that particular vat" [refers to one] within his grasp, and the one who said, "Even in a case in which he did not have a lien on that particular vat [the wine is deemed libation wine, refers to one] even beyond the man's reach [outside his immediate grasp]."

[Leiden MS and *editio princeps:* 4:12]

[**II**.A] *[And R. Simeon permits Israelites even to make use of it]* [M. A.Z. 4:11J]. R. Abin in the name of R. Samuel: "The law is in accord with the opinion of R. Simeon."

[B] R. Abin in the name of Samuel, "May I be atonement for R. Simeon: Either permit the wine for drinking, or prohibit it even for benefit."

[C] Said R. Jeremiah in the name of R. Abbahu, "There was a case and in respect even to drinking the wine they ruled in accord with the position of R. Simeon."

[**III**.A] [In reference to M. A.Z. 4:11K] R. Samuel in the name of R. Abbahu, "A gentile does not impart the status of libation wine through merely throwing."

[B] A gentile—what is the law as to imparting the status of libation wine through an action done when he is angry?

[C] Let us derive the law from the following:

[D] An Aramean has kegs in a storage house, and an Israelite came along and poured wine into them. The Aramean came along and brought his yoke and raised up the jugs in his anger and emptied them into the vat.

[E] Now the case came before the rabbis, who ruled, "A gentile does not impart the status of libation wine through an action done in anger."

[**IV**.A] R. Jeremiah in the name of R. Ḥiyya bar Ba, "This [wine,] which a gentile stirs into hot water, is prohibited [since it can have been used for a libation], but the wine that he mixes into cold water is permitted.

[B] "May a bad thing happen to me, if I have ever actually done so!"

[C] R. Yasa went to Tyre. He saw the Israelites drinking wine mixed with hot water, and an Aramean waiter was mixing the wine for them.

[D] He said to them, "Who in the world permitted you to do things in such a way?!"

The theory of the Mishnah's law is that if a gentile feels he has a stake in the wine, he will not hesitate to touch it, but if he does not, he will punctiliously observe the Jews' taboo. The opening unit amplifies the law by imposing yet another criterion. If we limit the rule of M. 4:11A–B to a case in which the gentile had a lien on that particular vat, then we also limit the application of the rule to a case in which the man was found standing within reach of that particular vat on which he had a lien. This second qualification still more severely limits the range of doubt concerning the status of the vat. The result is that if, in general, a gentile is found standing near a vat of wine, Israelites do not have to scruple about the gentile's having touched the wine. The limiting conditions place severe restrictions on the range of doubt that must be taken into account. Units **II**, **III**, and **IV** then take up practical decisions in sequence. First comes a ruling on Simeon's dissent (**II**). Then comes the issue of an act done in anger, surely to be read into M. A.Z. 4:11K. The Talmud gives a concrete illustration to the reference of the Mishnah to a case. Finally, at **IV**, there is a secondary case in which we find illustrated the principle that a gentile's contact with the wine does not invariably prohibit Israelite use of the wine.

4:12 [Leiden MS and *editio princeps:* 4:13]

[A] *He who prepares the wine belonging to a gentile in a condition of cleanness, and leaves it in his domain,*

[B] *in a house that is open to the public domain,*

[C] *in a town in which there are both gentiles and Israelites—[the wine] is permitted.*

[D] *[If it is] in a town in which all the residents are gentiles, [the wine] is prohibited*

[E] *unless he sets up a guard.*

[F] *And the guard need not sit there and watch [the room all the time].*

[G] *Even though he comes in and goes out, [the wine] is permitted.*

[H] *R. Simeon b. Eleazar says, "Whatever [was in] the domain of a gentile is subject to the same law [that a watchman is required whether or not the shop was open to the public domain, and whether or not the town was half-Israelite]."*

[I] *He who prepares the wine of a gentile in a condition of cleanness and leaves it in his domain,*

[J] *and the latter wrote for [the Israelite a receipt, saying], "I received its price from you"—it is permitted.*

[K] *But if an Israelite wants then to remove the wine, and [the gentile] would not let him do so unless he paid the price of the wine—*

[L] *this was a case in Beth Shean, and the sages declared [the wine] forbidden.*

[**I**.A] R. Abbahu in the name of R. Yosé b. R. Ḥaninah: "It is not the end of the matter that there be an open door [at M. 4:12B], but even if there is an open window, of a measurement of four by four by a height of ten cubits[, under the stated circumstances there must be a guard]."

[B] But this is on condition that it be roofed over and closed off.

[C] [Following Pené Moshe] [If] one had a [tree] growing [from which it was possible to see who entered and left a room, what is the law]?

[D] Let us rule: [If it is possible to] see [an Israelite] going up and coming down on it, [the wine] is permitted, and if not it is forbidden[, since in the former case the gentiles will know that the wine is periodically inspected].

[**II**.A] R. Ba in the name of R. Judah: "The Mishnah speaks of a city that has gates and a latch [so that only access is limited].

[B] "In such a case it has been taught, *'A guard—even though he comes only at intervals.'* "

[**III**.A] It has been taught: **A market to which an Israelite and a gentile bring wine, even though the guards are gentiles, even though the jars are open—[the wine in them] is permitted** [T. 7:10A–B], because that is not the way in which they make libations.

[**IV**.A] R. Hila in the name of R. Yannai: "He who purchases [a property for storing wine] has the same status as he who rents out [space in a gentile's house for the storage of wine]."

[B] And it has been taught in a Tannaitic tradition to the same effect:

[C] All the same are he who purchases and he who rents a place in the domain of a gentile [for the storage of wine].

[D] When the wine belongs to an Israelite, and the Israelite lives in the house, the wine is permitted.

[E] But that is the case when the Israelite has a lock and a seal [for the kegs of wine].

[F] Now when the wine belongs to a gentile, but an Israelite lives there [in the house, keeping watch on the wine, the wine still is] permitted.

[G] And that is the case when the Israelite has a lock and a seal for the kegs of wine [cf. T. A.Z. 7:9A–C].

[H] But if the Israelite does not dwell in the house [where the wine is stored, the wine is] prohibited.

[I] And that is the case even though he has a lock and a seal on the kegs of wine.

[**V**.A] R. Yaléy in the name of R. Yannai: "They took issue with R. Simeon b. Eleazar [M. A.Z. 4:12H].

[B] "It is not concerning this matter that the disagreement was expressed, but it was concerning the one that comes at the end: *He who prepares the wine of a gentile in a condition of cleanness and leaves it in his domain* [etc., M. A.Z. 4:12I]. [In this case, all types of gentile domain are subject to a single rule. This wine is of the sort on which a gentile has a lien, so he will feel free to touch it. In such a case the distinctions of the sages—M. 4:12A–G—apply, and Simeon b. Eleazar invokes a single rule.]"

Unit **I** takes up the matter of periodic inspections of wine that is accessible to the public. **I**.A–B speaks of a house open in public domain and refers to the house's having a door or even a window through which people can gain entry. In such a circumstance, in a town in which all residents are gentiles, the wine must be guarded. This then leads to the matter of guarding the wine. I rely on Pené Moshe for the reading of C and then the interpretation of D. If one has a tree nearby that one can climb, and if gentiles know it, then the wine is deemed to be suitably guarded. If this interpretation is correct, then C–D amplify M. 4:12E–G. Unit **II** goes forward in dealing with these same materials. Unit **III** leads nowhere. Unit **IV** then goes on to the storage of wine in a gentile's property. The main point is that whether the property is purchased or rented, the wine stored there is valid for Israelite use only when an Israelite is in constant attendance. The fact that the wine is within the gentile's control and domain, even if the Israelite owns the actual place in which the kegs are located, accounts for this strict requirement. Unit **V** proposes a rearrangement of the Mishnah's materials, as explained in the interpolated note.

5 Yerushalmi Abodah Zarah Chapter Five

5:1

[44c/A] *[A gentile] who hires an [Israelite] worker to work with him in the preparation of libation wine—*

[B] *[the Israelite's] salary is forbidden.*

[C] *[If] he hired him to do some other kind of work,*

[D] *even though he said to him, "Move a jar of libation wine from one place to another,"*

[E] *his salary is permitted.*

[**I**.A] [Now why, at M. 5:1A–B, should the Israelite's salary be forbidden to him?] Does [the gentile] not pay him his salary [for his labor]?

[B] R. Abbahu in the name of R. Yoḥanan: "[It is] a fine that [the sages] have imposed upon him."

[C] [But we have a ruling that in principle shows there is no such fine.] It has been taught: **Ass-drivers, porters, and all those who labor in connection with farming in the seventh year—their salary [may be in produce of] the seventh year** [T. Sheb. 6:26]. [The meaning is that they may accept payment out of produce of the seventh year. This then would appear to contradict the view that a fine is imposed in the present instance in which laborers work on a matter, like produce of the seventh year, forbidden to Israelites.]

[D] Said R. Zeira, "[The reason that in connection with labor in the seventh year the laborers may be paid as specified is that] the Mishnah [= Tosefta] speaks of a case in which [the laborers were working on] produce that was permitted [and not subject to the prohibitions of the seventh year at all, hence the two cases are to be differentiated from one another]."

[E] [What follows takes for granted knowledge of M. Sheb. 8:4: *"If one said to a laborer in the seventh year, 'Here is an issar for you. Harvest vegetables for me today,' the payment is permitted. But if he said, 'In return for the issar, harvest vegetables for me today,' the payment is forbidden. If a man bought from a baker a loaf worth a pundion, and said, 'When I have collected vegetables from the field, I shall bring them to you,' this is permitted. But if he bought it from him with no condition, he may not pay him with proceeds received for produce of the seventh year, since one may not pay a debt with proceeds received for the sale of produce of the seventh year."* Elsewhere Judah and Nehemiah prohibit the transaction with the baker, for the same reason as is given at the end.] Now [let us take up] that which R. Yoḥanan instructed the members of the house of Yannai, that they should not accept as their salary wine [having the status of produce of the seventh year] but rather coins. [It was] along the lines of the position of Judah and Nehemiah, [thus not utilizing the produce in payment of a debt] that he instructed them[, but the law follows the anonymous authority who permits this procedure, and hence there remains no contradiction between the two Mishnah rules, for, as said earlier, the right to use the legitimate produce of the seventh year paid as a salary is acceptable, while that same right does not extend to wine subject to the prohibition of libation wine].

[F] [Rejecting this interpretation of the case of T. Sheb. 6:26,] said R. Yalé, "The cited Mishnah passage refers to produce produced in transgression of the law of the seventh year [and yet permits the laborers to accept their wage, and the reason that the law here is different in principle simply is] in accord with that which R. Abbahu said in the name of R. Yoḥanan, 'As to libation wine['s not being a source of a salary to a laborer who has worked on it, the reason is that] it is a fine that [the sages] have imposed on him.' "

[**II**.A] [If the gentile employer employed the Israelite to] carry with a jug [of legitimate liquid, also] a jug [of wine used as libation,] as to his salary, one imposes a fine upon [the Israelite] to the extent [of the salary paid for carrying] a jug [of libation wine] [thus Pené Moshe in line with M. 5:1A–B].

[B] [If the gentile employer] paid [the Israelite's salary for carrying libation wine] in real estate[, the use of the property is prohibited to the Israelite].

[C] In every other context you have ruled that real estate is not subject to prohibition, but here it is subject to prohibition.

[D] [If the gentile employer] paid him [for work in libation wine] in a beast for his salary[, the use of the beast is prohibited to the Israelite].

[E] In every other context you have ruled that an animate creature [such as a beast] is not subject to prohibition, but here it is subject to prohibition.

[F] [If the gentile employer] paid him any [sort of object for work in libation wine] for his salary, is [the use of the whole of] any [sort of object prohibited], or does the prohibition extend only to that which is received as a salary [for working on libation wine] only? [This question receives no answer.]

[G] [If an Israelite] was working [for a gentile on libation wine] only in exchange for the pleasure [of doing the latter a favor, e.g., in hope for some future favor in return], you exact a pledge in recompense from the property of [the Israelite] to the amount [he would have received] for his salary [had he been paid in money].

[**III**.A] [If an Israelite] was working [for a gentile] for half of the day on that which was prohibited [that is, on libation wine], and for half a day on that which was permitted [any other sort of produce, may he keep half of his salary]?

[B] [The answer to this question is adduced from the following:] [If] one was selling unconsecrated food as well as food having the status of second tithe in a single sale, whichever part [the purchaser] wishes he treats as unconsecrated food, and whichever part he wishes he treats as produce having the status of second tithe.

[C] Here likewise [we rule that the salary for half a day is forbidden, and the salary for the other half is permitted, and that is the case, even though the employer who owed the salary paid the entire sum at one time].

[D] Let us [further] infer the law [about splitting up a single salary into fees for diverse acts] from the following:

[E] He who hires a worker to bring wine to a sick person—if [the worker] brought it to him, [the employer] is liable for paying him, and if not, [the employer] is not liable for paying him. But if he said to him, "Wine for a sick person [is to be brought] from such and such a place," or "an apple for a sick person [is to be brought] from such and such a place," [and the worker went to that place to retrieve the produce], whether [the worker then] brought [the produce to the sick person] or whether he did not, [the employer] is liable for paying [the worker]. [He pays him the] salary for his trip. [Thus there is a salary to be paid for the trouble of making the trip, even though the agent did not in fact carry out what was expected of him. The reasoning in the mind of the one who adduces this rule is that the salary paid for that part of the labor which is permitted is available for the benefit of the laborer, even though the other part of the salary is not. The important fact adduced from this case, then, is that one does make distinctions among parts of a salary, e.g., part of it covers bringing the produce to the sick person, and that part is not paid, but part of it is paid for making the trip, and that part is paid. Here too we make distinctions among parts of the labor performed by the Israelite for the gentile, and that segment of the labor in legitimate crops does produce a salary that the Israelite laborer may utilize.]

[**IV**.A] R. Jeremiah raised the question: "[If the gentile] hired [an Israelite] to destroy jugs containing libation wine[, even in such a case is his salary prohibited]?"

[B] Even in such a case his salary is prohibited.

[C] Assi said, "The proceeds received by a gentile for the sale of libation wine are prohibited." [This is in line with the fact that the proceeds received by a gentile for the sale of an idol, in the opinion of Yoḥanan, which follows, are prohibited.]

[D] The proceeds received by a gentile for the sale of an idol—

[E] R. Jonathan said, "[The proceeds] are permitted [for Israelite benefit]."

[F] R. Yoḥanan said, "[The proceeds] are forbidden [to Israelites for any purpose whatsoever]."

[G] The Mishnah teaching [*baraita*] may be cited as evidence in support of the position of this party, and the Mishnah teaching may be cited as evidence in support of the position of that party.

[H] The Mishnah teaching may be cited as evidence in support of the position of R. Yoḥanan:

[I] A gentile who owed money to an Israelite may not say to him, "Wait until I sell libation wine . . . ," ". . . until I sell my idol . . . ," "and I shall then pay you." For I maintain: Perhaps he may exchange [the funds received for the wine or idol for those set aside to be paid over to the Israelite, and an Israelite may not benefit from such funds].

[J] The Mishnah teaching may be cited as evidence in support of the position of R. Jonathan:

[K] A gentile who owed money to an Israelite—lo this one may sell libation wine and [then] pay the Israelite, or may sell an idol and pay the Israelite, [and that is] despite appearances.

[L] [44d] All [in any event] concur in the case of that which is exchanged for an idol or for libation wine, that [that which is given in exchange] is forbidden [for Israelite use or benefit].

[M] But what about what is exchanged [given] for what is received in exchange?

[N] Said R. Ḥaninah, "It is a matter of dispute between R. Ishmael and the rabbis."

[O] R. Ishmael b. R. Yosé said, "[The object received in exchange for what is received in exchange for an idol or libation wine] is prohibited."

[P] And the rabbis say, "It is permitted."

[Q] R. Eleazar bar Hoshaiah: "The scriptural basis for the position of the rabbis is as follows: '[And you shall not bring an abominable thing into your house] and become accursed like it; [you shall utterly detest and abhor it, for it is an accursed thing]' (Deut. 7:26).

"Whatever you can preserve from it—lo, this is like it [and prohibited]. [That is, what is exchanged for it, but not what is exchanged for what is exchanged for it.]"

[R] What is the basis [for Ishmael b. R. Yosé's position]?

[S] Said R. Yosé b. R. Bun, " 'like it,' 'like it' is stated two times, in line with the following: 'None of the devoted things shall cleave to your hand . . .' (Deut. 13:17)." [This then excludes even what is received in exchange for an idol or for libation wine.]

The Talmud systematically takes up first the Mishnah's specific law and second its general principle. Unit **I** presents an elegant argument in which a parallel case is adduced to clarify what is at issue in the present Mishnah law. The procedure itself is indirect and subtle. At the outset a reason is demanded and given: a fine, beyond the normal requirements of the law, because of the horrid character of libation wine. At that point, we are given the parallel problem yielding a contrary result (**I**.C). There are then two responses, first D, then E, which carries F in its wake. The flow of argument is smooth. The harmony achieved is natural, not contrived. Unit **II** presents a series of rules that indicate the full extent to which one fines a laborer for working in libation wine. Unit **III** then expands the range of discourse, depending upon the facts made available earlier, by raising a subtle question. If a laborer works part of the time in prohibited and part of the time in legitimate produce, is the salary split up accordingly, so that the laborer may utilize the part of the salary received for the legitimate work? The answer, achieved through a fairly convoluted exercise in adducing parallel materials, is that he may. Unit **IV** tends to become diffuse. It begins (**IV**.A–B, C) with two entirely relevant rules. These apply the principle of the Mishnah to related matters. D–L go on to a parallel case, treating proceeds of selling an idol as equivalent to proceeds of laboring in libation wine. Then L–S take up yet a tertiary matter, that is, what is received for what is received for idols or libation wine.

5:2

[A] *He who hires an ass to bring libation wine on it—*

[B] *its fee is forbidden.*

[C] *[If] he hired it to ride on it,*

[D] *even though the gentile [also] put a flagon [of libation wine] on it,*

[E] *its fee is permitted.*

[**I**.A] To what extent [is it permitted, in the case of M. 5:2 C–E, to add a flagon of libation wine to other things that a gentile has put on an ass driven by an Israelite driver, so that the Israelite nonetheless may retain his salary and not deem the salary the result of labor in connection with libation wine]?

[B] To such an extent that the ass-driver will not object [to the excess burden].

The Talmud provides a small clarification to the Mishnah's rule.

5:3

[A] *Libation wine that fell on grapes—*

[B] *one may rinse them off, and they are permitted.*

[C] *But if [the grapes] were split, they are prohibited.*

[D] *[The Talmud lacks:] [If] it fell on figs or dates, if there is sufficient [libation wine absorbed] to impart a flavor [to them], they are forbidden.*

[E] *MʿŚH B: Boethus b. Zonen brought dried figs by ship, and jars of libation wine broke open and dripped on them, and the case came to the sages, who permitted [the figs, once they had been rinsed].*

[F] *This is the governing principle: anything that bestows benefit through imparting a flavor is forbidden, and anything that does not bestow benefit through imparting a flavor is permitted—*

[G] *for example, vinegar [from libation wine] that falls on crushed beans.*

[**I**.A] The Mishnah's law treats a case in which the berries were not forcibly detached from the stalk [in which case there is no point of entry for the wine].

[B] But if the berries were forcibly detached from the stalk, the berries are treated as equivalent to split ones [and forbidden].

[C] How then do you treat such a case?

[D] Do you deem it as equivalent to a mixture of one wine with another wine, or as a mixture of wine in a cooked dish?

[E] If you treat such a case as equivalent to a mixture of wine in a cooked dish, then all parties will concur that the mixture is prohibited.

[F] But if you treat the mixture as a mixture of one wine in another wine, then there is a dispute between R. Meir and the sages. [The sages will permit, if the wine spoils the taste of the grapes, in line with M. 5:3F; under all circumstances Meir will prohibit.]

[**II**.A] Said R. Yoḥanan, "[In a case such as at M. 5:3G, in which vinegar from libation wine fell on crushed beans, the beans are permitted] in the case of hot crushed beans; but in the case of cold ones the mixture is prohibited.

[B] "For so it is the way of Sepphoris people to prepare beans in that way, and they call it cress-dish [made by pouring vinegar into cold split beans and then warming them; this improves the beans]."

[C] If they were warm and one cooled them off [what is the law? Do we rule that the bean-mush is prohibited when the vinegar fell into beans that to begin with were cold? Or do we maintain that even if the beans had been cooked and then allowed to cool off, once the vinegar having the status of libation wine has fallen into them, the beans are prohibited]?

[D] [It is obvious that we deal with beans that are cold and have not been heated up at all. In such a case the vinegar improves them. But if they had been heated and then cooled off, the vinegar does not improve them, and the mixture is permitted.] For if you do not take this position, then even in the case of vinegar's falling onto warm beans the mixture should be forbidden, since it is usual for the beans to cool off, at which point they will benefit from the vinegar!

[E] This is in line with that which is taught:

[F] **"All the same is that which bestows benefit through imparting a flavor and that which does damage through imparting a flavor—both are forbidden," the words of R. Meir.**

[G] **And the sages say, "If it is to the advantage [of the food], it is forbidden, but if it is damaging [to the food], it is permitted [T. Ter. 8:9].**

[H] [Citing Y. Orl. 2:5 and M. Ter. 10:2, Pené Moshe now supplies the following:] Said R. Simeon b. Laqish, "In what case do they differ? In a case in which [the prohibited substance] improved the character of the food and afterward damaged it, but if it damaged it and afterward improved it, even R. Meir will concur [that it is permitted]." R. Yoḥanan said, "There is no difference. Damaging or improving are equivalent to one another, as are improving then damaging. In all cases there is a dispute." [Thus, Pené Moshe goes on, R. Simeon b. Laqish maintains that R. Meir differs not in a case in which there is damage from beginning to end; here he will concur that the mixture is permitted. He differs where there is improvement at the outset, even though there is detriment caused at the end of the process. In such a case he declares the mixture forbidden. The criterion is what happens at the outset of the process of mixing, and if the improvement comes then, then the mixture is forbidden. In Yoḥanan's view, Meir more consistently will differ at whatever point the forbidden substance improves the mixture. Following Pené Moshe's version of the text, we proceed to the following, which carries forward G:] For we have learned *Barley [having the status of heave-offering] that fell into a vat of water—even though the barley polluted the water—the water is permitted [M. Ter. 10:2].*

[I] [Now does Meir concur in his case or does he differ?] Now what is the status of this Mishnah rule?

[J] R. Yoḥanan said, "It is subject to dispute. [Meir will prohibit the water.]"

[K] R. Simeon b. Laqish said, "It is the opinion of all parties."

[L] R. Yosé b. R. Bun said, "We have a tradition along these same lines. In accord with the view of R. Yoḥanan, it is subject to dispute, and in accord with the view of R. Simeon b. Laqish, it is the opinion of all parties." [In this case the water at the outset pollutes the water. There is no improvement therein. Yoḥanan maintains that Meir differs in this case as well, and there is no distinguishing the point at which the improvement comes, beginning or end, or the point at which the damage is done, beginning or end. Yoḥanan assigns to Meir a totally consistent view. Simeon b. Laqish then makes the distinctions introduced above and assigns them to Meir as much as to the sages.]

Unit **I** makes its own point and sets the stage for the protracted inquiry of unit **II**. In the former role it makes the point that a grape without its stem has a entry point for the liquid and so is equivalent to a split grape, with the consequences spelled out at A–B. Then the issue of the operative criterion for ruling on such a case (D) opens the matter of the dispute that is to follow (E–F), and that, for its part, is wholly comprehensible only when unit **II** is in hand. So the whole is the work of a single mind. The text of unit **II** follows Pené Moshe's judgment, ignoring several lines of what is printed before us. The interpolated language supplies the necessary information for understanding this passage, and further comment is not required.

5:4

[A] *A gentile who with an Israelite was moving jars of wine from place to place—*

[B] *if [the wine] was assumed to be watched, it is permitted.*

[C] *If [the Israelite] informed [the gentile] that he was going away, [the wine is prohibited if he was gone] for a time sufficient to bore a hole and stop it up and [for the clay] to dry.*

[D] *Rabban Simeon b. Gamaliel says, "[It is prohibited if he was gone for] a time sufficient to open [the jar] and stop it up and for the clay to dry."*

[**I**.A] Said R. Samuel, "MʿŚH B: A gentile with an Israelite was moving jugs of wine from one place to another. The case came before R. Abbahu who declared the wine prohibited."

[B] They say that the case involved open jars of wine.

[C] Said R. Zeriqan, "It is not the end of the matter that [the rule applies to jugs that are] filled up, but even if they lack [some wine, so it is hard to get at the wine, they will be prohibited,] for [the gentile is suspected of] putting the jug down, touching the wine with his hand, and putting the cork back on the wine."

[**II**.A] Do you maintain that the ruling of Rabban Simeon b. Gamaliel is to produce a lenient ruling? That is not the case, but it is to produce a strict ruling.

[B] For the time sufficient to bore a hole and stop it up and for the clay to dry, specified by the rabbis, is less than time sufficient to open the jar and stop it up and for the clay to dry.

[**III**.A] R. Judah bar Pazzi in the name of R. Ammi: "A roasted egg prepared by Samaritans, lo, this is permitted."

[B] R. Jacob bar Aḥa in the name of R. Eleazar: "Cooked foods prepared by Samaritans, lo, these are permitted."

[C] This rule you have given applies to a dish in which it is not usual to put wine or vinegar.

[D] Lo, [if] it is a matter of complete certainty that he put in wine or vinegar, it is prohibited, even for deriving benefit [e.g., sale by an Israelite].

[E] This is in line with the following teaching:

[F] At first they would rule, The wine of Zigdor [or: Ogedor, in Samaria]—why is it prohibited? Because of Kefar Pagash.

[G] And that of Borneta[, why is it forbidden]? Because of the town of Soriqah.

[H] And that of ʿEin Kushit? Because of Kefar Shalem.

[I] They reverted to rule as follows: If the jug of wine is uncorked, then in every location the wine is forbidden.

[J] If the jug of wine is sealed, in every place it is permitted.

[K] If the jug is pierced and then resealed, lo, this is tantamount to its having been left sealed.

[L] R. Isaac ben Ḥaqolah said, "Lo, this is equivalent to one that had been left open."

[M] Said R. Ḥaninah, "I can substantiate both rulings.

[N] "If there was on it a high price, it has not been opened.

[O] "And if not, it has been opened."

[P] This [prohibition of Samaritan food and wine] is in accord with the following teaching involving R. Simeon b. Eleazar:

[Q] He went to a certain town inhabited by Samaritans. A scribe came to him. He said to him, "Bring me a sealed jug of wine."

[R] [The scribe] said to him, "Lo, there is spring before you. Drink that." [Thus he was hinting not to drink the wine.]

[S] [Simeon] pressed him further, and he said to him, "Lo, there is a spring before you. Drink."

[T] [The scribe] saw him pressing him further, so he said to him, "Are you not master of your own desires? Lo, there is a spring before you, drink. But if you are not master of your own desires, then: '[When you sit down to eat with a ruler, observe carefully what is before you;] and put a knife to your throat if you are a man given to appetite' (Prov. 23:1)."

[U] [Thus the story proved that by that time] the Samaritans had already been ruined [and ceased to be reliable in observing the law].

[V] R. Ishmael b. R. Yosé went to the town of Neapolis [Nablus]. Samaritans came to him. He said to him, "I see that you do not bow down to that mountain itself, but rather to idols that are buried under it, as it is written, '[So they gave to Jacob all the foreign gods that they had, and the rings that were in their ears;] and Jacob hid them under the oak which was near Shechem' (Gen. 35:4)."

[W] He heard rumors that they were saying, "Let us get up earlier and take care of those thorns," and he knew that they planned to kill him. So he got up early and fled.

[X] R. Aḥa went to Emmaus, and he ate their dumplings.

[Y] R. Jeremiah ate leavened bread prepared by them.

[Z] R. Ḥezekiah ate their locusts prepared by them.

[AA] R. Abbahu prohibited Israelite use of wine prepared by them.

[BB] This was on the basis of instruction deriving from R. Ḥiyya, R. Assi, R. Ammi, who went up to the Royal Mountain and saw a gentile who was suspect by reason of having utilized their wine. They came back and told [Abbahu]. He said to them, "And [this is] not because of a rumor [but because of the fact of what you have seen]."

[CC] And there is he who proposes to state the reason [that the wine of Samaritans was prohibited for the following]: On a certain eve of the Sabbath, wine was not to be found in the entire town of Samartiqi. At the end of the Sabbath they found that the whole city was full of wine, which gentiles had brought, and which the Samaritans had purchased from them.

[DD] And there are those who wish to explain the reason as follows:

[EE] When Diocletian the king came up here, he issued a decree, saying, "Every nation must offer a libation, except for the Jews." So the Samaritans made a libation. [That is why the] sages prohibited their wine.

[FF] And there are those who wish to explain the prohibition on the following basis:

[GG] They have a kind of dove to which they offer libations[, so they really are idolators].

[HH] Samaritans in Caesarea asked R. Abbahu, "Your fathers would make ample use of things that we have prepared. Now why do you not make use of things that we have prepared?"

[II] He said to him, "Your fathers did not ruin themselves, but you have ruined yourselves through your deeds!"

[JJ] There we have learned:

[KK] *The land of Israel is clean, and its immersion pools are clean* [that is, not assumed to be filled with drawn water and so assumed to be valid for purification] [M. Miq. 8:1A].

[LL] **Samaritan territory is clean, and its immersion pools, dwellings, and paths are assumed to be clean [T. Miq. 7:1].**

[MM] It is assumed that they select a path for themselves only if it is known to be clean [and free of corpse matter].

[NN] **And its immersion pools are assumed to be clean [filled with valid, not drawn, water]:**

[OO] R. Eleazar b. R. Yosé, "It follows from what you have said that one must place credence in what they say, that the pools are not filled with drawn water. But lo, as to the full measure of forty *seahs,* they are not assumed to be filled [to that requisite volume].

[PP] "For the Samaritans interpret the relevant verse as follows: 'Nevertheless a spring or a cistern holding water shall be clean' (Lev. 11:36).

[QQ] "[Their exegesis is this:] The reference to a spring or a cistern is for the following purpose: Just as a spring effects purification, whatever the volume of its waters, so a cistern effects purification, whatever the volume of its waters [even if it contains less than the forty *seahs* of water that has not been drawn, such as is required by Israelite law]."

[RR] They asked R. Abbahu, "What is the law as to eating dumplings prepared by Samaritans?"

[SS] He said to them, "Would that we could impose a prohibition even on water drawn by them!"

[TT] R. Jacob bar Aḥa in the name of R. Ḥaninah: "As to the Samaritans of Caesarea, it is permitted to lend them money at interest[, for they are not regarded as Israelites at all]."

[UU] R. Yosé raised the question, "On that basis, then, one should not scruple about dough-offering separated from bread prepared by them [since this will be deemed no different from bread prepared by gentiles, which is not subject to the requirement of separating dough-offering for a priest], and yet we see that rabbis do scruple about separating dough-offering from dough prepared by Samaritans."

Units **I** and **II** amplify the Mishnah's rule. Unit **III** is relevant, so far as I can see, only at **III**.I–O. But these points are tangential to the center of interest of that vast anthology of whether or not Samaritans are deemed part of Israel. Only at UU is a contrary view suggested.

5:5

[A] *He who leaves his wine on a wagon or in a boat and went along by a shortcut, entered into a town and bathed—it is permitted.*

[B] *But if he informed [others] that he was going away,*

[C] *[the wine is prohibited if he was gone] for a time sufficient to bore a hole and stop it up and for the clay to dry.*

[D] *Rabban Simeon b. Gamaliel says, "Time sufficient to open [the jar] and stop it up and for the clay to dry."*

[**I**.A] Said R. Ḥaninah, MʿŚH B: [There was] a wagon belonging to the household of Rabbi from which the Israelite driver went away by more than four *mil*.

[B] The case came before the rabbis, who declared the wine to be acceptable to Israelites.

[C] They say that [this was because] it took place on a road near Sidon, and the whole of it was filled with Israelites.

[D] Said R. Ḥaninah, "There are times in which one sees hedges of thorns and thinks that they are people, and on that account [the gentile] is cautious [and will not make a libation and that accounts for B]."

The Talmud supplies a case illustrative of M. A.Z. 5:5A.

5:6

[A] *He who leaves a gentile in a store,*

[B] *even though he is going out and coming [in all the time]—*

[C] *[wine] is permitted.*

[D] *But if he informed him that he was going away,*

[E] *[the wine is prohibited if he was gone] for a time sufficient to bore a hole and stop it up and for the clay to dry.*

[F] *Rabban Simeon b. Gamaliel says, "Time sufficient to open [the jar] and stop it up and for the clay to dry."*

[**I**.A] And this ruling is in accord [even] with the view of R. Meir.

[B] For R. Meir said, *"[The wife of a haber who left the wife of an ʿam ha'areṣ grinding grain in her house—if the sound of the millstones ceased, the house is unclean. If the millstones did not cease, unclean is only the space up to the place to which she can reach out her hand and touch. If she left two women,] one way or the other [whether or not the grinding ceased], the house is unclean[, for one grinds, and the other snoops about],"* the words of R. Meir [M. Toh. 7:4].

[C] R. Ḥama in the name of R. Yosé bar Ḥaninah: "In the case of a courtyard that is divided up or partitioned,

[D] "in the matter of foods requiring preparing in conditions of cleanness, such foods will be deemed unclean.

[E] "But in respect to the issue of wine having been used for a libation, the wine is deemed clean."

[F] And lo, R. Meir imposes a strict ruling in the case of foods requiring preparation in conditions of cleanness [M. Toh. 7:4], but imposes a lenient ruling in the case of libation wine [as above].

[G] Also the rabbis impose a strict ruling in the case of food requiring preparation in conditions of cleanness, and impose a lenient ruling in the case of wine suspected of having been used for a libation.

The Talmud's interest in Meir is to distinguish his ruling at M. Toh. from the ruling given here, also assigned to him. So there will be no conflict between the two cases, the point is made that Meir rules more strictly with reference to one than the other; that is (F), he will accept the rule of M. A.Z. 5:6 while imposing a far stricter standard at M. Toh. 7:4. But G points out that that same distinction is possible for the anonymous authorities at both points. Even in a case in which there will be scruple for one sort of thing, there will be none for the other.

5:7

[A] *[If an Israelite] was eating with [a gentile] at the same time, and he put a flagon [of wine] on the table and a flagon on a side table, and he left it and went out—*

[B] *what is on the table is forbidden.*

[C] *But what is on the side table is permitted.*

[D] *But if he had said to him, "You mix and drink [wine]," even that which is on the side table is forbidden.*

[E] *Jars that are open are forbidden,*

[F] *and those that are sealed [are forbidden if he was gone] for a time sufficient to bore a hole and stop it up and for the clay to dry.*

[**I**.A] They proposed ruling that what is on the table is forbidden [M. A.Z. 5:7B] if it is within the space which a person can reach.

[B] And what is on the table is permitted if it is outside [45a] of the gentile's reach [M. A.Z. 5:7C].

[C] For did not R. Ba say in the name of R. Sheshet, "Just as they imposed the criterion of what lies within one's grasp in the case of foods requiring preparation in conditions of cleanness, so they imposed that same criterion in the case of wine suspected of having been used for a libation"?

[D] And that certainly is the rule:

[E] The one who ruled that what is on the table is forbidden [maintains that that is the case concerning food] within the gentile's grasp and what is on the side table is permitted, on condition that this lies outside of the person's grasp.

The Talmud introduces its desired criterion (C) into the interpretation of the Mishnah, with the result proposed at A–B and confirmed at E.

5:8

[A] *A band of gentile [raiders] that entered a town in peacetime—*

[B] *open jars are forbidden; closed ones permitted.*

[C] *[If it was] wartime, these and those are permitted*

[D] *because there is no time for making a libation.*

[**I**.A] [If] it was a time of persecution of Israelites, all [jars, open and sealed,] are prohibited, for it is not possible that there is a single Israelite who has refrained from performing an act of idolatrous worship under constraint.

[B] And this is in line with that rule which states: An idol that an Israelite has worshiped is never nullified [from its status as an idol].

[C] Said R. Yosé, "And you may infer from that statement [in addition] that an idol that an Israelite has worshiped under constraint also is never subject to nullification."

[**II**.A] [In reference to the statement, *If it was wartime, these and those are permitted,*] R. Yoḥanan said, "There is none here that is forbidden, but all are permitted [even if one left a keg sealed and found it opened]."

[B] Said R. Zeira, "There are here [in the case of wartime] also those that are forbidden, for [do you think that] if a gentile turns up the keg he is going to inform the Israelite, and if he does not turn up the keg he will not inform him? For the Israelite is not going to thank him [one way or the other, for it is wartime. Consequently, we have to scruple that a jug left sealed and found opened has been opened by a gentile and used in part for a libation]."

[**III**.A] R. Ammi in the name of R. Yoḥanan: "In time of peace there is a band of gentile raiders, and in time of war there is such a band[, and the issue of war or peace refers to the character of the band, not to the character of the times]."

[B] A snake was running after a [gentile], who fell [in his flight] into [a keg of wine]. The case came before the rabbis, and they declared the wine valid, saying, "[The snake] had not time to spit venom [into the keg]."

The Talmud's opening observation, unit **I**, greatly enriches the Mishnah. The next units serve as glosses. The dispute at unit **II** is clear as given, though to make sense of **II**.A we have to read in the conception of **II**.B. **III**.A is evidently meant to be illustrated by **III**.B.

5:9

[A] *Israelite craftsmen, to whom a gentile sent a jar of libation wine as their salary, are permitted to say to him, "Give us its value."*

[B] *But if it had already entered their possession, it is prohibited.*

[**I**.A] But would the proceeds of the keg of libation wine not be prohibited under the prohibition of libation wine?

[B] It was taught [by] Bar Qappara: "It is a case in which what was sent was for barter [for their labor, not the equivalent, in wine, of a specified sum. The wine was not subject to a valuation in specie, and, since they had not made acquisition of it, it is not a case of selling him the wine in exchange for money, but their specifying a different mode of payment for their work]."

The Talmud raises and answers the critical question.

5:10

[A] *He who sells his wine to a gentile [and] agreed on a price before he had measured it out—*

[B] *proceeds paid for it are permitted.*

[C] *[If] he had measured it out before he had fixed its price, proceeds paid for it are prohibited.*

[D] *[If] he took the funnel and measured it out into the flask of the gentile and then went and measured wine into the flask of an Israelite,*

[E] *if there remained [in the funnel] a drop of wine [from what had been poured into the gentile's flask, then what is in the Israelite's flask] is forbidden.*

[F] *He who pours [wine] from one utensil to another—*

[G] *[wine left in that] from which he emptied [the wine] is permitted.*

[H] *But [wine in] that [vessel, belonging to the gentile,] into which he emptied [the wine] is forbidden.*

[**I**.A] R. Ba, R. Huna in the name of Rab: "He who draws a skin of wine from his fellow [without having agreed on a price for it with him], and the skin was torn so that the wine poured out—the man does not owe him for it [because he had not made an agreement for its price, and therefore the purchaser had not come to a decision to acquire the skin, and the skin of wine did not yet stand in the domain of the prospective purchaser]."

[B] Said R. Yosé b. R. Bun, "Therefore it was necessary to teach [this obvious rule, A, to indicate that,] even if the prospective purchaser should raise the skin up to his own stall, [he is not liable should the skin break,] for his intention in doing so was only so that other people should make acquisition of the skin. [But it still has not fallen into his domain. Until a price has been agreed upon, the skin does not belong to the prospective purchaser (just as is indicated at M. A.Z. 5:10A–B).]"

[C] What is the law regarding the skin of wine having [automatically] been acquired by him at the lowest price [prevailing in the market at that time, even though there has been no agreement on any price at all? Do we say that, if he could have gotten the wine for the lowest prevailing price, he would have accepted it for that price? Or do we say that, since the skin of wine has not yet entered the prospective purchaser's domain, he is exempt of all liability for the wine]?

[D] Said R. Ḥaggai before R. Yosé, "The Mishnah itself has laid down the law that it is not [presumptively] acquired by the prospective purchaser for the lowest prevailing price.

[E] "For we have learned there: *He who sells his wine to a gentile [and] agreed on a price before he had measured it out—proceeds paid for it are permitted. If he had measured it out before he had fixed its price, proceeds paid for it are prohibited [M. A.Z. 5:10A–C].*

[F] "Now if you maintain that one should regard the wine as acquired by the prospective purchaser at the lowest prevailing price, then even a case in which he measured it out before he agreed upon a price should be treated as equivalent to a case in which he had agreed to a price before he had measured out the wine, [so that even in the case of C] the proceeds should be permitted. [For what difference will it make whether or not a price has been agreed upon if we maintain that there is a putative price, the lowest prevailing price in the market, which the prospective purchaser is assumed to be willing to accept under all conditions?]"

[**II**.A] What is *a drop of wine* [of M. A.Z. 5:10E]?

[B] It is that in the dregs, as you read in Scripture, "tracked with blood" (Hos. 6:8).

[**III**.A] It is self-evident [in the rule of M. A.Z. 5:10F–H] that an Israelite is holding on to the funnel and the gentile is pouring the skin of wine, so the opinion of all authorities is that the wine is forbidden.

[B] [If] a gentile is holding the funnel and an Israelite is pouring the wine—

[C] R. Assi declares [the wine] prohibited.

[D] And R. Ammi declares it permitted [since the gentile plays no part in pouring the wine].

[E] [If] a gentile is holding on to the mouth of the skin, but an Israelite is pouring the wine—

[F] R. Jeremiah in the name of R. Zeira, "This is a matter subject to dispute."

[G] R. Mana raised the question before R. Yosé, "What sort of dispute?"

[H] He said to him, "It is a dispute between R. Assi and R. Ammi [just as above at C–D]."

[I] If an Israelite is holding onto the skin, and a gentile is pouring the wine,

[J] they gave thought to ruling that, in the opinion of all parties, the wine is permitted.

[K] R. Samuel: "The very essence of the case is such as to rule that the wine is forbidden.

[L] "For sometimes an Israelite will stretch out his hands, and it will turn out that the entire act of pouring out is on account of the action of the gentile.

[M] "And this one who is guiding the flow from above to below—is he not subject to the consideration of pouring out from one utensil to another [in which case, that into which he emptied the wine is forbidden, as at M. A.Z. 5:10H]?" [If wine belonging to a gentile remains in the funnel, M. 5:10D–G, then that drop of wine is assumed to have been poured into the Israelite's flask. F–H go over a parallel case. The wine remaining in the upper jar, which is in an Israelite's hand, is permitted. That which is in the lower jar, held by a gentile, is prohibited.]

Unit **I** introduces into the interpretation of the Mishnah a secondary but fruitful question. May we not take for granted that a purchaser will agree on the lowest prevailing price? If we may do so, then the Mishnah's distinction falls away. This question is raised in an indirect way, by introducing Rab's statement, relevant elsewhere but not here, and adding to it Yosé b. R. Bun's explanation of the intent. It is at that point that the difficult problem is set for the present context (C). The answer, D–F, is clearly given and explicitly relevant in context. The exegesis of unit **II** adds little. Unit **III**, for its part, formulates a set of secondary questions, taking up the Mishnah's case and showing the potential complexities contained within it. The main issue is whether or not the flow of wine is guided by the force of a gentile's control, and that matter is not clearly contained within the formulation of M. 5:10F–H.

5:11

[A] *Libation wine is forbidden and imparts a prohibition [to wine with which it is mixed] in any measure at all.*

[B] *[If it is] wine [poured] into wine, or [libation] water [poured] into water, in any quantity whatever [it is forbidden].*

[C] *[If it is] wine [poured] into water or water [poured] into wine, [it is forbidden] if it imparts flavor.*

[D] *This is the governing principle: [If it is] one species [poured] into its own species [B], [it is forbidden] in any measure at all.*

[E] *[If it is] not [poured] into its own species [C], it is forbidden if it imparts flavor.*

[**I**.A] Hezekiah said, "This rule that you have stated [that if it is wine poured into water, or water poured into wine, it is forbidden if it imparts flavor (M. A.Z. 5:11C)], applies in a locale in which water is sold by measure. But in a locale in which water is not sold by measure, it is subject to the law pertaining to wine mixed with wine[, for in the latter case water is as valuable as wine]."

[B] Hezekiah said, "A cup of wine that one mixed with wine that was prohibited and with wine that was permitted,

[C] "[if] that which was prohibited fell in at the end, it is prohibited.

[D] "[If] that which was permitted fell in at the end, it is permitted."

[E] Said R. Samuel, "This teaching is that of R. Eliezer, for [in the following case: *If common leaven and heave-offering leaven fell into dough, and neither sufficed by itself, but together they leavened the dough], R. Eliezer says, "I should decide [whether the utensil was clean or unclean] by which of them came last."* [But the sages say, "By which came first"] [M. Orl. 2:11. Hezekiah, C–D follows what came last.]

[F] Said R. Jeremiah, "A stricter rule applies in the case of wine that has served for a libation. [Hezekiah does not necessarily accord with Eliezer.]"

[G] R. Yosé raised the question, "If a stricter rule applies in the case of wine that has served for a libation, then even if that wine which was permitted fell in last, it should be prohibited [entirely]."

[H] R. Assi in the name of R. Yoḥanan [differing from Hezekiah, B–D]: "A cup that one mixed from wine that was prohibited and from wine that was permitted—you regard the wine that was permitted as if it were not present.

[I] "And that which was prohibited—if it imparts flavor to the whole, the mixture is prohibited, and if not, it is permitted. [Thus we invoke the principle of M. A.Z. 5:11E.]"

[J] Said R. Hoshaiah, "And that rule applies in the case in which the wine that was permitted fell in at the end. [In this case we do not invoke the principle of M. 5:11B, D.]"

[K] R. Ammi in the name of R. Yoḥanan, "There is no real difference between the case in which the prohibited wine fell in at the outset and the permitted wine at the end, and one in which the permitted wine fell in at the outset, and the prohibited wine at the end.

[L] "Even if this is a case of water mixed with wine, and even if the mixture was fully stirred with permitted wine,

[M] "in any event you regard the permitted wine as if it were not present and, as to the prohibited wine, if it imparts a flavor, the mixture is forbidden, and if not, it is permitted."

[N] Said R. Zira, "As to what has been stated above, and as to all that we have learned [about R. Yoḥanan's thinking]—what would be a concrete case?"

[O] R. Yosé b. R. Bun, R. Abbahu in the name of R. Yoḥanan: "A flask of libation wine that fell into a jug of water, and afterward [the jug with the wine] fell into a cistern of water—you regard the permitted liquid as if it were not present, and, as to the forbidden liquid, if it is sufficient to impart a flavor, the whole is forbidden, and if not, it is permitted."

[**II**.A] [With regard to the Mishnah pericope of M. Orl. 2:11, cited above,] to this point we deal with a case in which one sort of leaven fell after the other. But what if the two fell at the same time?

[B] Let us learn the answer to that question from the following:

[C] **Leaven belonging to Samaritans—at what point is it permitted after Passover? That belonging to householders is permitted following three weeks of use in baking. And that belonging to bakers in little villages is permitted three days thereafter. And that belonging to bakers in large towns is permitted once [they have had an opportunity to prepare dough for] three [uses of their large] ovens. R. Simeon b. Eleazar says, "When they stated the rule concerning that belonging to householders, 'Following three weeks of use in baking'—if he was a householder, or was marrying off his son, and made use of his oven three times in succession, then it is permitted forthwith. And when they stated the rule concerning that belonging to bakers, 'In little villages, three days thereafter,' if he found the need and made use of his oven three times in succession, even on the very first day after Passover, it is permitted" [T. Pes. 2:1].**

[D] It was taught: **R. Simeon says, "Also when they stated the rule concerning that belonging to bakers in large towns, 'Once they have made use of their ovens three times'—nonetheless, it is prohibited for three days. For at dawn he would get the leaven for the whole of the rest of that day" [T. Pes. 2:2A–C].**

[E] That second piece of dough—has it not been leavened with leaven that was prohibited and with that which was permitted? [So the sages now concur with Eliezer that there is a prohibition when the two kinds of leaven work together.]

[F] R. Jeremiah said in the name of R. Simeon b. Laqish, "Who taught that Samaritan dough [is prohibited]? R. Eliezer."

[G] Said R. Yosé to R. Ḥaninah of Antonia, "I recall that you and R. Jeremiah in the name of R. Simeon b. Laqish were both teaching, 'Who taught that the leaven of Samaritans is prohibited? It is R. Eliezer.'

[H] "But R. Hila in the name of R. Simeon b. Laqish taught, '[The sages] went down [and adopted the prohibition of] leaven belonging to Samaritans, in accord with R. Eliezer.' [So the cited pericope accords with the sages, not solely with Eliezer.]"

[I] And furthermore, one must note the following, which R. Ḥaninah bar R. Abbahu said: "Father had a case. He sent and asked R. Ḥiyya and R. Ammi and R. Assi, and they instructed him to rule in accord with R. Eliezer [that leaven belonging to Samaritans is prohibited immediately after Passover]."

[J] Now what follows from that? Do people give instruction on the basis of the opinion of an individual [as against the sages as a group]? [Obviously not!]

[K] No, it was because [the sages] went down [and adopted the prohibition of] leaven belonging to Samaritans, in accord with the opinion of R. Eliezer.

[L] Said R. Mana before R. Yosé, "Just as you ruled there, 'The law is in accord with the opinion of R. Eliezer,' so you should rule [45b] here, 'The law is in accord with R. Eliezer.' "

[M] He said to him, "And [in fact] for the entire law that applies in this case [the law is in accord with him]."

The Mishnah's point is expressed twice, in the contrast of B–C, then in the generalization at D–E. When the two substances are of the same species, then the mixture of any volume at all of a prohibited one with a permitted one prohibits the latter. But if they are not of the same species, then, as at C and E, we take account of whether or not the prohibited substance (liquid) has changed the character of the permitted one, because, the substances being different from one another, the mixture to begin with is not complete and pervasive. Once matters are framed in this way, the principal concern will be the mixture of prohibited wine with permitted wine. The first initiative of unit

I is to examine the ideas of Hezekiah, who has a comment on the Mishnah. The segment at **I**.B–D is what is under analysis. What is at issue is whether or not Hezekiah's comment on the Mishnah places him into agreement with Eliezer, M. Orl. 2:11, as against the sages. If it does, then Hezekiah sides with the minority, as against the majority, view. This matter plays itself out at E–G. Then (H) Yoḥanan takes a position altogether different from Hezekiah's. What is important in the interpretation of the Mishnah is not the order in which the prohibited or permitted elements joined the mixture, but the principle expressed, to begin with, in the Mishnah itself. Yoḥanan thus wishes to treat prohibited and permitted wine in accord with the stated principle of M. 5:11E. Hoshaiah (J) explicitly excludes Hezekiah's principle, but Ammi in Yoḥanan's name (K–L) shows how to harmonize what Hezekiah thinks is important with what Yoḥanan wishes to stress in the Mishnah. Zira then asks for a concrete case to exemplify Yoḥanan's view of the matter, and this is given at O. The concrete case leaves no problems; all the elements of the antecedent discussion are covered in it. Carrying forward unit **I**, unit **II** returns to analyze the cited pericope, M. Orl 2:11. Once more at issue is whether or not the law follows Eliezer, and **II**.E shows that, so far as all parties are concerned, the sages will concur that, when there is a mixture of prohibited and permitted leaven, in which the leavening process is possible only because of the presence of both the prohibited and the permitted kinds, then the dough is prohibited, a view with which the sages, as much as Eliezer, will concur. The only point under dispute is that specified at M. Orl. 2:11, a case in which one enters the mixture, and then the other comes in later on.

5:12

[A] *These are forbidden and impose a prohibition in any measure at all:*

[B] *[1] libation wine, [2] an idol, [3] hides with a hole at the heart, [4] an ox condemned to be stoned, [5] a heifer, the neck of which is to be broken, [6] the birds to be offered by a "meṣoraᶜ," [7] the hair cut off a Nazir (Num. 6:18), [8] the [unredeemed] first born of an ass (Ex. 13:13), [9] meat in milk,*

[10] the scape goat, [11] unconsecrated beasts that have been slaughtered in the temple courtyard—

[C] *lo, these are forbidden and impose a prohibition in any measure at all.*

[**I**.A] *Libation wine, an idol, and hides with a hole at the heart* [are prohibited] on the count of the following verse of Scripture: "None of the devoted things shall cleave to your hand" (Deut. 13:17).

[B] An ox that is condemned to be stoned [is prohibited] from what is implied by the verse "the ox shall be stoned[, and its flesh shall not be eaten]" (Ex. 21:28).

[C] Does one not know that [the meat] is not to be eaten [for it is carrion]?

[D] So why does Scripture state, "It shall not be eaten"?

[E] On this basis, [we must rule] that the corpse of the ox is prohibited also as to benefit.

[F] As to the heifer, the neck of which is to be broken? It is on the basis of the recurrence of the word "there" in the following two verses: "and they shall break the heifer's neck there in the valley" (Deut. 21:4); "And [she] was buried there" (Num. 20:1).

[G] Just as "there" in the latter context [referring to a corpse] means that there is a prohibition against deriving benefit [from things pertaining to the corpse], so "there" in the present context means that there is a prohibition against deriving benefit [from things deriving from the heifer whose neck is to be broken].

[H] As to the birds to be offered by a *meṣoraʿ* [prohibited when slaughtered]? "Of all clean birds you may eat" (Deut. 14:11)—this refers to the bird that is set free. "But these are they of which you shall not eat" (Deut. 14:12)—this refers to the bird that is slaughtered.

[I] Or perhaps matters are just the opposite [and the slaughtered one is permitted]?

[J] R. Yoḥanan in the name of R. Ishmael: "The Torah does not impose a prohibition against benefit [as well as against eating] upon something that is alive."

[K] And the hair of a Nazirite? "And he shall take the hair from his consecrated head and put it on the fire which is under the sacrifice of the peace offering" (Num. 6:18).

[L] The firstling of an ass? The breaking of the neck is written in that connection, ["Every firstling of an ass you shall redeem with a lamb, or if you will not redeem it, you will break its neck" (Ex. 13:13)], and the breaking of a neck is written in connection with the heifer [Deut. 21:4, cited above]. Just as in the latter connection, one must bury the heifer, and it is prohibited as to the benefit, so in this connection one must bury the firstling, and it is prohibited as to benefit.

[M] Meat in milk? It has been taught: "You shall not seethe a kid in its mother's milk" is stated three times (Ex. 23:19, 34:26, Deut. 14:21). One is meant to prohibit eating it, one is to prohibit deriving benefit from it, and one is to prohibit cooking.

[N] And as to unconsecrated beasts that have been slaughtered in the temple courtyard—

[O] R. Yoḥanan in the name of R. Ishmael: "The Torah has decreed, 'Slaughter what belongs to me in an area that belongs to me, and what belongs to you in an area that belongs to you. Just as what of mine is slaughtered in an area that belongs to you is prohibited, so what of yours is slaughtered in an area belonging to me [is prohibited].'"

[P] [If so, should not one who does so be] subject to the penalty of extirpation?

[Q] And did not R. Ishmael state, "They may learn a rule from an argument *a fortiori*, but they do not inflict a punishment on the basis of an argument *a fortiori?*" [So P's proposal is rejected.]

[**II**.A] And why do we not learn that carrion belongs to this same list?

[B] Said R. Yosé b. R. Bun, "The Tannaitic tradition repeats only matters that are prohibited as to benefit. But carrion is permitted as to benefit."

[C] They objected, "Lo, there is leaven on Passover [that is prohibited as to benefit, and which is not listed]."

[D] Leaven on Passover is subject to extirpation, but violation of these does not produce the penalty of extirpation.

[**III**.A] R. Yosé in the name of R. Ḥanina raised the question, "Matters that are prohibited for enjoyment—what is the rule as to their being deemed null when joined [with small bits of permitted matter]?"

[B] And have we not learned on the list of the Mishnah: *an ox that is condemned to be stoned* [, so how can the huge volume of prohibited meat ever be nullified in a volume of permitted]?

[C] Apply the rule of the Mishnah to a case in which we deal with small bits of such an ox.

[D] And have we not learned on the Mishnah's list, *"The birds to be offered by a meṣoraᶜ"?*

[E] Interpret the law of the Mishnah to speak of a bird among a larger group of birds [among which it is indistinguishable].

[F] And have we not learned in the Mishnah's list, *The hair of a Nazirite?*

[G] Can you now claim that we deal with a case parallel to "a bird among birds"?

[H] When you come to [the following passage in] tractate Orlah [you will find the anwer to A, as indicated below].

[I] R. Jacob objected before R. Yosé, "Have we not learned: *He who weaves into a garment one sit's length of wool from a firstling—the garment must be burned. If he wove into a sack a Nazirite's hair or hair from the first born of an ass, the sack must be burned* [M. Orl. 3:3]. [So the answer to A is negative.]"

[J] He said to him, "If you had given this answer [when we were dealing with Orlah], it would have been fine."

Unit **I** provides scriptural bases for M. A.Z. 5:12B[1–9] and an argument to explain no. 11. Why no. 10 is omitted entirely I do not know. The proofs are conventional, and within the system, pose no problems. Unit **II** then carries out a secondary exegetical exercise, asking in a desultory way about items that might have been included but are omitted. The purpose is effected at **II**.D, which tells us why we have what we have and do not have what is omitted. Unit **III** then raises a question expanding the rule of the Mishnah: Is it possible that the items listed will be deemed null, by reason of their unimportance, when they are chopped to bits and mixed with permitted substances? The answer comes in the citation of M. Orl. 3:3 at **III**.I. I am not entirely clear on the force of J.

5:13

[A] *Libation wine that fell into a vat—*

[B] *the whole of [the vat] is forbidden for benefit.*

[C] *Rabban Simeon b. Gamaliel says, "Let the whole of it be sold to a gentile, except for the value of that volume of libation wine that is in it."*

[**I**.A] R. Yosé, R. Yoḥanan in the name of Ben Beterah: "*Libation wine that fell into a vat—let the whole of it be sold to a gentile, except for the value of the libation wine [that is in the vat].*"

[B] R. Samuel bar Nathan in the name of R. Ḥama: "The law is in accord with the opinion of Rabban Simeon b. Gamaliel."

[C] Said R. Yasa, "One of the rabbis went out of the meeting-house. He stated, 'R. Yoḥanan and R. Simeon b. Laqish differed from one another.

[D] " 'One of them said, "The law is in accord with the opinion of Rabban Simeon b. Gamaliel,' and one of them said, 'The law is not in accord with the position of Rabban Simeon b. Gamaliel.' "

[**II**.A] But Rabban Simeon b. Gamaliel concurs in the case of [libation] wine mixed into a cooked dish, that the dish is prohibited [since the wine improves the dish].

[B] R. Bun in the name of Rab: "The sages concur with Rabban Simeon b. Gamaliel in the case of a jug of [libation] wine situated among other jugs, [which someone had in hand, that he is permitted to] sell the whole of the set of jugs to a gentile, [receiving in exchange all of the proceeds] except for the proceeds of the [jug of] libation wine that is in the lot[, for the suitable wine is not mixed with the prohibited wine, so one can distinguish one from the other]."

[C] Said R. Zira before R. Ammi, "If you had not made this statement, we should not have known that that is the case.

[D] "Had you said only, 'The sages concur with Rabban Simeon b. Gamaliel,' or had you said only, 'Rabban Simeon b. Gamaliel concurs with the sages,' [we should not have had access to either statement]."

[E] Said R. Yudan, "R. Zira knew full well that matters are thus, but he pretended to be a person who heard something for the first time in order to raise questions about it [for the sake of discussion]."

Unit **I** presents diverse traditions on the state of the law. **II**.A has Simeon b. Gamaliel concur with the sages' principle in one sort of case, the sages with Simeon in another. In the former there is no way of distinguishing the proportion of the prohibited wine in the cooked dish, since the wine improves the taste of the whole. In the latter there is a way of distinguishing the proportion of prohibited wine from permitted wine, so the sages concur with Simeon's picture of matters.

5:14

[A] *A stone winepress that a gentile covered with pitch—*

[B] *one dries it off, and it is clean.*

[C] *And one of wood—*

[D] *Rabbi says, "Let him dry it off."*

[E] *And the sages say, "Let him scale off the pitch."*

[F] *And one of earthenware—*

[G] *even though one has scaled off the pitch, lo, this is forbidden.*

[**I**.A] [The opening clause of the] Mishnah [M. 5:14A–B] is in accord with the view of Rabbi.

[B] *As to one of wood, Rabbi says, "Let him dry it off." And the sages say, "Let him scale off the pitch."*

[C] *And as to one of earthenware[, even though one has scaled off the pitch, lo, this is forbidden]*—this is not in accord with the view of Rabbi.

[D] For it has been taught:

[E] **A vat, ladle, and siphon of gentiles [made of earthenware]—**

[F] **Rabbi permits [Israelites to use them].**

[G] **And the sages prohibit.**

[H] **But Rabbi concedes in the case of jars that they are prohibited [T. A.Z. 8:1A–G].**

[I] On what account are these forbidden and those permitted?

[J] Into these one puts wine, and into the others one does not put wine.

[K] R. Yosé in the name of R. Yoḥanan, "The law is in accord with Rabbi."

[L] As to utensils made of papyrus that a gentile has covered with pitch—

[M] there is a dispute between Rabbi and the sages [since these are equivalent to wooden utensils].

[N] R. Yosé b. R. Bun in the name of Samuel: "The law is in accord with the view of Rabbi."

[**II**.A] **It has been taught: "[If] one's wine vats [and olive presses] were [cultically] unclean and one wanted to clean them—**

[B] **the boards and the two posts supporting the beams of the press and the troughs does he dry, and they are clean.**

[C] **The cylinders of twigs and of hemp [he must dry].**

[D] **As to those of bast and of reeds, he must leave them unused.**

[E] **[And how long does he leave them unused?] Twelve months.**

[F] **Rabban Simeon b. Gamaliel says, "From one wine vintage to the next, or from one pressing season of olives to the next."**

[G] **It was taught: Said Rabban Simeon b. Gamaliel, "If he wants immediately to purify them, he places them for a whole season in a river whose waters flow or under the spout whose waters flow."**

[H] **And just as you dry them for cleanness, so you dry off wine used for idolatrous purposes [T. A.Z. 8:3].**

[I] And how long is "a whole season"[G]?

[J] R. Yosé in the name of R. Yoḥanan says, "Half a day and half a night."

[K] It was taught: R. Ḥiyya says, "A day or a night."

[L] Now does he differ?

[M] No. In one case, the day and night are of equal length, and in the other, the day and night are not of equal length.

Rabbi's view is that merely drying off a stone or wood object suffices to render it suitable for Israelite use. His opinion is the center of unit **I**. I have rearranged the order of K–M. Unit **II** presents and provides a gloss of a pericope on the same matter as the Mishnah. The point of contact is at **II**.A–C: merely drying off wooden objects suffices.

5:15

[A] *He who purchases utensils [for use with food] from a gentile—*

[B] *that which is usually immersed one must immerse.*

[C] *That which is usually scalded one must scald.*

[D] *That which is usually heated to a white-hot flame one must heat to a white-hot flame.*

[E] *A spit or gridiron one must heat to a white-hot flame.*

[F] *A knife one [merely] polishes, and it is clean.*

[**I**.A] *He who purchases utensils from a gentile—*

[B] **in the case of things that one knows [have not been used] for preparing food, for instance, cups—one rinses them [in cold water] and they are clean.**

[C] **But as to pitchers and water kettles, one scalds them in boiling water.**

[D] **And in the case of all of them that have been used, even if one has not immersed, scalded, polished, or heated them to white heat, lo, these are clean [cf. T. A.Z. 8:2].**

[E] It was taught: R. Hoshaiah [said], "One has to immerse [cups or other utensils for food]."

[F] This is in line with the following:

[G] R. Ammi went up with R. Yudan the Patriarch to the hot springs of Gedar.

[H] They borrowed silver from certain gentile money-lenders [to make the silver into utensils].

[I] They asked R. Jeremiah [whether even the silver had to be immersed]. He instructed them to immerse the coins, for they had come forth from the uncleanness pertaining to a gentile and had entered the sanctification pertaining to an Israelite.

[J] When [R. Jeremiah] went out to give instruction, they went out and heard R. Jacob b. Aḥa, Simeon bar Ba in the name of R. Yoḥanan: "The teaching of the Mishnah [M. A.Z. 5:15] applies only to one who purchases [such objects,] but he who borrows [such objects]—it is permitted [without such a process of purification]."

[K] If so, then even in the case of utensils [one should say the same as J states and apply Yoḥanan's view to M. 5:15's cases].

[L] R. Hoshaiah would purchase utensils and immerse them [but not borrowed ones].

[**II**.A] There you say [at M. Zeb. 11:7F(5), in regard to a spit and a grill, that to clean those used for a sin-offering,] one puts them into scalding water [to clean them], and they are clean, and here you say one must heat them to a white-hot flame [M. 5:15E]. [Why is a more stringent procedure required here than at M. Zeb. 11:7?]

[B] A stricter rule applies to objects that gentiles have scalded.

[**III**.A] As to a knife, one sticks it into the ground three times and that suffices.

[B] R. Ba in the name of R. Judah: "That rule which you have stated applies to a small knife.

[C] "But in the case of a large knife, one has to heat it to a white heat, and the heating up must be such that sparks fly from the knife."

The important point, following the citation of the Tosefta's supplementary materials, is in the story of G ff. The distinction between borrowing and purchasing means that these procedures are in no way meant merely to remove uncleanness, whether cultic or culinary. **I**.I contains the main point. When an object enters Israelite possession it must be "remanufactured," as it were. Merely borrowing the object does not impose a similar consideration. Unit **II** contrasts the treatment required for a spit and grill here and in the cult. Unit **III**, finally, adds an item to the information provided by the Mishnah. So in this instance we move from secondary to primary materials.

Abbreviations and Bibliography

A.Z.: Abodah Zarah

b.: *Babli,* Babylonian Talmud; *ben,* "son of."

Bekh.: Bekhorot

B.Q.: Baba Qamma

Dem.: Demai

Ed.: Eduyyot

Editio princeps: Talmud Yerushalmi . . . Venezia. Reprinted without place or date. Originally printed by Daniel Bomberg, 1523–24.

Git.: Gittin

Hal.: Hallah

Hul.: Hullin

Jastrow: Jastrow, Marcus. *A Dictionary of the Targumim, the Talmud Babli and Yerushalmi, and the Midrashic Literature.* 2 vols. Reprint. New York: Pardes Publishing House, 1950.

Kel.: Kelim

Ket.: Ketubot

Kil.: Kilayim

Leiden MS: *The Palestinian Talmud, Leiden MS. Cod Scal. 3. A facsimile of the original manuscript.* 4 vols. Jerusalem: Kedem Publishing, 1970.

M.: Mishnah

Ma.: Maaserot

Miq.: Miqvaot

Oh.: Ohalot

Orl.: Orlah

Par.: Parah

Pené Moshe: *Pene Moshe.* Moses Margolies (d. 1780). *Pene Moshe.* Amsterdam: 1754; Leghorn: 1770. Reprinted in the Yerushalmi Talmud.

Pes.: Pesahim

Qid.: Qiddushin

R.: Rabbi

Shab.: Shabbat

Sheb.: Shebiit

T.: Tosefta

Ter.: Terumot

Toh.: Tohorot

Zeb.: Zebahim

Index of Biblical and Talmudic References

Biblical References

Amos
4:4, 7, 9
4:5, 9

1 Chronicles
14:12, 122
21:19, 131

2 Chronicles
7:3, 156
15:11, 54
15:16, 122

Daniel
1:8, 98

Deuteronomy
2:6, 97–98
4:14, 93
7:1–5, 2
7:2, 44
7:3, 47
7:25, 126, 163
7:25–26, 2
7:26, 48, 132, 135, 192
7:28, 125, 130
9:21, 121
12:2, 162
12:2–3, 3, 163
12:3, 123, 134, 166
13:1, 91
13:7, 193
13:17, 214
13:18, 120, 123
14:3, 132
14:11, 214
14:12, 214
14:21, 215
17:11, 91
20:16, 169
21:1, 10
21:4, 214–15
23:21–23, 9
27:15, 162, 164
31:10–11, 11
31:16, 93
32:35, 19

Ecclesiastes
10:8, 67, 90

Exodus
13:13, 213, 215
17:19, 92
18:4, 116
21:1, 93
21:28, 214
22:31, 73
23:13, 1
23:18, 8–9
23:19, 215
23:24, 1
23:32–33, 1
23:45, 72
25:33, 92
32:20, 121
34:12–16, 2
34:26, 215

Genesis
3:15, 20
4:7, 92
18:18, 53
27:41, 22
30:27, 118
33:14, 58
33:17, 58
34:6–7, 93
34:15, 20
35:4, 199
40:20, 23
49:6, 92
49:7, 92

Hosea
5:1–2, 12
6:8, 207
7:5, 9–10
7:6, 9
7:7, 10

Isaiah
7:5–6, 8
8:21–22, 168
10:14, 115
24:23, 171
27:3, 128
27:9, 166
30:22, 132, 135–36
43:9, 19
49:4, 113
49:23, 59
50:4, 20
57:6, 128
60:7, 52–53

Jeremiah
34:5, 23

Joshua
7:2, 135
7:10, 156

Judges
8:27, 136
8:33, 135

1 Kings
12:27–28, 11
12:29, 11
12:31, 8
12:32, 12
15:13, 122
22:47, 23

2 Kings
17:30, 117–118
17:31, 118
18:4, 122

Leviticus
5:16, 118
11:36, 201
14:45, 134

18:5, 67
18:19, 132
18:29, 132
19:4, 111
22:17ff, 55
22:25, 55
23:23, 12
26:1, 155, 166

Malachi
1:8, 33

Micah
2:6, 91
2:11, 91

Nehemiah
9:1–2, 17

Numbers
6:18, 213, 215
18:28, 178
20:1, 214

Obadiah
1:21, 58

Proverbs
12:18, 46
23:1, 199
27:26–27, 93

Psalms
1:1–2, 42
2:2, 54
5:11, 113
31:19, 113
32:6, 113
37:34, 111
58:5, 11
97:7, 171
106:28, 69, 133
115:8, 171
129:8, 180–81
139:12, 20
146:5, 115
146:6, 115

1 Samuel
2:28, 8
5:5, 119
6:14, 55
6:15, 54
15:15, 55

2 Samuel
15:32, 155
24:21–24, 55
24:23, 55

Song of Solomon
1:2, 88, 90, 93
1:3, 88
7:9, 90

Zechariah
11:12, 53

Zephaniah
1:9, 119
3:9, 54

Mishnaic References

Abodah Zarah
1:1, 8, 13, 15–16, 18–19, 24
1:2, 19, 23
1:4, 30
1:5, 32–34
1:6, 35, 37–40
1:7, 33
1:9, 47–48
1:10, 49
2:1, 34, 51, 56–59
2:2, 68
2:3, 70, 77–78, 80, 89
2:4, 82
2:5, 85
2:7, 88, 92–94, 103
2:8, 96–98, 104–5, 107–8
2:9, 103, 108
3:1, 115–16
3:2, 119
3:3, 120–21
3:5, 128–30
3:6, 136–39
3:7, 141, 42
3:8, 145, 167
3:9, 146
3:10, 147
3:11, 149
3:12, 151
3:13, 151
3:14, 149, 152
4:1, 153, 156–57
4:3, 161
4:4, 144, 161–62, 164, 166–67
4:5, 168
4:6, 164–65
4:7, 170–71
4:8, 85, 173, 175
4:9, 176, 178
4:10, 179
4:11, 182–84
4:12, 185–87
5:1, 188–89
5:2, 194
5:3, 195
5:5, 202
5:6, 203
5:7, 204
5:10, 207–9
5:11, 209–10, 213
5:12, 216
5:14, 218
5:15, 221
7:8, 99

Bekhorot
1:1, 38

Berakhot
1:3, 90

Beṣah
1:1, 94

Demai
3:4, 75

Eduyyot
1:5, 99

Giṭṭin
4:6, 68

Ḥallah
3:2, 177–79

Ḥullin
8:5, 89–90

Kelim
9:5, 85
22:1, 108

Ketubot
2:9, 51

Kilayim
7:4, 126–27

Maaserot
3:5, 49

Moʿed Qaṭan
1:7, 14

Ohalot
7:6, 66

Orlah
2:11, 210–11, 213
3:3, 216–17

Parah
2:1, 50–51, 54, 59
5:7, 137

Pesaḥim
2:2, 45

Qiddushin
4:12, 57

Sanhedrin
11:3, 91
11:4, 90, 94

Shabbat
14:4, 61
17:2, 62

Shebiit
5:9, 179–81
6:26, 188
8:4, 189

Shebuʿot
2:3, 156

Terumot
10:2, 196
11:1, 86–97

Toharot
7:4, 202–3
8:9, 173, 175

Zebaḥim
11:7, 221

Toseftan References

Abodah Zarah
1:1, 8
1:2, 29
1:3, 16
1:8, 13, 27
1:15, 28
1:21, 31
2:3, 40
2:4, 57
2:5, 42
2:7, 42
3:1, 57
3:2, 56
3:4, 58
3:5, 67
3:6, 67
3:19, 122
4:10, 81
4:11, 86, 96–97
4:13, 107
5:1, 116
5:2, 116
6:4, 135
6:7, 171
7:1, 176–78
7:5, 172
7:6, 174
7:9, 186
7:10, 185
8:1, 219
8:2, 220
8:3, 219

Baba' Qamma'
6:18, 85
7:8, 24

Bekhorot
2:1, 37

Giṭṭin
3:13–14, 25

Ḥullin
8:12, 89

Miqvaot
7:1, 200
8:1, 200

Pesaḥim
2:1, 211
2:2, 211
2:15, 45
2:16, 46

Qiddushin
5:9, 57
5:10, 57

Shebiit
6:26, 189

Terumot
8:9, 196

Palestinian Talmudic References

Abodah Zarah
1:1, 3, 7–19
1:1–2:7, 3–4
1:2, 3, 19–23
1:2–4, 3
1:3, 23–26
1:4, 26–31
1:5, 3, 31–34
1:5–2:2, 3–4
1:6, 3, 34–41, 44
1:7, 3, 41–43
1:8, 43–44
1:8–10, 4
1:9, 44–48
1:10, 48–49
2:1, 4, 50–60
2:2, 4, 60–68
2:3, 4, 69–80
2:3–9, 4
2:4, 80–84
2:4–6, 4
2:5, 85
2:6, 86–87
2:7, 4, 88–95
2:8, 4, 95–103
2:9, 4, 103–9
3:1, 4, 110–17, 119
3:1–9, 4
3:1–4:7, 4–5
3:2, 117–19
3:2–3, 4
3:3, 119–23
3:4, 4, 123–25
3:5, 4, 125–31
3:6, 4, 132–41
3:7, 141–43
3:7–9, 4
3:8, 143–45, 165
3:9, 145–46
3:10, 4, 146–48
3:10–14, 4
3:11, 148–50
3:11–13, 4
3:12, 150–51
3:13, 151–52
3:14, 4, 152
4:1, 153–59
4:1–2, 5
4:2, 160
4:3, 5, 160–61
4:3–7, 5
4:4, 161–67
4:4–6, 5
4:5, 167–69
4:6, 169–70
4:7, 5, 170–71
4:8, 5, 171–76
4:8–5:15, 5–6
4:9, 5, 176–79
4:10, 179–81
4:10–11, 5
4:11, 181–84
4:12, 184–87
5:1, 188–93
5:1–2, 5
5:2, 193–94
5:3, 5, 194–97
5:4, 197–201
5:4–6, 5
5:5, 201–2
5:6, 202–3
5:7, 5, 203–4
5:8, 5, 204–5
5:9, 205–6
5:9–10, 5
5:10, 206–9
5:11, 209–13
5:11–12, 5
5:12, 213–17
5:13, 217–18
5:14, 218–20
5:14–15, 6
5:15, 220–22

Beṣah
1:1, 94

Giṭṭin
1:1, 106

Orlah
2:5, 196

Terumot
Ch. 2, 87

General Index

Abba, on gentiles and commercial relationships, 8, 44
Abba bar Ḥana, on gentiles and commercial relationships, 29
Abba bar Zebdda, on gentiles and commercial relationships, 61
Abbahu: on asherah, merkolis, and idolatry, 155–56, 158–59; on gentiles and commercial relationships, 13, 21, 28, 31, 45–47, 50, 55, 60, 62–63, 71, 74, 81, 84, 100; on idols and idolatry, 113, 115, 133, 137, 155–56, 158–59; on libation wine and gentiles, 174–75, 183, 185, 188–89, 197, 199–201, 211
Abin: on gentiles and commercial relationships, 38, 49, 53, 57, 62; on idols and idolatry, 119, 149; on libation wine and gentiles, 183
Abina, on gentiles and commercial relationships, 78
Abin bar Kahana, on gentiles and commercial relationships, 12
Ada, on libation wine and gentiles, 170
Aḥa, on gentiles and commercial relationships, 16, 49, 64, 99, 107, 199; on idols and idolatry, 112, 155
Ahai, on idols and idolatry, 155
Aḥi, on gentiles and commercial relationships, 102
Ami (Ammi): on asherah, merkolis, and idolatry, 146, 153, 155–56; on gentiles and commercial relationships, 25, 36, 47, 54, 57, 70–71, 73, 83, 102; on idols and idolatry, 146, 153, 155–56; on libation wine and gentiles, 180–81, 198–99, 205, 208, 210, 212–13, 217, 221
Aqiba: on gentiles and commercial relationships, 69, 79, 82; on idols and idolatry, 125, 130–33, 135–36, 140
Asherah, merkolis, and idolatry, 4, 145–160
Asi (Assi): on gentiles and commercial relationships, 74, 83, 89, 105; on libation wine and gentiles, 199, 208, 210, 212
Asyan, on idols and idolatry, 112

Ba: on asherah, merkolis, and idolatry, 153, 157; on gentiles and commercial relationships, 16–17, 22, 25, 34, 50, 61, 63, 76–77, 81–83, 85, 102, 105–6; on idols and idolatry, 120, 126, 137, 143, 153, 157; on libation wine and gentiles, 173, 182, 185, 204, 206, 221
Ba b. Ḥiyya, on gentiles and commercial relationships, 46
Ba bar Kohen, on gentiles and commercial relationships, 90
Ba b. R. Judah, on gentiles and commercial relationships, 95
Ba bar Ṭablai, on gentiles and commercial relationships, 14

Ba bar Zabeda, on gentiles and commercial relationships, 61, 89, 105
Ba bar Zutra, on gentiles and commercial relationships, 61, 62
Bar bar Mamal, on gentiles and commercial relationships, 71, 102
Bar Qappara: on gentiles and commercial relationships, 100; on idols and idolatry, 164; on libation wine and gentiles, 206
Ben Beterah. *See* Judah b. Beterah
Benjamin bar Ledai, on gentiles and commercial relationships, 104
Bibi, on gentiles and commercial relationships, 22, 71
Bisna, on gentiles and commercial relationships, 40
Boreqai, on idols and idolatry, 130
Bun, on libation wine and gentiles, 217
Bun bar Ḥiyya: on gentiles and commercial relationships, 32–34, 43; on idols and idolatry, 127–28, 166
Bun bar Kahana, on gentiles and commercial relationships, 70

Commerce with gentiles, 3–4, 7–109

Dosa, on gentiles and commercial relationships, 106

Eleazar: on asherah, merkolis, and idolatry, 146; on gentiles and commercial relationships, 42, 51, 65, 71–72, 75–77, 87, 104–5; on idols and idolatry, 115, 130, 133, 135, 142–45, 146, 166; on libation wine and gentiles, 174, 198, 212
Eleazar bar Ḥoshaiah, on libation wine and gentiles, 192
Eleazar b. R. Ṣadoq, on gentiles and commercial relationships, 100
Eleazar b. R. Simeon: on gentiles and commercial relationships, 86; on idols and idolatry, 116
Eleazar b. R. Yosé, on gentiles and commercial relationships, 33, 49, 67
Eliezer: on asherah, merkolis, and idolatry, 150–51; on gentiles and commercial relationships, 34, 50–54, 56, 59, 77–78, 89, 94; on idols and idolatry, 114, 150–51; on libation wine and gentiles, 210–13

Festivals and fairs of gentiles, 3, 7–31

Gamaliel: on gentiles and commercial relationships, 13, 45–46, 48, 67; on idols and idolatry, 123–25
Geniba, on gentiles and commercial relationships, 101
Gentiles: and commmercial relationships, 3–4, 7–109; and libation wine, 5–6, 171–222

Haggai: on asherah, merkolis, and idolatry, 151–52; on gentiles and commercial relationships, 38, 47, 56, 93, 99, 105; on idols and idolatry, 129, 137, 140, 151–52; on libation wine and gentiles, 207
Ḥama, on libation wine and gentiles, 203, 217
Ḥama bar Gurion, on idols and idolatry, 134
Ḥama bar Ḥanina, on gentiles and commercial relationships, 68
Ḥama bar ʿUqbah, on gentiles and commercial relationships, 7, 33, 92
Ḥama b. Yosé, on idols and idolatry, 124
Ḥanan: on idols and idolatry, 112; on libation wine and gentiles, 172
Ḥanan bar Ba, on gentiles and commercial relationships, 40, 105
Ḥanina: on idols and idolatry, 112, 139; on libation wine and gentiles, 202, 216
Ḥaninah: on gentiles and commercial relationships, 15, 29, 47, 61–63, 70–73, 75–76, 83, 91, 99, 105; on idols and idolatry, 129–30, 133–34, 168; on libation wine and gentiles, 174, 192, 198, 201–2
Ḥaninah bar R. Abbahu, on libation wine and gentiles, 212
Ḥaninah of Antonia, on libation wine and gentiles, 212
Ḥaninah b. Gamaliel, on idols and idolatry, 116

Haninah b. R. Hillel, on idols and idolatry, 138
Ḥaninah bar Pappa, on libation wine and gentiles, 180
Ḥaninah bar Yasa, on idols and idolatry, 128
Ḥaninia b. Gamaliel, on gentiles and commercial relationships, 108
Hezekiah: on gentiles and commercial relationships, 62, 100; on idols and idolatry, 121, 128–29, 166; on libation wine and gentiles, 199, 209–10, 213
Hila: on asherah, merkolis, and idolatry, 145; on idols and idolatry, 143–45, 162, 166, 168; on libation wine and gentiles, 177, 179, 186, 212
Hillel, house of, on gentiles and commercial relationships, 90, 94
Ḥisda: on gentiles and commercial relationships, 28, 31, 66; on idols and idolatry, 133, 147–48, 151
Ḥiyya: on gentiles and commercial relationships, 25, 32, 44, 47, 70, 73, 76–78, 83, 104, 108; on idols and idolatry, 158; on libation wine and gentiles, 180, 199, 212, 220
Ḥiyya bar Ada, on idols and idolatry, 158
Ḥiyya bar Ashi, on idols and idolatry, 163
Ḥiyya bar Ba: on gentiles and commercial relationships, 73, 86, 89, 93–94, 101; on idols and idolatry, 110, 119, 121, 156, 166; on libation wine and gentiles, 183
Ḥiyya the Great: on gentiles and commercial relationships, 97–98; on idols and idolatry, 158
Ḥiyya bar Luliani, on gentiles and commercial relationships, 54
Ḥiyya bar Madayya, on gentiles and commercial relationships, 62
Ḥiyya bar Rab, on libation wine and gentiles, 174
Ḥiyya bar Vada: on gentiles and commercial relationships, 29; on idols and idolatry, 158
Ḥoniah, on gentiles and commercial relationships, 18, 92
Ḥoshaiah: on gentiles and commercial relationships, 53–54; on idols and idolatry, 112, 124, 126, 166; on libation wine and gentiles, 210, 213, 220–21
Huna: on gentiles and commercial relationships, 11–12, 22, 39, 53, 58, 64, 77, 102; on idols and idolatry, 128, 135, 137; on libation wine and gentiles, 173–74, 206

Idi, on gentiles and commercial relationships, 91
Idols and idolatry, 4–5, 110–87
Ilai: on gentiles and commercial relationships, 45, 70; on idols and idolatry, 127
Isaac: on gentiles and commercial relationships, 54, 71, 93, 106; on idols and idolatry, 149
Isaac b. R. Eleazar, on gentiles and commercial relationships, 22, 102
Isaac b. Eliasheb, on idols and idolatry, 112
Isaac bar Goptah, on gentiles and commercial relationships, 47
Isaac bar Naḥman: on gentiles and commercial relationships, 29, 65, 69, 71; on idols and idolatry, 133, 163, 166
Isaac ben Ḥaqolah, on libation wine and gentiles, 198
Ishmael: on gentiles and commercial relationships, 3, 7, 16, 57, 66, 88, 91–92; on idols and idolatry, 5, 153; on libation wine and gentiles, 214–15
Ishmael b. R. Yosé, on libation wine and gentiles, 192, 199–200

Jacob: on gentiles and commercial relationships, 64; on libation wine and gentiles, 216
Jacob bar Aḥa: on gentiles and commercial relationships, 12, 29, 58, 60, 63, 71, 76, 82–83, 88, 91, 96–97, 104–5; on idols and idolatry, 151–52, 168; on libation wine and gentiles, 198, 201, 221
Jacob of Hefar Ḥanan, on idols and idolatry, 136

Jacob bar Idi: on gentiles and commercial relationships, 65, 107; on idols and idolatry, 149
Jacob bar Zabeda, on gentiles and commercial relationships, 45, 106
Jeremiah: on gentiles and commercial relationships, 51, 62–63, 66, 73, 75–78, 80, 84, 86, 96; on idols and idolatry, 119, 143–44, 168; on libation wine and gentiles, 174–75, 183, 191, 199, 208, 212, 221
Jonah: on gentiles and commercial relationships, 34, 50–51, 62, 64; on idols and idolatry, 115, 130, 155; on libation wine and gentiles, 176–79
Jonathan: on gentiles and commercial relationships, 63, 74, 96, 98; on idols and idolatry, 160; on libation wine and gentiles, 191–92
Joseph, on idols and idolatry, 135
Joshua, on gentiles and commercial relationships, 70, 88
Joshua b. Levi: on gentiles and commercial relationships, 22, 47, 63, 69, 71, 76, 88, 91, 95, 99, 107; on idols and idolatry, 113–14, 123–24, 149
Joshua b. Zeidel, on gentiles and commercial relationships, 69–70
Josiah: on idols and idolatry, 129, on libation wine and gentiles, 174
Judah: on gentiles and commercial relationships, 7, 14–15, 31, 34, 36–37, 40, 43, 49, 85, 87–88, 98–99, 105–6; on idols and idolatry, 111, 116, 126–28; on libation wine and gentiles, 185, 189, 221
Judah b. Beterah: on gentiles and commercial relationships, 31, 34, 39–41, 74; on libation wine and gentiles, 217
Judah b. Gamaliel, on gentiles and commercial relationships, 108
Judah the Patriarch: on gentiles and commercial relationships, 8, 10, 16, 39–40, 61, 86, 93, 98–101, 105; on libation wine and gentiles, 218–20
Judah bar Pazzi, on libation wine and gentiles, 198
Judah b. Shammua, on gentiles and commercial relationships, 90

Kahana, on idols and idolatry, 129–30
Kahana bar Taḥekipa, on gentiles and commercial relationships, 105

Levi: on gentiles and commercial relationships, 10, 22, 61, 66; on idols and idolatry, 138
Libation wine and gentiles, 5–6, 171–222

Mana: on gentiles and commercial relationships, 15, 42, 47, 53, 64, 76, 83, 97, 100; on idols and idolatry, 130, 134, 156, 171; on libation wine and gentiles, 208, 212
Mana bar Tanḥum, on gentiles and commercial relationships, 86, 101
Mani, on gentiles and commercial relationships, 75, 84
Matteniah: on gentiles and commercial relationships, 9; on idols and idolatry, 118, 124, 129, 157
Meir: on gentiles and commercial relationships, 4, 19, 23, 31, 33, 42, 44, 49, 60, 76–77, 80–82, 85–86, 88–89, 91; on idols and idolatry, 4, 110–111, 124, 126; on libation wine and gentiles, 195–97, 202–3

Naḥman: on gentiles and commercial relationships, 53; on idols and idolatry, 171
Naḥman b. Jacob: on gentiles and commercial relationships, 22; on libation wine and gentiles, 173
Naḥum, on idols and idolatry, 149
Naḥum the Mede, on gentiles and commercial relationships, 7
Naḥum bar Simai, on idols and idolatry, 111–12
Nathan, on gentiles and commercial relationships, 39, 42
Nathan bar Ba, on gentiles and commercial relationships, 106
Nehemiah, on libation wine and gentiles, 189
Nullifying an idol, 5, 160–71

Pazzi, on idols and idolatry, 114